Solve Every Problem In Your Life

Secret Ancient Principles Guaranteed to Grant You Wisdom

Jose & Edith -
Thank you for being
wonderful neighbors.
I admire your family -
Go catch your dreams!

Ellory Grant

Published by

Granted Wisdom International, Inc.
Tel: 704-SOLVE-IT (704-765-8348)
Fax: 704-765-8631
Internet: SolveEveryProblem.com
Email: info@ SolveEveryProblem.com

Editing, design and layout:
Baron Phoenix Media
1042 East Fort Union Blvd #346
Midvale UT 84047
baronphoenix@journalist.com

About this Book:

People occasionally ask why I left my well established, carpentry business to write books and do training speaking, and consulting. I typically respond, "Because I am so frustrated with the enormous increase of problems—everywhere I look— and the tidal wave of imprudent attempts to address them. People have so much potential and yet so little awareness of and perceived access to that potential that it is scary. For about 20 years, I searched for this book because, with it, I could have discovered how to solve all my own problems. When I discovered it did not exist, I was given the charge write it." That got me thinking, however, so, with that question and response in mind, I wrote the following:

The ability to reason—to think and act in pursuit of higher ideals—is encoded in the DNA of all human souls.

The Declaration of Independence was the gateway to The Constitution and The Bill of Rights. These inspired documents reflect the wisdom of the ages. They made the USA, the most sought after place to live earth's history and turned us into the most powerful nation the world has ever seen. Not so much because we wanted to be better or more powerful than others, but simply because living these principles maximized our intrinsic potential and inadvertently created *The Great American Dream.*

Today, these documents, have proven a blueprint of freedom around the globe. They empower governments to vanquish their evil adversaries and encourage people to preserve, protect and defend their unalienable (that is, God-given) rights. Thus, governments and people are empowered to evolve together and perpetuate liberty, harmony, prosperity & enlightenment.

Today our freedoms and independence are being threatened on almost every side. Not only from outside but inside our boarders. Not only by our enemies but our own citizens and even more disturbing, by many of our leaders and politicians. Granted, not all intentionally, but the results are the same.

Abraham Lincoln said, "...I am bound to stand with anyone who stands right and part company with him when he goes wrong." Such is our responsibility and sacred honor to secure and preserve this freedom and independence. Therein alone lies our ability to build an enlightened society—even an interdependence where there are no poor among us and a limitless potential beyond.

This is my quest.

What Leaders are saying about Eldon and his message:

"There is some amazing information in this manuscript and I learned a lot by reading it, even though I have spent the last decade of my life studying this very subject intensely. I frequently had to set the book aside and just think about the things I had read in order to enjoy the many inspirations and revelations that came to me as a result of the words on the page. While self-help books have become more popular, this manuscript is unique. Reading it can be life changing for those who prefer action to dreaming..."

— Cassandra Legge, Professional Writer and Editor

"I've had the honor to work with Eldon Grant on a professional level for the past year and have found him to have a unique understanding of life's problems that sheds light on solutions that escape most people. He can see past the peripheral issues and zero in on the best way to isolate and remove obstacles that stand in the way. He's a gifted speaker and a man who's message has the ability to transform the way companies do business. I highly recommend Eldon Grant."

— Tamra Nashman Richardt, Celebrity Speaker,
Marketing Consultant and author coach
www.Extra-OrdinaryImage.com

There is a spreading sickness in our society that is creating many problems, divorces, unhappy marriages and failed relationships of all kinds.

When I first met Eldon Grant it was immediately evident that he has a centered and calm spirit. Within a very short time, it was also obvious that he is very intelligent but without a grandiose ego. His energy and presence resonate in balance with the Chinese Taoist philosophy of Yin and Yang.

The more I got to know Eldon, the more I understood that his message, teaching and spirit, along with his great aura of kindness, intelligence and humility is part of his blessing and gift to heal this sickness. It's my intention to surround myself with as many people as possible who can enlighten me, be a mentor and help me, both in my personal and business pursuits. Eldon definitely has that gift. I encourage you to listen very carefully to him.

— Michael Doucett, Internationally acclaimed photographer
MichaelDoucettSeattleInstagram

Early in 2016, I got a call from Eldon Grant, whom I'd met the previous year. He'd written a book called *Solve Every Problem in Your Life*, and he hired me to edit it. This project became one of the highlights of my professional life. Like me, you've probably heard of hundreds of self-help books and, I hope, you're very skeptical about advice other people give you.

This one is different. I've been a lay minister in my church; served as a director of two national non-profits; was secretary to the board of trustees for a small university; run my own small business and served in the military. During all this time, I've seen examples of brilliant, atrocious, and even indifferent leadership, and I've looked carefully for what I call the *universal constants*—the ideas that apply to every individual and situation; educational, corporate, family, etc. In some respects, this book is like an action movie; a non-stop adventure into your life, with new ideas—actually, old ideas, most of which will probably feel familiar. When you reach the end, I can see you saying, "Yeah, that's what I've always thought, I just didn't know how to put it into words."

Eldon has laid the foundation for a lifelong self-training, self-discovery journey with one simple premise: *You're in control of your life; get in the groove with the stuff that always works and life will be better.* No one can guarantee great wealth, a worry-free life or that your wildest fantasies will come true. But, after three decades of serious examination, I can guarantee you'll find value in Eldon's writing, and, who knows, you might even find some advice that leads you to achieve that wild fantasy!

— Phoenix Roberts, Professional writer, editor and entrepreneur

Like his victorious dance with a world class dancer, Eldon now demonstrates how to dance in rhythm with universal law to excite and embellish life's performance. His book "Solve Every Problem in Your Life" is an invitation to be guided through the chaotic turbulence of life's straits and chart a successful course to harbors of unconventional wisdom and the simplicity on the other side of complexity.

— Del Whetstone D.O.

Eldon, I really enjoyed reading the first part of your book. I can see from the brief glimpse into it that you have a treasure of insights that this world needs. I can't wait to read the entire book when you are complete.

Terri L Stecher CPC, CFC, NLPP, PDPA, SPHR,
www.terristecher.com

I've known Eldon for a number of years and benefited personally from his example and teachings. I was thrilled to see him finally share his story and compile the simple guiding principles that have made him successful. As a person, Eldon is an honest and true friend to all. As a teacher his is kind, compassionate, extremely knowledgeable about his subject matter and yet ever the student himself. This book is well thought out and the culmination of tens of thousands of hours of work to make simple the wisdom of the ages. To those looking to make significant changes in their lives to find greater peace, joy and success, this book is a must.

Jon Thompson, President and CEO Atlas Development Corp.

"I am a full time teacher; I am also Eldon's brother. I have been in conversation with thousands of brilliant men and women and shared Insights about the secrets of success and the purpose of life. I have dedicated my life to this great cause. However, with all that I have heard and gleaned, listening to Eldon is like having the manor's curtains opened to vistas of perspectives, landscapes of learning and cathedrals of thought that few men and women have ever conceived.

Eldon provides a paradigm on life that is refreshingly hopeful and invigorating for anyone and trains you how to measure your success along the way. Once introduced to the time honored principles that he shares, your purpose and perspective will never be the same. Your life will begin to produce sustenance and fragrance that you may have thought not to be in existence or only found in the minds of dreamers.

I assure you [his teaching] is worth your investment of time and study... It is a vehicle that offers vision for a brighter future, validity in universal law, and vitality to propel you into a divine pursuit of real happiness. God bless you in your efforts."

— David Carter Grant, high school and college religious educator.

Eldon, First, thank you for your time and efforts you put into our training... People were engaged and interested in your thoughts. Several stated they wished you had more time but that you have successfully planted seeds of new thoughts and ideas of how to make real change in who we are and what we accomplish. You were recognized as a great speaker and personality. You inspired us and I greatly appreciate you, your spirit and your thinking. Thanks again,

Gary Howell, CEO Integral Software

Comments from high school/college staff & students:

"You were a wonderful change of pace from our other speakers."

"It was so eye-opening to see how most people work for success in a direction that can never produce it."

"It was really cool to see someone without a PHD with such wise insights"

"Our students walked a little taller the next day."

"Your points were very clear; I especially like the point of not allowing anyone else to break your spirit."

"Your 'pick me up' story was captivating and encouraging."

"I liked how interactive your talk was."

"Your country humor cracked me up."

"You gave us a very different way to look at life."

"It was scary to realize how much impact our friends have on us."

"The lessons you provided were personally informative...and helped me understand how to be extraordinary."

"Your SPESIFC's of life was a great lesson."

"That certainly was a different perspective to how schools teach."

"It will save us a life time of finding out for ourselves that universal laws are unbreakable."

"Your advice about risk taking really hit home."

"I loved your SPESIFC's example."

"I found your principles thought-provoking."

"It's great to know that someone can still dig themselves from tragedy and make themselves better."

"I enjoyed the bike metaphor... but even more interesting were your ideas about friends."

"I will remember to raise my goals and expectations."

"You are a very generous and inspiring speaker."

"Your presentation reinforced ideas we are learning [here]."

"The notes I have taken from your speech will be beneficial for time to come."

"We hope you come back."

Dedication

To my wife, Jackie.

You carried and raised our children;
you made our house a home;
you put up with more idiocy from me than a wife should have to;
through all our good times and all our hard times,
you made it all worthwhile.

I am honored to share this journey of life with you
Thank you for being my angel and the love of my life.

Acknowledgements

There have been so many people who have ultimately made it possible for me to write this book that I could not list them all if I tried. There are a few however who have been so influential that without you, this would either still be a figment of my imagination or not even fathomed.

First, as you might expect God has to come at the top of the list. Not only is He responsible for my being here on earth but has unquestionably prompted, directed and guided me to make this a reality.

Second, has to be my amazing and sweet wife. I am well aware that you could have rightly refused to put up with this incessant obsession. Even through so many of your frustrations, you believed in me. At times, it could have been easier for you to demand a change, but you chose to exercise faith in me instead. As a result, my love, respect, appreciation and gratitude for you has grown by leaps and bounds. I have discovered through life and being married to you that genuine "soulmates" are never really *found*, but they can be *created*.

Third, would have to be my brother Carter. So many times I called you with new ideas and insights and even when you had other important things to do, you were willing to listen and give me good feedback. At times you stayed on the phone with me for much longer than you probably should have. So many of our talks helped me to clarify my ideas. I admire how super smart you are, you are one of the most selfless people I know.

Then Robert G. Allen. You introduced me to this whole world. Then your amazing character and commitment to live with integrity helped to keep me here. I understand that if you hadn't been there, God would have provided someone else, but the fact is that you put yourself in a position where God trusted you to be my initial, ideal guide and mentor and I will forever be grateful to you.

And Denis Waitley. Your tape *Seeds of Greatness*, then later what I discovered about your character and your many other programs, effectively and completely hooked me on a lifetime of personal and professional development study and practice.

I could write an entire book about how my parents and each one of my 11 siblings (and their spouses now) have personally helped to shape my life for good. At times I feel like "the black sheep of the family" who was given this unbelievable gift to have each one of you in my life for different reasons. I hope this book can perhaps, in some small fashion, help you understand how much I love and admire you and perhaps can make at least a small scratch on the surface to let you know how much I have learned from you and am honored to be part of your family.

My three sons have also been very supportive. Sometimes you have been rightly frustrated about my time and attention with you being out of balance. But you continue to believe in me and my love for each one of you has significantly grown.

I have to express extreme gratitude also to Anne McIndoo. Even though you don't know me (yet). Without your book and program, *So You Want To Write*, I still may be trying to figure out how to get this all started. Or perhaps even given up.

Then Cassandra Legge and Phoenix Roberts who both rode in on their white steeds, just in the nick of time, as my "Knights in Shining Armor." Thank you for helping me to edit these ideas into a coherent and meaningful way.

There are so many more individuals that I would love to acknowledge here, like other family, friends, mentors, role models and coaches who have added directly and indirectly to not only writing this book but also to my life's success and happiness. My gratitude to you is forever.

Then to each of you who pick up this book. I must say "thank you so very much." Again, I genuinely believe in you and send a personal blessing directly into your life:

God Bless You, Enjoy and Go Catch Your Dreams.

Table of Contents

ABOUT THIS BOOK: I

What Leaders are saying about Eldon and his message: ii

Comments from high school/college staff & students: v

Dedication.. vi

Acknowledgements vii

PART 1 1

CHAPTER 1: CONVENTIONAL WISDOM — THE GREAT ILLUSION 1

How to Use This Book 3

CHAPTER 2: THE SPESIFC'S OF LIFE.. 8

Conclusion.. 16

CHAPTER 3 THE TRUTH ABOUT TRUTH 17

CHAPTER 4 UNIVERSAL LAWS AND PRINCIPLES 23

Summary... 26

CHAPTER 5 THE CORE HUMAN OBJECTIVE: OUR QUEST FOR PERFECTION 27

CHAPTER 6 HOW TO ACTIVATE THE GIFT OF GRACE............................ 34

"God wants You to be Blessed so You can be a Blessing."................... 34

The Investment Mindset 36

CHAPTER 7 HOW AND WHY THESE PRINCIPLES REMAIN SECRET 39

PART 2 44

INTRODUCTION: THE MOST TALKED ABOUT SECRET THAT IS STILL A SECRET 44

CHAPTER 1 THE ALPHA AND OMEGA PRINCIPLE.................................. 46

You Are a Creator 46

Thoughts: The Building Blocks of Reality 46

Information vs. Principles 47

Faith and Miraculous Results... 54

Consumer Mentality vs. Investor Mentality.................................... 57

Personal Accountability 58

A Bold Statement... 60

Conclusion.. 61

Summary.. 62

CHAPTER 2 THE OMEGA & ALPHA PRINCIPLE.................................... 66

The Laws of Recreation... 66

Activities: The Cement of Reality 66

Information vs. Principles 67

Faith and Miraculous Results... 68

Recreation Mentality vs. Re-Creation Mentality 69

Personal Holidays 71

A Not-So-Bold Statement.. 71

Some Final, Miscellaneous Thoughts.. 73

Conclusion..74

Summary...75

CHAPTER 3 THE OWNER'S MANUALS PRINCIPLE 77

One: The Spiritual Owner's Manual..77

Two: Your Historical Owner's Manual 80

Three: Your Role Models and Mentors Owner's Manual 81

Four: Your Personal Experience Owner's Manual............................83

Five: Your Nature and Environmental Owner's Manual 83

Conclusion..85

Summary...86

CHAPTER 4 THE APPRENTICESHIP PRINCIPLE.....................................88

What is Education?...88

The Five Concepts of True Education 89

The Mentor/Apprentice Relationship 98

Conclusion..101

Summary...102

CHAPTER 5 THE JOY-IN-THE-JOURNEY PRINCIPLE 105

Maintenance is a Myth...105

Enjoying the Journey, no Matter What..108

Know Your Resources...110

Moving Ever Forward..110

Become as a Little Child...111

Choosing Your Path..112

Which Road Are You Travelling Now? 114

Taking Stock of Your Current Location..116

Always be Grateful for the Good in your Life but Never Lose the Committment to
Make it Better...118

Conclusion..119

Summary...120

CHAPTER 6 THE NEXT-BEST-GUESS PRINCIPLE 122

Application of the Apprenticeship Principle...................................122

"Spock, That's Extraordinary!"..124

Understanding the Difference between Needs and Wants 125

Conclusion..127

Summary...128

CHAPTER 7 THE SHORTCUT PRINCIPLE 130

My Business was Cut Short...130

Shortcuts vs. Cutting Corners...131

The Real World 132

There's Nothing Wrong with a Good Shortcut 135

Hand-outs vs. Hand-ups 137

Conclusion 139

Summary 139

CHAPTER 8 THE MEASUREMENT PRINCIPLE 141

How important is Measuring Results? 141

Standards of Measure 141

Universal Law Governs All 143

Finding the Standard for Measurement 144

If you don't Write it down, it didn't Happen 146

Don't Run Faster than You are Able 147

Take the Long View 148

Conclusion 149

Summary 149

CHAPTER 9 THE ASSOCIATION PRINCIPLE 151

Role Models 151

Symptoms of Associations 153

Conclusion 158

Summary 159

CHAPTER 10 THE LEADERSHIP PRINCIPLE 161

Leadership of Self 161

Leadership by Following 163

Leadership of Others 166

Leadership by Precept 167

Leadership by Example 168

Conclusion 170

Summary 171

CHAPTER 11 THE COMMUNICATION PRINCIPLE 173

Speak! 174

Perception is Mostly Illusion 175

Listening vs. Hearing 176

Non-verbal Communication 177

Defining Our World 177

Understanding 180

Conclusion 181

Summary 181

CHAPTER 12 THE DESTINY PRINCIPLE 184

The Highest Path 184

Finding the Path 186

Following the (sometimes bumpy) Path 188

The Path of Magnificent Obsession 189

The Loyal Opposition 190

Conclusion 191

Summary 192

CHAPTER 13 THE FIRE PRINCIPLE 194

Fear — the Fire on the Mind 194

Passion — the Fire in the Heart 201

Conclusion 205

Summary 206

CHAPTER 14 THE REAL-ECONOMICS PRINCIPLE 208

The Law of the Harvest 209

Valuta 212

Liberty 214

Responsibility 215

Hand-outs vs. Hand-ups 216

Wealth and the Wealthy 217

1+1=2 Only If You Want A Settle-For Life 220

Scarce Resources 221

One More Quick Note 222

Conclusion 223

Summary 224

CHAPTER 15 THE EXPONENTIAL RETURNS PRINCIPLE 226

Tithes and Offerings 226

Conclusion 230

Summary 231

CHAPTER 16 THE TEMPLE PRINCIPLE 232

What is a Temple? 232

Why Are They Built? 233

The Dove-tailed Being 234

Spiritual Health 239

Conclusion 243

Summary 244

CHAPTER 17 THE SYNERGISM PRINCIPLE 246

Belief 247

Vision 248

Plan 249

Faith 251

Hope 251

Charity *253*

Passion..*254*

Miracles *255*

Conclusion...*256*

ABOUT THE AUTHOR: 258

Solve Every Problem in your Life
Secret, Ancient Principles Guaranteed to Grant You Wisdom

Part 1

Chapter 1:
Conventional Wisdom — The Great Illusion

Everyone has heard the term "conventional wisdom". Like many terms in our everyday vocabulary today, "conventional wisdom" is an oxymoron. There is no such thing as conventional wisdom, and even to mention it as having any legitimate context is completely absurd. There is not a trace of wisdom in conventionalism and not a hint of conventionalism in wisdom. In fact, the two are opposites. If we have the courage to state it properly, we would call it "conventional naivety" or "unconventional wisdom." At extremes, we could even and rightly call it "conventional stupidity."

To do something conventionally means to follow well-established methods or socially accepted customs. This is where the masses reside; doing things the way they have always been done and/or following the widely accepted thinking of the day. All of us are guilty of being conventional sometimes simply because that's the way we were raised and trained. Even when we are advised to change what we are doing or feel the need to do try something new, it's often too much effort and too scary to venture out on an unknown path. We don't call it "the comfort zone" for nothing!

Doing things the conventional way never produces extraordinary results, let alone miracles. Where's the wisdom in doing things the conventional way only to end up with conventional — or in other words — poor to mediocre results?

Although much of what we discuss in this book will likely be familiar to you and your everyday experience, it is all grounded in core principles. As you discover the efficacy of these principles for yourself, the wisdom you gain will unveil the truth that conventionalism is a route to nothing but pain and regret. The study of these principles comes from the wisest people who have ever lived and who have proven their wisdom beyond question by producing the finest results in one or more areas of life. If you have any notions of a truly happy and fulfilled life, you, like they, must get over your own prejudice and be extremely careful believing what others say until you have proven that their formulas are founded in correct principles.

Conventionalism, at best, produces mediocrity; but often, the results are far worse than mere mediocrity. The trouble lies in assuming you know more than you actually do. Understanding these principles is a life-long process. Understanding these principles includes both understanding the concepts and their eternal-reaching effects as well as what principles actually are. Discovering the principles themselves and how to apply them to create your own unique and ultimate life is the objective. There is a lifetime of increase and evolution awaiting you as you continue to learn, grow and evolve in order to produce over-the-top, miraculous results on a consistent basis and understand exactly why you are getting those results.

So take a brave step away from conventionalism and learn to ask better questions, dig deeper for more creative and better solutions, climb higher, practice more and longer and pay better attention to what you are doing compared to what you are getting. If you are not doing these things, you are missing out on crucial insights that would drastically improve your life.

Robert G. Allen, best-selling author and wealth-creation guru, was the first person to help open my eyes to the fact that when the masses are headed in any particular direction, I should run as fast as I can in the opposite direction — unless, of course, I happen to be in a burning building heading for the only exit, and even then, it can be wise to reconsider.

This was a very difficult concept for me to grasp and accept in the beginning. As soon as I began to understand the damage caused by conventionalism, I also began to recognize the same counsel from Jesus when He said, "…strait is the gate and narrow is the way and few there be that find it." Hundreds of the wisest men and women who ever lived have echoed that same counsel — Buddha, Confucius, Solomon, Aristotle, Benjamin Franklin, Andrew Carnegie and Earl Nightingale, among many others. Along the way, I've also learned from my own very painful and costly mistakes that this advice pertains to every single area of life — bar none!

You will find the perspectives and truths in this book to be unconventional, even according to the majority of self-help literature. This book also includes several principles which are rarely taught, and we'll delve into them to a deeper degree than I'll bet you ever have before, regardless of how much you have studied them. We'll take a good, hard look at these convention-defying principles because they are the only way to build structural integrity into the foundation and framing of your life.

Since what you'll read here is most likely different from anything you've previously read or heard before, you may feel a tendency to discount the information or create controversy around it in your own mind. That is absolutely normal, but I challenge you with the same challenge I accepted from another of my cherished mentors, M. Scott Peck, who wrote, "Spiritual growth demands that you actively seek the threatening and unfamiliar and deliberately challenge all you have been taught and hold dear. The road to holiness lies through questioning everything."

Likewise, Albert Einstein's counsel, "A man should look for what is and not for what he thinks should be."

In this book, I want to encourage you to think critically about every piece of so-called "conventional wisdom" that you feel compelled to believe. As you replace the delusion of conventional wisdom with the factual evidence of positive results that flow from applying these principles, you will be able to place your own knowledge structure into much more productive perspectives and paradigms, thus breaking the chains of illusion and set yourself free. You will begin to replace the so-called-truths others have imposed on you and see truth as it has always existed. Seeing the reality of your life and the world around you — which includes not trying to force the world to be what you think it should be — is a big step toward solving every problem in your life.

How to Use This Book

I encourage you to read this book as if it is a college textbook. Underline things that have special meaning to you; take notes in the margins to remind you of inspired thoughts and "A-ha!" moments; keep a note pad with you for more in-depth ideas, questions, lists and so on. If you are not used to reading and studying in this way, it's a good habit to get into anyway, even if it feels strange at first or seems to take too much time. You may even feel like it is a sacrilege to mark up a book like that, but I guarantee that these kinds of efforts will skyrocket your results.

It's important to note that virtually all the great and wise people of the world took notes as a crucial part of their study. I am a true believer in taking notes because, for the past almost 25 years, I virtually *always* studied with a notebook and still do. This was counsel from almost all of my most cherished mentors, some of the wisest people who ever lived. I have learned more, gained deeper insights and received more inspiration from taking notes than from virtually any other thing I have ever done...even more than prayer, meditation, pondering, etc., and it has dramatically increased my understanding of everything I've studied, but then again my note taking is often a combination of all of that.

Taking notes and writing down my "A-ha!" insights and inspirations has had several positives for me: First, writing down an inspired thought shows I am grateful for it. Second, writing down an inspired thought assists in retaining the message. Third, writing down an inspired thought encourages me to do something with it. Forth, writing down your inspired thoughts and then acting on them will bring you additional inspiration.

Trying to absorb this entire book all at once would be impossible. As Winston Churchill famously said, "Never give-up!" Likewise, Jesus said, "Let not your heart be troubled, neither let it be afraid." but, "be of good cheer." Franklin-Covey co-founder Hyrum Smith is fond of saying, "You haven't learned anything unless you've forgotten it twice."

To assist your studies, this book is designed more like an encyclopedia — every part is important, but you don't have to understand it all at first, nor must it be understood in the exact order as written. Every small piece you comprehend will change your life for the better and will lead to better understanding the rest of the book. One beautiful thing about the structure of the world, your life and your mind is that just at the right time, opportunities will be presented to you in order to understand what you need to understand. The responsibility to make sure you understand however, is 100 percent yours, but the opportunity will be extended. You didn't pick up this book by accident. Herein lies an opportunity that will bring new recognition, enlightenment and expansion to every other opportunity for the rest of your life.

The more you study this book, the more opportunities you'll have to understand these crucial principles. The more you apply what you study, the quicker you will see your life change for the better. I write this book to bring insights into these principles so that you (first) understand better what these principles are and (second) learn how to make principles the focus of everything you do. At work, at church, at school, on vacation, at home with your family, struggling through problems or enjoying confidence and peace of mind, this book can help you expand your strengths and strengthen your weaknesses. Just remember that all growth is a process. So be patient but also doggedly persistent.

If you ever start feeling overwhelmed, just sit back, take some deep breaths, look up toward the sky, smile and say, "I don't need to do it all right now, I can do at least one more thing, even if it is a small thing, and I'll be that much closer. Forget all the rest. When that is done, I can do one more thing. If you are willing to take baby steps in the beginning and understand some of the deeper meanings, realize a little broader reality, discover how to look for and discover principles in all that you do, life will begin to make more sense, be more meaningful and very soon you will be having those "A-ha!" moments and making bigger steps and, then, quantum leaps. They will take you by surprise and bring you the greatest thrills of your life because everything in life will take on more profound and exciting meaning.

If you are feeling stuck, asking the right question of the right people will get you on your way again. Of course, each time you begin a new area of study, there will be some baby steps again. You've heard people say that "we learn more every day." Unfortunately, that is not true most of the time. Only if you pay attention and deliberately try to learn are you actually better off for having experienced the day. Otherwise, you are worse off because you have lost a day that you could have invested for a handsome return. I look forward to being part of your journey of learn and sharing your gifts with the world.

The more you study this book and the other books and the people referenced herein, the stronger habits and grander perspectives you will develop. This book offers you the chance to recognize more reality, be happier, develop a brighter future and you will do it all naturally because life will become more and more logical and easier to predict. Even things that now bring you frustration, struggle and even crushing sorrows will transform into genuine peace of mind. So much so that you'll want to shout from the roof tops about how others can ease their pain by seeing through the illusions and deeper into principles/reality.

Read this book once, wait a (short) while and then read it again. As you do, add new thoughts and insights to your previous notes. The new insights and freedom you will gain through your second and third readings will blow your mind! They will also enable you to better measure how much is really changing for you. Even things you were not intentionally working on will improve and sooner or later, you will begin to awaken to your own "state of constant, total amazement," like Joe and Patricia talked about in the movie *Joe vs. the Volcano*. (an idea we will address in more depth later in the book).

In addition to these notes, also write down your questions on a separate sheet of paper. Even the process of keeping track of your questions is a great measurement of your growth. Review them often and send the questions you struggle most with to me at <AskEldon@SolveEveryProblem.com>. There, I will invite you to participate in other programs where I specifically address these questions.

More than any other piece of advice, I encourage you to track your insights, thoughts and questions. This book's core objective is to facilitate your journey and enable you to understand the principles that will allow you to *"fall…" so that "the one [you] want, the one [you] will become, will catch [you]."* (Thanks, Josh Groban, for singing and sharing such an inspiring song *Let Me Fall*!) You will consistently and systematically solve every problem in your life by learning to utilize a few secret, simple and ancient principles and, when it begins to happen, you will be amazed and wonder why it's taken so long to figure things out because they are so simple.

In fact, because you have picked up this book and read this far, I invite you to log on to our website <www.SolveEveryProblem.com> and share with us a couple of your top dreams and goals along with why they are so important to you. I also encourage you to share the problems you currently find are most in your way. When you do, I have a gift for you.

I've had a lot to say about "conventional wisdom", so I need to explain what real wisdom actually is. I don't know about you but when I was young, the definition I heard most about wisdom, even from respected teachers and leaders was that "wisdom is the correct application of knowledge."

Without really giving it much thought (actually no thought at all) I accepted that as truth and repeated it myself whenever I needed a definition for wisdom. Then after I had actually been studying many of the wisest people on earth, it didn't take long to discover that if a person stands on an assembly line and screws nuts onto bolts, that is definitely the correct application of knowledge but it has nothing to do wisdom. Jim Rohn, an American entrepreneur, author and motivational speaker, was right when he said that we can go almost anywhere and find lots of people filling every profession, they are "…a dime a dozen but good one's are hard to find." That's because most people go through school and their entire work lives, just going through the motions but never dig deep enough to discover real core principles and become truly wise. When someone does apply wisdom, it is always the correct application of knowledge, but the vast majority of correct application of knowledge has nothing to do with wisdom.

The more I studied, the more I began to see similarities in all these wise people's paradigms. Even though they came from extremely diverse backgrounds and even entirely different eras, I saw similarities in the way they thought, the way they interacted with others, and the way they solved problems. That's when I began to discover these things called principles. These principles enable people to think much deeper than the masses around them and that's why they were almost always in high demand for counseling and rose to leadership positions, even from the lowliest beginnings.

So, below is the definition of wisdom that I have deciphered and diagramed over the years from my study of the truly wise.

Wisdom is comprised of four distinct components. If any one or more of these are lacking or even not the right quantity, it is not real wisdom but only an imitation or illusion that, if left unattended, will collapse. Trying to design and build any kind of success on any other foundation will create major problems. Like leaving any ingredient out of a concrete mix will leave it useless for its intended purposes. Sooner or later it will fail and whatever you have built on it will also fail. On the other hand all four ingredients of wisdom, combined correctly together, will create a powerful synergy that will stand strong, virtually forever.

- **Superior Intelligence** This is much broader and more comprehensive than mere knowledge. Knowledge is based on information and can be taught, memorized and handed down from one person to another. Intelligence, on the other hand, is founded in principles. No one can teach you principles. Worthy mentors can instruct and guide you toward principles but you must discover them for yourself, by your own due diligence. I call them "The principles that lead to wisdom and enable you to harness the laws of creation."

1) **Extreme Skills.** Study and research is never enough. You must be willing to consistently push yourself beyond your comfort zone and never be contented

with your current skill levels. Even if you are at the top of your class. There are always improvements to make and even major breakthroughs to discover. The greatest masters of earth are the ones who are unconditionally committed to continually improving their skills. These are the extreme-high-end, hard and soft skills of life, leadership and success, which includes technical skills. How-to's. A deep understanding of the correct application of principles.

2) **Powerful Character.** All the intelligence and skills on earth will only lead you to a dead-end of pain and regret unless you also develop the character to hold the integrity of that intelligence and those skills intact. I often say that great leadership is not dependent on knowledge and skills but on character and wisdom. It's not about what you do but about why you choose to do it. Stress is one of, if not the biggest killer of people. Doing things for the right reasons and having solidarity between who you really are and what you do, not only releases stress, but heals you. It is also the one and only worthy example you can set for others. Integrity and charity are the core or right character.

• **Ultimate Insight**. Even with all the above, until you discover your own true potential and learn to see into the true potential of others, it is impossible to hold yourself or anyone else to an optimal or even reasonable standard. If you push too hard, you will break, burn out or burn up. If you do not push enough, you will undercut your potential and never come close to what you could have accomplished.

As Buddha counseled, "Enlightenment is in the middle way. It is the center between all opposite extremes. Finding and living within that center is the only space, time and environment in which true wisdom can exist. This book will help you discover that center.

Chapter 2:
The SPESIFC's of Life

It hit me, one day, like the proverbial ton of bricks — if I divided my life up into its fundamental areas, I could create a system that would perfectly measure how I was doing at any given point of my life. I had studied several different peoples' ideas about the basic areas of life, but most of their theories had holes in them, and, I had a hard time remembering the good theories. So I decided to come up with something that was all-inclusive and easy to remember. After brainstorming for almost a year, this acronym popped into my head as an inspiration. I now refer to them as the *SPESIFCs of Life*.

People often laugh about my spelling of *specific* until I remind them that Mark Twain said that he didn't have much use for any person who could only spell a word one way. Besides, it works for the acronym, it's easy to remember and fits my unconventional, backwoods cowboy style. Most importantly though, it's my choice, I like it and I'm keepin' it!

S

Spiritual must come first because it is the foundation to all other areas of life. There is an actual spiritual realm in which we live but which we cannot perceive with our physical senses. I understand there are many different perceptions about the universe, including many who don't believe things outside the physical world exist. That is their right and I allow them their beliefs, whatever those may be. However, this book is about truth, so: God is real, spiritual realms exist and we are part of a Greater Universe. If you decline to accept this truth, you can still improve your life but you will be severely handicapped. Only closer harmony with reality brings growth. Illusions on the other hand, as grand as they may seem in the moment will only leave you worse off, the further you chase them.

Writing this I was just reminded of a quote I heard some time ago by Arthur Schopenhauer that, "All truth passes through three stages. First, it is ridiculed. Second, it is violently opposed. Third, it is accepted as being self-evident." (That is at least, and especially when it is introduced contrary to the status quo, both with the individual and the bigger collective).

To continue: When you consider how drastically the physical world has been misunderstood, even by the best minds of their respective ages, and how difficult it has been to uncover truth about the physical world and get that truth to be accepted by the world in general — the whole "Earth is flat" and "The sun revolves around the earth" concepts, as glaring examples — it is only logical to realize that the spirit world is much more seriously misunderstood.

Since we can't perceive the spiritual world the way we perceive the physical world, spirituality is, in part, the extent to which you recognize spirituality and allow spiritual guidance to have a significant, positive and consistent effect on you.

That there is more to the universe than what meets the eye is now established scientific truth — you need only review recent discussions of "dark matter" and "dark energy" on the Internet to see how weird the universe has become since Isaac Newton's apple fell. That discussion aside, the more seriously you delve into history, ancient and recent, the more obvious it is that this concept of a spiritual realm is a universal thread in philosophy. Virtually every culture has a fierce reverence for, and an accountability to, the principles and inhabitants of the unseen world.

If spiritual things are so hard to perceive, how can one measure spiritual growth? One of the simplest and most powerful measurements lies in your stewardship of the other six **SPESIFC**s. To create any structure, an adequate foundation must first be designed and laid. Since the physical world is built on the foundation of the spiritual realm, your stewardship of the other SPECIFCs of Life becomes a solid benchmark. The more you reverence and take good care of these other areas, the greater your potential to be in touch with and understand the spiritual realm will be.

P

Physical health is essential to good health in other areas. I heard a quote a while back that: "When a man has his health, he has a thousand dreams. When he does not have his health, he has but one." I divide physical health into seven fundamentals, I needed the best way to remember them so I came up with the acronym, NEAREST. Although most of these should not surprise you, I believe some will and all of which we will discuss later in greater detail. I have asked 100's of educated people, even lots of doctors, fitness trainers and health professionals and so far, not one of them has been able to give me a complete list, by memory, of what it takes to stay healthy,. So, don't take this lightly.

If you do not know all of these by memory, it is impossible for you to stay in good health because the ones you don't consistently pay attention to will create a weak link in your chain of life and cost you dearly in time, money, lost production, etc. when your chain breaks — and it will break — earlier than it needs to. The fact is that virtually every unhealthy person, got that way because they did not pay attention to some or all of these areas of health. Whether they knew about them or not is irrelevant. If you pay the very small price to memorize this acronym and remember what it stands for, the better you will inadvertently keep them in mind and develop better and better habits with them. Take even small steps toward each one now and they will return huge dividends to you in the future.

Nutrition: Your food needs to be well-balanced and clean; that is free from pesticides, harmful bacteria, added hormones, anti-biotics, etc. your consumption needs to be neither too little nor too much. Avoid processed foods. Eat as many single ingredient foods as possible and stay hydrated.

Exercise: Your fitness program needs to balance stretching, strength, endurance and tone and be appropriate for your age and overall health. Remember, work out gyms for the general public are virtually new to the world in only the past few years. Even though science has learned to keep us alive longer, we are by enlarge, unhealthier today than ever before because of our drastic change in lifestyles. Productive and meaningful activities can be better for you than exercise, just for exercise sake.

Activity: Your activity calendar needs to balance physical, intellectual and emotional endeavors. Even those who are independently wealthy need to contribute to society and all of us need to play. A little adventure spices up life and relationships. Family and friendships need to be cultivated, but solitude is equally essential. Also you can often find activities that you love that can take the place and even be better for your all-around health than going to the gym.

Rest: Your down time needs to balance sleep with diversion. Everybody needs to dream (even day-dream), but we also need to do sometime different, relaxing, and cleansing now and then.

Environment: The most important thing you can do about your environment is to be aware of toxins in the air they breathe and on surfaces they contact. It's good to keep your environment clean, but that doesn't mean sterile nor even too clean. A very big problem we see in the world today is that children and adults often stay too clean. One of the healthiest things you can do is to dig in the dirt with your bare hands, like planting, cultivating and harvesting a garden. It's healthy to sweat with your own labor.

Get outside in nature for fun and for productive tasks. Among many other things, those activities, in that environment will improve your immune system and nothing else will take its place. You must also consider the frequencies and energies around you. Also the attitudes (positive and negative) of the people in your circles at work, in your home and socially. If you cannot change the environment around you and it is to unhealthy, As Jim Rohn reminds us, "You can move. You're not a tree!"

Solidarity: In this one crucial area, we seek a different balance: Though we need to be accepting of the philosophies and opinions of others, we must be firm in our own belief system. Do you honestly and wholeheartedly believe what you accept as your personal philosophy, political agenda, religion, etc.? Everyone wants to belong, to be part of a collective bigger than themselves, in which they have the sustaining support and acceptance of others. When the group paradigms represent reality/truth and encourage an upward reach in all, your convictions form the firm foundation which keeps you safe as the world becomes ever less sane. Obviously, the truer the paradigms, the stronger, more unified and solid your foundation becomes.

The less congruent you are within yourself and within your environment, whether you consciously recognize it or not, the more unhealthy stress you will experience and unhealthy stress, as you probably realize is the largest contributor to a compromised immune system, disease and even death.

Thought: Other than solidarity, mental health is the most overlooked of all fundamentals to good physical health (and visa-versa). Some must deal with real challenges and disabilities and most people can thrive in spite of and even because of such trials. Though most people believe they have good mental health, if they are burdened with sub-par results, that's a clue that the mental health is not as good as they believe. Results never lie, they are the measurement of the quality of your formulas. The only way to improve your results is to improve the formulas you used to create them. Proper self-accountable thinking habits will contribute powerfully to your health and wellness.

Likewise, the old "positive thinking" ideals are also largely misunderstood. Interestingly, the majority of people believe, other than occasional bouts of negativity, that they are mostly positive thinkers. However, results follow thinking. Since the vast majority of our results are poor to mediocre, that is a good measurement to determine how positive our thoughts really are.

E

Emotional stability is essential to happiness. What is your self-talk like? What pictures are habitually on the television screen of your mind? When Jesus was asked "What is the greatest commandment?" He gave two — love God and love your neighbor as yourself. Included in the second however is a deliberate hint; In order to love anyone or anything else, you must first love yourself.

Lots of people have a problem with loving themselves. They suffer under the delusion that loving oneself would be selfish, self-centered, or, somehow, self-righteous. The fact is that you are only capable of giving away that which you already possess. The extent of the love you have for yourself is the only extent to which you have capacity to love God or anyone else. It is impossible to give anything more than you possess to anyone else.

So many people believe that doing service for others is the highest form of character and love. However, the hardest and most important work you will ever do in your life is to put yourself on a path and trajectory of consistent self-evolution. Discover your own unique value and then go about consistently and deliberately aligning yourself with it. This will absolutely require that you give up the limiting illusions you currently have about yourself.

Again Jim Rohn, correctly stated that, "our emotions need to be as educated and our intellect." And also that "Self-sacrifice is *not* noble," in the sense that putting your own development below anyone else's is a very bad thing. Putting yourself even 2nd place after anyone else, is a guaranteed formula for personal decay. It is also an example that you unwittingly pass on to others around you, such as your children; that it is okay to treat others better than you treat yourself. Any sacrifice of your personal self-development causes extensive damage. When it is done in the name of service to others, it is actually a disservice to you and to them. If you do not develop yourself first, your ability to help others develop is virtually lost. You become a teller and no longer a teacher. You lose your integrity and cannot, therefore, truly serve others. You can only teach others to develop themselves by your own example to develop yourself.

S

Social skills are also essential to success in life. How well do you deal with other people — spouse, children, neighbors, friends, colleagues, superiors, subordinates, mentors, and strangers? Are you nice to be around? What about your relationships in business, the community, your government, and so on? Some time ago, I was little upset and said some harsh words to my wife. Later that day she came in with a gift and a smile. As I opened the package, it was a plaque that said simply, "It's nice to be important but it's more important to be nice." My heart melted and that plaque continues to remind me about the importance of patience and kindness.

Life is all about developing leadership skills and leadership is a social skill. Everything you will have, or ever hope to have, must come to you by way of other people. The people you surround yourself with the most, and how well or poorly you relate to them will dictate your ultimate success or failure in every one of these areas of your life.

Human nature is such and thus the world is designed — — that we are compelled to gather in groups and form alliances. The more people you have working toward the same goals and dreams, the faster a society rises to greatness. The more those societies continue to support each individual in the group, and the individuals support society, the stronger and more capable they become. The moment any person attempts to get ahead by using others unfairly is the moment society either needs to discipline or remove that person or the society will decline.

I discovered this personally several years ago, and I wrote, "The secret to real happiness is to forget about trying to collect it (even though you can only give it to yourself) and concentrate on giving it to others (even though they can never get it from you)." Now, this might sound contrary to what I just said above about how self-sacrifice is not noble, but it is actually in perfect harmony. This concept enables you to understand that the greater a desire you have to bless others' lives, the more you are absolutely accountable to intentionally and consistently improve your own. The better you learn to deal with others, the more you will grow. The more you grow the greater ability you have to give. The more you give, with the right intentions, the more you will receive in return.

This also includes understanding which behaviors we encourage in ourselves and in others that have naturally self-evolving results (this is called living) and which behaviors we discourage that create an end to evolution (this is called dying). Thus we can properly understand how to best offer "hand-ups" and avoid the trap of "hand-outs".

I will always remember a quote from one of my favorite mentors, Denis Waitley, "...when other's say to you, 'you know, I like me best when I'm with you.' And when you say to them, "I'll make you glad you stopped with me. I'll give you all the value I can, unconditional value by choice." When you have that kind of genuine character and results to prove it, you'll know your social skills are beginning to excel.

I

Intellectual exercise is as vital to progress as physical exercise. Do you routinely challenge and expand your creativity, your memory, your critical thinking capacity? Studying from the great books and brilliant leaders (avoiding those who just *think* they are brilliant) is a crucial skill and should be a habit throughout all your life. How are your problem solving skills? Are you merely a memorizer or do you continually dig deeper for the why's and lessons beneath the surface and then beneath the depths? Are you prone to being satisfied with answers or do you continually look for better questions? By the way, one of the keys to intellectual or any other area of health lies in *never* believing you have arrived. The layers beneath the surface are infinitely deep. They will keep you growing for as long as you are willing to chase and discover them. The deeper you go, the more you become aware that everything is intrinsically connected and effects everything else — in every way.

You are the only person who can advance your own knowledge and increase your own wisdom. There is a reality to the universe and it will never change. Using your cognitive reasoning capacity and your innate humanity, you can learn to recognize the principles that provide access to and allow you to accurately interact with the laws of the universe. The more you discover about those principles and the results they bring, the more your life will naturally produce the sustenance and environments that will bring you genuine and fulfilling happiness.

F

Financial health is essential. When you are worried about feeding your family, little else matters — in extreme cases, laws against theft don't matter, as Jean Valjean found out (I loved how Hugh Jackman portrayed that character in the latest version of Les Miserables). You may want to be a billionaire or you may have very modest financial goals, such details are insignificant. It is a very safe bet that you want financial security during your working life and financial independence for retirement and maybe a little something to leave to the children and your favorite charities.

In *Citizen Kane*, John Foster Kane (Orson Welles in one of his finest performances) says, "The best way to help the poor is to not be one of them." If you want to be financially secure or independent, just as in any other area of life, there are immutable laws; know and follow these laws and as sure as night time follows day, you will "win." Cheat, take short cuts, play loose with the rules and you may find short term gains, but long-lasting security is out of the question, especially if you are ever willing to give into dishonesty, even in tiny matters.

Also, it is wise to understand that if you are not achieving your financial goals, something is wrong with your formula. Just beware that most of the so-called "experts" willing to give you advice, do not understand core economics and financial principles. Also people who do understand these principles may have a hard time explaining how you can apply them because they have never been where you are. It is very important to be completely grateful for what we are currently able to earn but the moment you become contented with that, you have immediately lost the ability to earn more. Like everything else, your ability to earn is nothing more than your willingness to learn. But that means learning the right principles, from the right people. Your economy has everything to do with what is between your ears and nothing to do with anything outside yourself.

I have heard so many complaints and rants about how terrible our economic system is because it revolves around money. I challenge such people to show me a better system. Our current monetary system is flawed, but free market capitalism is the only system that has ever or can ever end poverty! It provides the greatest incentive for people to take educated risks and the leaps of faith that create a booming economy.

You've heard the old saying, "money can't buy happiness", but what kind of a naïve and foolish notion is that? In the area in which money works, noting will take its place. Where there is enough money, you will find life more comfortable, people more educated and more willing and able to share with others. Where people exist in grinding poverty, you will find far more misery and hopelessness, crime and abuse of others. That doesn't mean that more money always brings more happiness, nor does poverty always bring misery. Those kind of thoughts are foolish and only keep the poor and conventional minded declining.

People will be grateful and happy or sad and miserable based on their character and money will only magnify that character — be that character prideful or charitable; mean or kind; demeaning or ennobling; compassionate or cruel; influential or selfish. The bottom line is this: Money is a tool; more money is a tool that does more things and less money restricts your freedom to do more of what you want to do and become more of what you can become. In particular, it can empower you to control your situation, to take advantage of more opportunities to protect yourself and your family and help others in times of need. There is no such thing as too much money for anyone to have, only too little/undeveloped character. Why would anyone decide to settle for less and intentionally cut themselves off from helping more? That is a cop-out and only an excuse to be lazy and cut off your potential. Having money is no different than having friends. Why would anyone decide to have less of the right kind of friends? Understanding the principles that govern money it is all it takes. As financial guru Dave Ramsey likes to remind his fans, "if you are willing to live like no one else, you'll be able to live like no one else."

C

Chronology is a constant over which you have no control. As Hyrum Smith, co-founder of Franklin-Covey, has taught, you can't manage time, you can only manage yourself. You do this by regulating the time and energy you put into any given effort. That regulation (or management, if you prefer) is crucial to maximizing your return on investment (ROI).

Time and energy are the dynamic duo of SPESIFCs — they are the most basic resources you invest in any effort and they are the most valuable resource in the universe, simply because they are absolutely irreplaceable. They are required for everything you hope to do and hope to become. They are never stagnant but are ever-fleeting and, once they are gone, it is impossible to get them back. This is where "the rubber meets the road." What you choose to do with these resources is the unfailing standard by which you can easily measure your priorities in life and your effectiveness and efficiency in all areas. By this you can reasonably predict where you will be at any given point in the future.

Your "chronological health", therefore, consists of how effectively you allocate the time and energy (or priorities) for each task in each **SPESIFC** area of your life. Are you on a trajectory of decline and decrease or incline and increase?

Conclusion

Everything you will ever deal with in the length of your life is covered in these seven areas. Although there is a lot to learn about each area, they are all based on simple principles. With your past choices, you have created the exact results you are now experiencing in each of these areas.

As we go along, you will notice how your life can become simpler and more manageable by giving proper priority to the SPESIFCs. Instead of countless things to keep track of, you now only have seven basic areas to manage and this makes measuring your progress much simpler.

So, is your overall spiritual health poor, mediocre, extraordinary or miraculous? What about your physical, emotional, social, intellectual, financial and chronological health? Would you like to significantly increase your abilities, wisdom and miraculous results in one or more of these areas?

Many great speakers and writers have compared our lives to a chain. Each area of life or success is one individual link in the chain. Regardless of how strong you may be in other areas; you are only as strong as your weakest link. The problems in your life are actually blessings because they show you your weak links and provide incentives and direction to strengthen them. As you continue to learn about and apply the principles upon which all results are based, you will be able to systematically solve every problem in your life by turning those weak links into powerful ones.

Chapter 3
The Truth about Truth

I am sure you have heard many people explain how one person's truth is different from another person's truth. This is called "relativism". It's been taught in public schools and universities across our country for generations and is a total, absolute *lie*! The difficulty in recognizing the fallacy of this claim is compounded by the fact that the ego does everything it can to convince you that you are right, even when you are dead wrong and have no reasonable or logical explanation or solid understanding of why you believe as you do. I have had conversations with many people about this subject, and I need to deal with it here in the beginning.

To repeat, the idea that truth is relative is absolutely and unequivocally wrong. For the most part, it isn't your fault if you have been taught and believe that truth is relative, but to persist in believing such a fallacy is deadly. It makes people naïve at best or willfully ignorant at worst. It's not easy to shake off what you have been taught for years by teachers, parents and other authority figures, and I understand that. People use the concept of relative truth to justify their own insecurities and lack of achievement, and they want to convince you of it as well so they have license to continue to accept it for themselves. People don't like to be personally and uncomfortably accountable for the truth, when to do so would force them to change their thoughts, habits, and behaviors. Belief in relativity is the easy way out in the moment, but if you buy into it, it will confine you to an unfulfilled and very frustrating life of ultimate failure.

My advice to you is to love the people who believe in and teach relative truth but be wary of them. If they are teachable, encourage and help them see reality, realizing always that you cannot do it for them. Give them a copy of this book. If they are not teachable, continue to be friendly toward them, but don't let them influence your life and that will take significantly limiting your time with them. They are probably decent, well-meaning, wonderful people (and, of course, they are God's children), but they cannot help you discover and thrive within the truth when they are stagnating outside the truth.

Now, it is obviously true that individuals possess different pieces of truth. That is a no-brainer. The ultimate truth, however, the truth underlying the kind of success I am talking about, can never be different from one person to another. People can do different things and follow different formulas to create success, but if a formula produces true success, it is a part of the ultimate truth or, at least steps in the right direction. The more truth you understand, the better you will see the big picture of reality and how every piece of truth harmonizes with every other piece to create the whole, just like a jigsaw puzzle.

Ultimately, no two different formulas can create the exact same results. If two people are working for the same result with two different formulas, one will be more effective and efficient than the other. When I was in Jr. High School, I took a job on a logging crew. My first job was harnessing our work horse and skidding the cut and trimmed logs to the road so they were ready for loading on the trucks. Years later we purchased a big skidder/tractor. Even though there were advantages with the horse, all in all the big skidder could pull far more logs in a quicker time, was easier to maintain and made the work with horses obsolete.

I was teaching this concept in a class several years ago when a lady spoke up indignantly. "That is NOT true. I have several children (I think it was 6) and I promise you that there is not one formula that works best with all of them. They are all different so I have to use different formulas on each of them. "I responded with something like, "I'm glad you recognize that. Of course you have to treat them different, but that is the point, they are all different people with different needs and desires. If they were all exactly the same, you would need to treat them the same. But because they are all different, there is a different formula that will work ideally with each one. However, they are also consistently changing as people and so you need to continue to change your formulas to best suit each of them as they change."

Specifically, for one of your children, there is an ideal way to treat that particular child. You may or may not have found that one group of formulae that works absolute best for that specific child. The trick to being a good parent is to understand each child's unique personality, gifts and weaknesses and do your best to facilitate their growth in optimal ways accordingly.

I like to relate this subject to John Godfrey Saxe's version of the ancient parable about the blind men and the elephant:

It was six men of Indostan
To learning much inclined,
Who went to see the Elephant
(Though all of them were blind),
That each by observation
Might satisfy his mind.

The First approached the Elephant
And happening to fall
Against his broad and sturdy side,
At once began to bawl:
"God bless me! But the Elephant
Is very like a *wall*!"

The Second, feeling of the tusk,
Cried, "Ho, what have we here,
So very round and smooth and sharp?
To me 'tis mighty clear

This wonder of an Elephant
Is very like a *spear*!"

The Third approached the animal
And happening to take
The squirming trunk within his hands,
Thus boldly up and spake:
"I see," quoth he, "the Elephant
Is very like a *snake*!"

The Fourth reached out an eager hand
And felt about the knee
"What most this wondrous beast is like
Is mighty plain," quoth he:
"'Tis clear enough the Elephant
Is very like a *tree*!"

The Fifth, who chanced to touch the ear,
Said: "E'en the blindest man
Can tell what this resembles most;
Deny the fact who can,
The marvel of this Elephant
Is very like a *fan*!"

The Sixth no sooner had begun
About the beast to grope,
Then seizing on the swinging tail
That fell within his scope,
"I see," quoth he, "the Elephant
Is very like a *rope*!"

And so these men of Indostan
Disputed loud and long,
Each in his own opinion
Exceeding stiff and strong.
Though each was partly in the right
And all were in the wrong!

For my own purposes, I rewrote the last verse into two verses to portray this message in a way that makes it less likely to be misunderstood, to reflect reality, and to dispel the myths about it so it is easier to draw out of it its intrinsic value:

And so these men of Indostan
Disputed loud and long,
Each in his own opinion
Exceeding stiff and strong.

Though each believed that he was right
Were all completely wrong!

For an elephant's an elephant,
Not a wall, a rope or tree,
And certainly not like a spear
Or fan or snake, you see.
So none were right
'Cause all were wrong.
As wrong as wrong can be.

Every time I've ever heard this story, it was told by someone trying to show how we all have pieces of the truth but miss the big picture. They conclude their "lesson" (actually falsehood) by teaching that we are all right but are simply limited in our understanding of the big picture. They use that idea to convince us that everyone is right in our own way. But that is complete foolishness. Are we all right in our own way? Of course not! The idea is absurd. But that is our political correct "conventional wisdom." "We can't hurt anyone's feelings, so we need to show everybody how they are all right." Right? No, Wrong!

You see, if two or more people disagree on any one specific thing (like what an elephant is for example) either one of them is right and all the rest are wrong or they are all wrong. Here is the reality, an elephant has absolutely zero intrinsic value to anyone who perceives it as anything other than it really is. On the other hand, the more you understand the truth about elephants, the more valuable elephants will be to you and to those you serve with them. And isn't that the bottom line? What good does it do you to have a bunch of information in your head that is of no value? If you can't use it to improve your life, it's called "trivia," and trivia, by its definition, has no intrinsic value.

An elephant is not even close to being like a rope. It is an elephant. If you believe it is a rope, or anything remotely like a rope, you will only become discouraged and stop trying to use the elephant because it can never function adequately for you. Or, you'll continue to try and use the elephant as a rope and you'll only end up with a very angry elephant (and that would be bad, not good)! The only accurate standard to measure how much a person actually understands is through the results they produce for themselves and others around them as well as how long those results will self-perpetuate. The more truth you understand, the better you are in creating success in every area of your life, and the better the results you produce — period.

Truth alone puts you in control of your own life results. The only reason people have problems is because they have not discovered or at least did not live by the principles that surround the problem. If you try to live an illusion, your life will have problems to the exact degree of the illusion. All of us have some understanding of the truth but all our understandings are incomplete. This is not a negative, it is just the reality of mortal life. You have two choices — you can keep striving to obtain greater truth or you will continue in semi-ignorance, which is actually worse than complete ignorance.

Without the truth, you are in bondage, never able to accomplish what's possible. Jesus, among many other sages, said "and the truth shall make you free." He might as easily have said, "Only with the truth are you free but without the truth, you are in bondage." Genuine happiness comes from personal fulfillment and, until you are free to fulfill your own personal destiny, the happiness you seek will be forever beyond your reach. The price for freedom is your personal commitment to deliberately discover the truth — "the whole truth and nothing but the truth" as we say in court. Consistently applying that truth — with specific intent so that it actually improves your life — is what we mean when we say "living a principled life".

Confucius said, "They must often change who would be constant in happiness or wisdom." First, in order to achieve a true state of happiness, you must become wise, for genuine, lasting happiness can only be found in wisdom. Second, in order to be consistently happy, your wisdom must increase on a consistent basis. Third, in order to routinely become wiser, you must be willing to face and embrace and even learn to love the process of consistent change (that mostly means changing your mind from error to truth).

As you really discover truth, you will be excited to also see that your behaviors, habits, thoughts, paradigms and even your character changes, many times effortlessly, to reflect the greater truth you now understand which in turn can also increase your wisdom and happiness. The choice to remain in a static state of habit and refuse to be flexible will bring misery and frustration because you will only continue to create the same problems over and over again — and those problems will continue to escalate as they create more and more decay in your life. (That's called dying, not living).

The scriptures teach us that God does not change, therefore, truth is unchangeable. While God is perfect and does not change, we humans have a long way to go. The closer you come to discovering that ultimate truth, the better, easier, and more exciting your life becomes. These are the truths upon which principles are founded.

All you need to do is look back over the past few hundred years. Once upon a time, in the not-so-distant past, most people on earth believed the world was flat and the center of the universe. Reality was never affected in the smallest degree by those false beliefs. The world just went on being exactly what it is.

Once people began to understand the truth about the world, they immediately began to develop a greater awareness about the truth in different areas as well, and this blossoming of knowledge led to the period of history known as the

Renaissance. That is the way of life, one truth always provides opportunity to learn more which has led us to today and which, if we continue in that mode, we will soon find ourselves in a future that will make today seem like the Dark Ages. The opposite is also true: one illusion or falsehood, if not corrected, leads to others, until we really do regress to the Dark Ages of the past. That cycle is prevalent throughout history.

Do you make the most of learning opportunities or do you let them pass by? Fortunately, even if you fall prey to an illusion — again, we all do it at times — if you habitually take advantage of learning the next lesson made available to you, you will discover the truth sooner or later. On the other hand, if you do not habitually question the supposed truths you have been taught, the resulting falsehoods will take over your life, and you will one day experience a mighty painful crash onto the rocks of reality.

Chapter 4
Universal Laws and Principles

Universal laws are the cornerstones on which the universe was created and the foundation upon which all existence functions — on which matter, energy, time and intelligence act and react. These are the laws of physics and mathematics, the law of the harvest, the unchanging roles of gender, and on and on. Aware of them or not, you are constantly interacting with these laws every day of your life. You cannot change them or break them. As Zig Ziglar often said, "If you step out of a tenth story window, you don't defy the law of gravity, you confirm it."

Principles are processes that follow from these laws and give us access to them. For example, gravity says humans can't fly, however, if you apply correct principles, such as "When thrust plus lift is greater than gravity plus drag, any object can fly". You aren't *breaking* the law of gravity; you are applying principles to harness and *harmonize with* the laws of gravity and aerodynamics to obtain the desired result. Let's bring it down to a simple, real life example:

Several years ago, as a custom cabinet maker, I received a blueprint and specification sheet from a general contractor who asked me to build and install a custom, built-in entertainment center and a China hutch for his client. I had never met the contractor or his client before. I had never seen the home where my pieces would be installed. I had never seen this particular style of furniture before. About two weeks after the project was completed, I received a very nice thank you and bonus because what I had built was beautiful and functional beyond their expectations.

Now, as impressed as my clients were, this experience really isn't particularly special. The construction and installation of quality furniture does require skill, but skill is essentially a product of education — which includes the right kind of practice. I got the accolades and bonus because I understood a few laws and correctly applied the principles that produced a result even better than my clients expected. In the simplest possible terms, I did my job well. In any industry or endeavor, the better you understand the laws (the deeper your intelligence) and apply the right principles (the higher level of skills you have) of that industry, the greater ability you have to be more flexible and creative while maintaining the structural integrity of the things that you create.

In addition, if you use that intelligence and those skills in win-win endeavors, and truly operate on the cutting edge of your potential, you are in the process of becoming wiser. Wisdom is the great key that produces genuine fulfillment, happiness and success — the wiser you are, the greater miracles you will create.

On the other hand, the less you understand about these laws and principles, the more you will inadvertently behave contrary to them. If you justify cutting-corners, being selfish, dishonest or sacrifice your integrity in any other way, you inadvertently decay instead of grow. It isn't always evident in the beginning, but time and truth are inseparable companions and always edify each other in the long run. Time will, sooner or later, bring you face to face with the consequences of your decisions

For example, if you decided to grow tomatoes, how successful will your harvest be if you lived in North Dakota and started planting in August? Under normal outdoor garden and climate conditions, even if the ground, fertilizer, cultivating and watering systems were ideal, you wouldn't harvest any tomatoes in the middle of a northern winter regardless of how much you believed you would. All the contrary feelings in the world are irrelevant. Only reality is relevant. In the beginning, you might believe you are making great progress as you see the sprouts shoot from the ground and begin to grow. But, when that first freeze comes, you come face to face with the cold, hard facts (only a little pun intended) that your efforts and resources will not pay off, at least not this year. There is one possible success at this point: You can learn from this experience that planting tomatoes in the spring works better. If you decide to raise sheep, build a factory, dig a ditch or build a friendship, if you operate contrary to universal law, you will never realize the kind of harvest you want.

By the same token, every single problem that has ever bothered you is the result of some failure to understand universal laws and adequately apply the principles attached to them. You cannot control your life unless you have a clear and correct understanding of laws and principles. This may concern some readers, thinking they have to master every law and principle to be effective and happy. That is not true. No one on earth is perfect and yet many people are genuinely effective and happy. On the other hand, you do have potential to get better and the quicker you do, the more effective and happy you will be. You just have to learn the truth and avoid the illusions of truth.

Everyone is born with a conscience and if you learn to recognize and follow yours, it will guide you to the truth. The more you ignore it, the more you will have painful, natural consequences. Not out of some kind of punishment but from simple cause and effect. Life also brings opportunities to learn from practical experience, unfortunately, most of the time we don't pay enough attention or try to blame our problems on someone or something else and so we miss the lessons. We also make false assumptions because of our limited understanding which also keeps us from the results we want. But if we simply understand that if we don't have the result, we either don't have the right formula or we haven't followed it long enough, which is only part of the formula.

If we remain or return to being diligent, we begin to see how principles are the action arms of the laws and understand how the laws apply to all situations. If you truly seek wisdom, you will consistently experiment to discover more about how laws and principles work and thus how to improve your results. The more you grasp principles, the more you will understand how to solve problems and improve results, even when events take you far outside your experience. So if you find yourself discouraged when things don't work like you want. Just know that if you persist, it is impossible for you not to discover the truth/the right formula. Then the results you create will speak for themselves that you have found and applied the right formula.

It reminds me of my first real girlfriend. We were both in Jr High School. She was a beautiful Native American girl and I thought I would be *In Love forever.* We dated for about a year until she started getting interested in another guy. How dare her? How could that happen? I was doing everything right and so this was not fair, right? But what is the right formula? What is fair? Is that according to my rules or her rules that I didn't understand or was not willing to live by? Even relationships function or not, according to cause and effect. And nothing to do with luck or fate or chance or meeting someone else or money or any other lame excuses we come up with. If I had really put enough energy and creativity into understanding her and how she felt and what made her feel valuable and loved and stopped my stupid thinking that only how I was the victim, that wouldn't have happened. Any relationship can keep growing forever as long as the other person is important enough to you. I'll bet you have your own stories about that. ☺.

Those who do not seek continual improvement can expect failures to compound themselves, bringing more pain and struggle. This is one of the biggest reasons we see individuals, families, businesses, organizations, governments, etc., start off and do well but in time crash and burn.

The world and its limitless abundance is your birthright but, like anything worthwhile, it takes the right intelligence and skills and character and insight to obtain it and then to keep it. Sadly, many advertisers and marketers deceitfully try to talk us into buying things by telling us that we "deserve" something better than we have. The reality is that no one in the world "deserves" what they do not have. The universe has no choice but to follow these laws of cause-and-effect. What you deserve is exactly what you have, nothing less, and nothing more. If you want something different, you have to do something different, only then will you deserve something different.

Now, I can already hear many people saying, "That's not true! What about child abuse, slavery, all kinds of oppression, murder and all manner of other evils. 1st, I will address all that in some upcoming chapters but just for a tiny insight, It is true that many people are too immature or powerless to control some of the circumstances others impose on them. In many of those cases, it is yours and my responsibility to change things. We just have to be wise enough to make sure the changes we make are in everyone's best interest and will not make things worse. If we do not have to fight to solve our own problems, we will never have the strength or the wisdom to solve our future problems and become powerful leaders for positive change.

You absolutely CAN deserve what you want, but only after you apply the principles (consistently) that create what you want. (We'll talk much more about that later in this book). Again, all consequences, including both prosperity and lack, are governed by law, not by luck. You create your own results by your decisions. Specifically, your decisions either clash against and offend or harmonize with and honor these laws and principles and create the results of your life. Those results are the measure of the fallacy or correctness of your decisions. To enjoy abundance, therefore, you must continue to diligently discover what makes things die and what makes them grow and then act accordingly. As you do this consistently, grace will flow more and more freely into your life.

It is all about accessing the right laws by way of the right principles — cause and effect rules the universe and everyone in it. It brings new meaning and power to the challenge, "wake up and live!"

Summary

Universal laws have existed forever. They never began. They will never change. They are the great constants in the universe. Correct principles enable us to make use of the universal laws in practical situations. The more you understand both, the better your results will be.

As Ralph Waldo Emerson so aptly wrote, "Let him learn a prudence of higher strain. Let him learn that everything in nature, even dust and feathers, go by law and not by luck, and what he sows, he reaps."

You alone have capacity to make these laws your enemies or your allies:

If you make them your enemies, you will bring yourself pain. It may not be immediate, but it is certain. (This is a problem this book is designed to solve.) All the pleading, wishing, hoping, excuses, justifications and prayers in the world won't solve your problem. As Abraham Lincoln wisely affirmed, "If the end brings me out all right, then what is said against me won't amount to anything. If the end brings me out wrong, then ten angels swearing I was right would make no difference."

If you make them your allies, you will consistently find more and more relief from the pains and sorrows of life. The deliberate process of harmonizing yourself with universal laws will open you to ever greater success. As you also consistently cultivate right character, these laws will bring you better health, more happiness and greater peace. The process isn't always easy, in fact, sometimes the cure may be more painful than the disease — but the pain of the cure is temporary, whereas the pain of the disease will sooner or later kill you if you continue. This process is sometimes referenced as the universal laws of "repentance" and "forgiveness."

Chapter 5
The Core Human Objective: Our Quest for Perfection

The great Og Mandino, in his book *The Greatest Salesman in the World,* stated, "I will always aim my spear at the moon, for is it not better to aim at the moon and strike only an eagle, than to aim at an eagle and strike only a rock?"

I used to say I can show you not only how to aim at the moon but to hit the moon. However, I have recently changed that because, today, we've already hit the moon. We've already landed on Mars — far past the moon. We need goals that force us to reach way beyond our potential, so now I say let's hit the stars! To hit the stars within an optimal time frame requires a quest for perfection, and perfection demands a deeper understanding of the truth. I believe for the most part, people want to know the truth. I know that anything less than a goal of perfection will stop you short of your potential, and stopping short of your potential will keep you aiming for eagles and leaving you with mostly rocks.

Striving for perfection is a scary prospect for most people. "Nobody's perfect" is a cliché because it's true. Unfortunately, most teachers (who should know better) water down this quest for perfection to a quest for excellence. How often have you heard phrases like these?

"Forget perfection, there is no such thing."

"You will never reach perfection, so will always be disappointed if you try."

"Reach for progress, not for perfection."

And so on. Each of us is given a short span of life. Some choose to take 20 years to learn something they could've learned in six months. Learning it (whatever it is) in 20 years is progress, and you should be grateful for it, but is that really cause for celebration, or cause to kick yourself in the rear and re-evaluate your priorities? You need to recognize how much time and resources you wasted along the way. That kind of progress certainly doesn't make miracles or achieve great dreams. It only keeps us wallowing in mediocrity and failure.

What is the difference between shooting for excellence and shooting for perfection?

For the purposes of this discussion, I'm defining *excellence* as "performing at the optimal level of your current capability". That's not a worthy goal. Excellence is what you ought to be right now. Why would we set a goal to do something in the future that we should be doing now? I understand that The "Pursuit of Excellence" means being better today than yesterday and better tomorrow than today. But that still falls very short of optimal potential if it does not include perfection as soon as possible. Without the perfection part, there is far too much license for misunderstanding and underestimating your real potential and falling into the fatal habit of procrastination.

Likewise, for this discussion, I'm defining *perfection* as "performing at the optimal level". Not *your* optimal level, *the* optimal level, there's a difference. Perfection is your potential and pursuing it is where miracles happen. One quick example, by way of explanation: Samuel F. B. Morse developed a working electrical telegraph in 1837. People could suddenly communicate over vast distances using coded messages. It worked, and it worked really well; everybody was happy with it. Then, Alexander Graham Bell asked himself, wouldn't it be more efficient if the electricity could move real voices over wires? In 1876, Bell patented the telephone. It worked, and it worked really well; everybody (except parents of teenagers) was very happy with it. Then, a few people got the idea that phones without wires would be better. It's almost scary to think about what people are thinking up for the next generation.

The point is obvious: Morse tried to make communications perfect and he stretched the technology of his decade to its limit. Telegraph was excellent, not optimal. Bell took the foundation Morse laid and build on it, trying to making communication perfect, stretching the technology of his decade to its limit Landline telephones were excellent, not optimal. Cell phones are excellent, but are they optimal? Of course not! The difference was a simple question crazy people kept asking and answering: "Is this good enough?" And the answer is "no, so what is?" We must be grateful for the progress we've made, but we must never be content with it!

Another important point — shooting for excellence gives you license to compare your performance against someone else's, much like the comparisons we see every day in competitive sports and in business. But like Zig Ziglar said, "Success can never be measured by what you have done compared to what someone else has done. You might have ten times the ability. Success can only be measured by what *you have done*, compared to what *you could have done* with what God gave you" (emphasis added).

Our culture is obsessed with rewarding winners of competitions. This is understandable, the simplest method of measuring success from the outside is to compare one thing to another, based on some standard (possibly a very arbitrary standard) to define "the winner". It is far more difficult to quantifiably measure a person's heart, character and potential and how far they have progressed.

Unfortunately, most competition today is only about beating another person or team, regardless of how we performed according to our potential. We would be infinitely better off if we really analyzed "what is our ultimate potential and how can we push past that, regardless of the competition?"

The measurement of a person's heart, character and potential is to see what intrinsic value has actually been added to their life and to the world. What progress have you made compared to what you could have made? Victory over yourself is the only victory worthy of accolades because that personal victory is the only thing you get to keep once the momentary thrill of competition fades with the lights, the cheering and the dwindling crowds. Once you are back with yourself, what have you become? Once you step back into the real world, what do you have to offer?

How can you lift yourself and encourage others to achieve that sense of fulfillment and genuine peace of mind and happiness that never ends? Many top athletes, actors and other celebrity types command huge salaries, yet give very little to the world in terms of real value. This is *not* just about celebrities; the vast majority of typical citizens rarely get out of their own way long enough to make an impact that makes the world a better place. Conversely, a few amazing celebrities and business people are some of the most philanthropic people in the world and there are a few men and women who quietly, consistently produce miraculous results far from the camera's greedy eye — no fame, no fortune, just ordinary people who make extra-ordinary, even miraculous contributions.

The only realistic and important measurement is how you are doing compared to how you were doing last year, last quarter, last month, last week, yesterday or this morning. Measuring your current progress against your past progress frees you from competing against anyone else with different abilities and trials. This is a system that works beautifully for every person in every situation.

I am often asked, "So what is my best," or, "When is 'good enough' good enough?"

For you, I have no idea. You are the only person who can answer that about you. The processes in this book will help you optimize your activities but the best results you can obtain from any activity will result from your continued quest for superior intelligence. Your determination to improve your skills by paying closer attention to the details and results of your activities. Your willingness to always challenge your motives and intentions to love and show compassion and live every day with courage and how well you learn to (pardon the cliché) think outside the box to maximize that activity like only your unique potential can, like no one ever did it before. If you want to live a happy and fulfilled life, there is no such thing as "good enough" for those high-priority activities.

As a young carpenter, I used to joke, "Oh, it's good enough for who it's for." Then I started building and doing high-end finish work in church houses. While I always tried to do a good job, that experience pushed me to take a more sober look at my performance. Whether it was a mobile home, a commercial building or a mansion, the owners deserved my respect and best effort. I decided to never say that again on any project and to always push my abilities and results to the next level.

What a tragedy it is to stop at being merely excellent when miracles are just around the corner. Imagine that you succeeded in blessing the lives of a hundred people in need, especially when the norm was only being able to bless five. Would that be excellent? Would that make you happy and fulfilled? Possibly, but like all questions, these come with an answer, "It depends." That evokes another question, "What if, with just a little more effort, I could've blessed the lives of a thousand people in need?" Where is the contentment now? How hollow are accolades that echo in the caverns of regret? Especially if you knew you could have done just that little more but justified quitting because you were tired or board or afraid or because you had already done more than others, even if you didn't realize the result could have been that much bigger. You may be able to hide the fact that you missed your mark from those who applaud you, but the thought of what you could have done will haunt you forever unless you are willing to drink from that bitter cup, gather your courage and guarantee that your next efforts are more worthy of your potential.

My dad's words will forever ring in my ears when I used to complain about things being difficult. "The real difficult things we can do immediately. The impossible just takes a little longer."

You might recall I mentioned repentance a few pages back. Some people assume repentance is only a religious concept, turning away from sin and back to God. It is that, but repentance is a much bigger principle as it applies to every situation in every part of your life. It is the realization that you came short of perfection and the commitment to eventually discover what perfect looks like.

Setting true perfection as your goal will drive you to your very best performance. Compounding those best efforts over the course of years and, ultimately, a lifetime, is the difference between owning a wheel barrow full of gold and owning gold mines around the world (literally or metaphorically speaking).

You will never know how high your efforts can take you until you pursue perfection with a passion and a firm resolve to achieve it. Perfection is my ultimate goal and it wasn't until I mustered the courage to diligently pursue it that my life finally blossomed into the most passionate of journeys.

Almost every person I have ever studied encourages people to forget about perfection — even people from whom I have learned much and to whom I owe many of my amazing transformations. So why am I telling you to shoot for perfection in the face of almost total rejection of that principle? In one way, they are right to turn you away from perfection, but only if you are prone to short-term thinking. In the most important ways however they are dead wrong as the right kind of long-term thinking has the power to keep you on track with your potential

At this point in your journey, you obviously don't know what perfection looks and feels like (no one on Earth really does), but the closer you get, the more your vision of it clarifies, and that is a good thing. Within every experience is a new awareness and clues to what and how you can do better next time. Go with the changes and get excited because that is a clue you are getting closer.

Besides, a desire for perfection is a core human emotion. Virtually everyone wishes they could be perfect, at least at something. As long as you don't get tripped up and waste time and energy trying to make something perfect before you have the capacity to make it perfect, why would you try to suppress that desire and get inferior results instead of using it to your advantage for optimal results?

I call this the difference between *perfectionism* and *pursuing perfection*.

Perfectionism is chasing an impossible standard and that will kill you. It will cost you enormous amounts of wasted time, energy and personal growth. It is the attempt — even a compulsion — to hang onto a task until it is absolutely perfect when you do not have the ability to make it perfect. Then you really have failed because you can't make it perfect. Perfectionism will keep you from starting tasks because you are afraid you don't have the knowledge, skills or resources to create an absolutely perfect outcome.

Pursuing perfection, on the other hand, is an ultimate long-term goal. It is something that will take major time, focus and energy to achieve. It also means that you don't have to be perfect right now. Only pursuing perfection holds you to an optimal standard that enables you to put your very best effort into any project and deliberately learning from each experience to the maximum degree.

I use "pursuing perfection" as a catalyst to give me what some in the world of self-help refer to as "the advantage of a slight edge." It is that little extra that makes the difference between the gold medal and the bronze — or, more likely, between the gold medal and no medal at all. It is the difference between creating poor, mediocre, or even extraordinary results vs. miraculous results. It will keep you focused on expanding what and how you do things in order to gain maximum benefits from each experience. You can take pride in what and how you do things now because everything you do is in a state of evolution, an improvement over your last experience. In the meantime, you are finding a balance between doing your best and not wasting time. At the same time, you are still holding your feet to the fire so you can't make excuses and justifications for failure or for less than your best. It will enable you to be completely grateful and happy with today's excellent results while simultaneously not dulling your cutting edge so that tomorrow's effort will be as much better as possible.

I have heard so many people say that it is depressing, and even debilitating, to your psyche to keep reaching for things you cannot hope to achieve. But those people do not understand the "pursuit of perfection." They are also mistaken about the true expanse of human potential. I personally promise you that this is a crucial perspective that has enabled me to push through years of countless setbacks —

going from poverty to abundance in every area of my life. This pursuit also keeps me jazzed every day with a passion to create a bigger and better tomorrow.

So how do you know when you've done your best? When is good enough, good enough? How do you know you couldn't have done any more? Isn't it all right to be pleased with what you've accomplished — especially if it has turned out to be an excellent result? What really is your best?

Those are great questions. Achievements absolutely should be celebrated but now you can also use what you have learned to strive for better results next time. No goal or objective will push your limits and maximize your potential like the ultimate pursuit of perfection. Everything else leaves you wondering if you could have been better or done more.

When it comes to making improvements, I have a simple plan: First, I examine what worked and what didn't — you have to be brutally honest with yourself here. Second, I make note of why things didn't end better and how I could have given more and done better with what I already had. Finally, I commit to make those improvements next time — but based on my unlimited potential for perfection, nothing less. My after-action report for project A becomes part of my plan for project B. Sounds simple? It is, that is the beauty of the system. It really is that simple and it has enabled me to get closer to really doing my best, and, eventually (even if it is after this life), to win the ultimate prize of perfection.

If you make mistakes (which we all do) just make sure you learn as much as possible from them. It is even okay to beat yourself up sometimes when you have allowed yourself to become distracted and messed up, but it's never okay to leave yourself wounded. There is an element of forgiveness here, also, that perfectionists harbor negative feelings for not being perfect and therefore damage their health in every SPESIFC area of life because they don't forgive themselves. Those pursuing perfection on the other hand have much less need to forgive themselves because they understand that mistakes are simply part of learning. As long as they are doing their best, they have not done anything wrong but in fact have done things right. When they are in need of forgiveness, they are much more able to forgive themselves and others quickly and get back to living.

So, never let go of your goal of perfection. Aim for the stars. Remember that every result you ever produce will bring with it opportunities to learn, reach higher and achieve more. Expect that, learn to love the lessons, and that paradigm will propel you into accomplishing your divine purpose and potential.

Now, I know that I talk in pretty grandiose terms, but only because your future can be incredibly grandiose. At the same time, I also see how striving for perfection can be overwhelming. But I offer to you the words of the Master from the plains of Galilee. Have you ever noticed that every single time someone came to him with a problem, even huge, seemingly impossible problems, He always offered comfort and counsel such as: "Fear not." "Why weepest thou?" "Let not your heart be troubled, neither let it be afraid." "Oh ye of little faith, be of good cheer." "Peace be unto you." "As ye believe, so shall it be done unto you," Etc. His mission was a constant stream of encouragement. All growth happens "line upon line, precept upon precept… [and] by small and simple things, are great things brought to pass."

Why did He offer such comfort? Because He knows that people's problems are not as big as they think they are. He understood that there is always a way. He can see solutions where we cannot. He realizes that if we discover how to "have faith as a grain of mustard seed," (I'll define faith later in this book in a way that will surprise and delight you) that we can solve our own problems by learning and growing and understanding these secret ancient principles. In other words, exercise your faith, be persistent, stop focusing on problems and start focusing on solutions and rewards.

Chapter 6
How to Activate the Gift of Grace

Grace is that hand-up that enables us to accomplish worthy goals and objectives that are bigger than ourselves. "Grace" is defined, among other things, as "a manifestation of favor, especially by a superior." Generally, most of us think in terms of the "grace of God" meaning divine intervention on our behalf. Certainly, there's a lot of that in the world (and there could be much more), but grace can also be given by humans — mentors, friends, strangers, etc. — sometimes openly and publicly, sometimes silently and anonymously.

Grace bridges the gap between our best efforts and our commitment to achieve self-evolution and eventual perfection. It is given (by God, angels or our fellow humans) for the express purpose that the receiver of grace also eventually becomes the giver — that is what the "pay it forward" concept is also based on. The more you push yourself to grow and increase — with integrity — while learning to offer to others what you have been given, the more grace is extended to you.

Although we know about the basics of this gift of grace, we do not understand exactly how it works. Grace is a dynamic that interweaves throughout every aspect of our lives. Every person receives some significant portions of grace, from the air we breathe, to the people who provided our food, clothing, shelter and education when we are too young to do so for ourselves, to the very Earth itself that sustains our lives.

You can learn how to prepare for grace and activate it. You cannot tell exactly when or how it will manifest itself, but we do know, as Benjamin Disraeli, a British conservative politician and writer (who twice served as Prime Minister) discovered, that as we push ourselves to grow, "Nothing can resist the human will that will stake even its existence on its stated purpose."

"God wants You to be Blessed so You can be a Blessing."

Grace takes care of you while you are in the process of learning to apply correct principles. Applying false principles literally causes physical and spiritual damage to your body and soul, and that's why there is death in the world. In this life principles are miraculously accompanied with a provision of grace. This grace enables you to gather the information you need to learn and make corrections along your journey without being destroyed against the laws you accidentally break in the process.

Whenever anyone accepts grace without investing and growing from it, they have just changed it from a hand-*up* to a hand-*out* and as a result, the next time they want it, it requires a higher price. Every time someone gets something for nothing, someone else had to get nothing for something, and in the process, both become more of nothing than something. Essentially, refusing to use grace as a way to grow in abilities and character means you will restrict or even cut yourself off from the ability to receive grace in the future.

There are five crucial keys to prepare yourself for grace. The more you neglect these five keys, the more grace is restricted from you. The better you get at these, the more grace will be there for you when you at the right time:

G

Gratitude is consistently acknowledging and sincerely expressing thanks for the grace you receive.

R

Resolve is a commitment to achieve your worthy goals in spite of all opposition. It is not "if I can"; it is "whatever it takes!"

A

Action is your commitment to start now. Not only with study and preparation but with personal experience and practical application. It take humility and courage to be willing to be vulnerable and be bad at something until you get good and then great, then become a master and beyond.

C

Charity is your own love of self, measured by an absolute commitment to expand your own potential along with the love and compassion to share your wins with others around you as hand-ups, never hand-outs.

E

Education is continually learning as much as you can from the best mentors you can as often as you can and making sure you are learning what will assist you most in achieving your full potential.

This principle of grace reminds me of a story I heard long ago about a preacher driving down the road. As he came around a bend, he was taken by surprise with the most beautiful farm he had ever seen. The buildings were kept in neat and clean condition, the fences freshly painted. The furrows in the fields near perfectly straight and cultivated to a tee. The animals in prime health.

Full of awe, he pulled his car to the side of the road, just to take a more careful look and noticed the farmer working his way toward him in the field. We waited till the farmer arrived and offered a friendly hello. The preacher shook the farmers hand and said, "God has blessed you with a beautiful farm!" The farmer replied

"Yes He has and I thank Him every day for it. But you should have seen this place when God had it all to himself."

The farmer understood well that it was his own labor of love, his own pursuit of perfection combined with God's grace that created his farm. The farmer understood well that God would never have done it without him and that he could have never done it without God.

There are those who would have us believe that people who assume the greater risks and choose delayed gratification have a harder, less joyful life. That is one of the great lies of modern culture. Mediocrity — living below your potential, never reaping the grand rewards that could have been yours — is far harder and virtually completely void of real joy.

If you fail to make plans or fail to follow through with the plans you make, understand that your life will have a lot of unnecessary, extended struggle and pain. Think of the people who live paycheck to paycheck — once their money is gone, they have to start all over and work to collect more resources so they can survive another short period of time. They never get ahead because they consume all they produce. Even if they save up, they still only have that much more to consume at a later date because they cannot or will not practice and improve mindsets and strategies that move their economics upward.

The Investment Mindset

Just for the record, even though I talk about money while talking about this Investment Mindset, cultivating this principle will bring you the same effects in every other area of your life.

The opposite of an Investment Mindset is a Consumer Mindset. There are many who think they are investors but are really only glorified consumers. Even the majority who earn money in the stock and commodities markets or other areas of "earning money from money." Those who mistakenly believe they are investors might save up a nest egg and then buy something with it in order to resell it for a profit. This is a linear transaction and is not self-sustainable. Even though this allows a person to collect more than simply trading time for dollars or to make a profit, he or she is not truly investing, regardless of where the capital comes from.

Even if things go well with these Consumer Mindset transactions, even if they have more capital to use next time, once they collect, they have to start all over again to find another transaction to create another chunk of profit. Money or resources used this way among the masses who call themselves "investors" because they are in the stock market, commodities and similar things are in the same boat. This mindset brings about a whole slew of other problems and issues that I will address in the future.

If you think about it, everyone is trying to get a "return of investment" in some form, through everything they do. Most actually make poor investments because they end up with less than they started with.

People with a true Investor Mindset, however, think differently. They don't save what they can, they save part of everything they collect and intelligently invest it in something that will bring a long-term return on investment. (In the best case scenario, it will be a perpetual return.) Passive return investing, as it is called, can even bring perpetual and compound increase, if applied wisely. This principle has application to every SPESIFC area of life.

Only people with this kind of investment mentality ever experience the greatest benefits of grace. Certainly not all investors understand how to activate grace. In fact, only a tiny fraction of even real investors understands this principle. If you do not make worthy investments, you may gain profit in one area while simultaneously losing in other areas — i.e., make lots of money but ruin relationships or develop strong relationships but live paycheck to paycheck until you die. Continuing to cultivate an investment mentality is crucial.

Giving back goes hand-in-hand with the Investment Mindset and receiving grace. All great successful men and women understand that giving is key to receiving. Receiving is not their motive, but they do recognize it as an irrefutable universal law. Charity is that process of consistently giving and receiving grace, which we will discuss later in this book.

When you are on a deliberate track — traveling in the right direction and traveling fast enough to keep from getting run over — the universe sees your efforts and automatically sends grace to assist you in those deliberate efforts.

William Hutchison "W. H." Murray, a Scottish mountaineer and writer, said, "Until one is committed, there is hesitancy, the chance to draw back. Concerning all acts of initiative (and creation), there is one elementary truth that ignorance of which kills countless ideas and splendid plans: that the moment one definitely commits oneself, then Providence moves, too. All sorts of things occur to help one that would never otherwise have occurred. A whole stream of events issues from the decision, raising in one's favor all manner of unforeseen incidents and meetings and material assistance, which no man could have dreamed would have come his way. Whatever you can do, or dream you can do, begin it. Boldness has genius, power, and magic in it."

This element of grace has been a topic of great interest and focus for many throughout history. It is the essence of miracles, which are the physical and spiritual manifestations of grace. They do not defy universal law but are simply a higher form of cause-and-effect than we currently understand. All miracles are in complete and total harmony with universal law and are activated to a finite degree by our qualifying for grace — that is, living by principles.

Struggle, frustration, problems, fatigue and fear are the guardians of grace. These guardians keep those unwilling to conquer the trials of their faith from gaining the most precious treasures on earth, treasures that you can only access through grace. Defeating these guardians requires you to go as far as you can see and then take those significant leaps of faith beyond, into the darkness. This does not mean it always takes a lot of time. On the contrary, the more background (research, experience and planning) you invest, the quicker and more correct are the decisions you can make for your next leap of faith.

The following song "Let Me Fall" was originally written for a Cirque du Soleil performance at the 25th anniversary of the Montreal International Jazz Festival 2009 and sang by Mathiew Lavoie. It provides a wonderful description of the paradigms and attitudes that qualify you for grace. I heard it first sung by Josh Groban with the lyrics changed slightly. It is one of my favorite songs and I recommend it to you:

Let me fall. Let me climb.
There's a moment when fear and dreams must collide.
Someone I am is waiting for courage.
The one I want, the one I will become will catch me
So let me fall if I must fall. I won't heed your warnings, I won't hear them.
Let me fall if I fall, though the phoenix may or may not rise.
I will dance so freely, holding on to no one.
You can hold me only if you, too, will fall away from all these useless fears and chains.
Someone I am is waiting for my courage. The one I want, the one I will become will catch me.
So let me fall if I must fall. I won't heed your warnings. I won't hear.
Let me fall, if I fall. There's no reason to miss this one chance this perfect moment.
Just let me fall.

The core objective of this book is to facilitate your journey of life and enable you to understand the principles that will allow you to fall so that the one you want, the one you will become, will catch you. Every time you let yourself fall, your capacity to exercise faith, create miracles and prove your worthiness for greater and greater grace increases. In this way you will consistently and systematically solve every problem in your life as you discover and apply these secret, ancient principles guaranteed to grant you wisdom and enable you to better harness those universal and never changing laws of creation.

Chapter 7
How and Why These Principles Remain Secret

You have definitely heard of many of these secret and ancient principles. You may even believe that you already understand and live by some of them. In fact, you may have experienced some extraordinary benefits — even miracles — by way of them. However, they are still secrets.

Why are they secrets? Because from about two and a half decades of deliberate and focused study of the wisest people in history, I have begun to recognize the truth; that almost everyone lives far beneath his/her potential. I've also discovered that the primary cause of this underachievement is an innate predisposition in all human beings to believe that we understand more than we actually do. This predisposition is a self-preserving but debilitating trick of the ego to ensure that we feel enough of a sense of self-worth to preserve and perpetuate life. When you get your ego in check and working for you instead of against you, the goal of perfection never becomes harmful or a source of negative stress. Instead, it becomes an exciting and exhilarating adventure.

So, I give you a strong word of caution — like all principle-based writing, this is a *sealed document*. That simply means that although there is a lot of information and knowledge to gain at more shallow levels, the true wisdom that brings miracles into your life can only be discovered by training yourself to see through the camouflage of the words and the delusion of empty space between the lines. You must find and mine the nuggets of treasure locked tightly within the principles from which wisdom comes. In other words, the real message of any principle based writing or spoken word is a secret because there are no words to instill them into your heart and mind and habits and character.

Sadly, we have almost lost the mechanism in the world that brought the majority to self-discover principles, which was the agrarian and entrepreneurial society in the world for about 6,000 years. Also sadly, within our new "conventional wisdom" — this new trend of conventional thinking (which is the absence of thinking), people are not willing to push themselves past their current comfort levels — through the complexity of things to eventually set themselves up for grace and begin to discover the simplicity beyond complexity, which is real wisdom.

Knowledge comes from information written, spoken, explained, memorized, practiced and passed from one person to another. Wisdom is founded in principles, and you can no more attain wisdom or understand principles from words, examples or even typical experiences than you can dissect and examine emotions on a slide under a microscope. Principles must be excavated and mined with great care and by diligent persistence and continued discovery. Only then can you refine those principles in the furnace of deliberate, calculated and evaluated experiment and then temper them in the furnace of right character into wisdom. When you adequately educate your ego (which will initially try to convince you that you know enough already and discourage you from the effort it takes to do that mining and refining) the real journey begins.

Also, beware that this is not a formula you can simply memorize and follow to produce the result. Formulas, in and of themselves, leave you with no capacity to discover principles on your own. There are infinite variables that could never be accurately accounted for in our current state of limited awareness. To gaze into and understand principles is a gift, and access will only be granted after you have done "all you can do" and then take those next "leaps of faith." That doesn't mean being foolish or reckless; it means taking deliberate, intelligent, calculated risks. Those are the tolls and passwords required to bypass the guardians of truth and grace so that the principles are opened to you. This is one of the higher extensions of grace.

Principles are the most cleverly hidden and most valuable treasures on earth. They lead us to and teach us wisdom that allows us to harness and harmonize with universal laws to our best advantage. They are difficult to find; but, then, as Tom Hanks' character said in the movie *Extremely Loud and Incredibly Close*, "If it were easy to find, it wouldn't be worth finding." The wise can guide and point the way, but no one can show you where principles are or how to use them; that part is entirely up to your own powers of discovery, practice and deliberately activating the powers of grace.

Every truth and principle is surrounded and camouflaged by illusions designed to safeguard them from people who would use them selfishly and dishonestly, and who are not willing to do the appropriate work to discover them for themselves.

What you memorize can make you smart, but only what you discover has the potential to make you wise. The world is full of smart people who are financially, physically, emotionally, socially and/or spiritually broken. Wisdom alone has the power — not just to bring you what you want but to enable you to consistently improve upon what you already have.

The wise in every era have taught about this major road block of ego, and yet it is rarely mentioned by the masses, so it is tough at best to recognize, let alone overcome. Here are a few examples of some pretty wise people who understood this truth:

Mark Twain said, "It ain't what you don't know that gets you into [the most] trouble. It's what you know for sure that just ain't so."

I completely rewrote the following verse from an unknown author to illustrate the same point:

You don't know what you don't know.

You don't even know what you think you know.

On the other hand, you actually know things that you don't know that you know.

And that's why you don't have.

Because if you actually did know and knew that you knew, you would have.

Because if you think you know but do not do,

And/or do not continue to upgrade what you do,

That is a sure-fire guarantee that you don't have a clue.

Albert Einstein observed, "You can't solve a problem with the same mind that created it."

Several years ago, I heard a talk about "The 11th Commandment — Thou Shalt Not Fake Thyself Out." I cannot, unfortunately, remember who gave it. I chuckled about it at first, but have since come to embrace it as my 11th Commandment because I see the devastation everywhere caused by its disregard. Whoever came up with it understood well this great temptation to fake yourself out by convincing yourself that you know far more than you actually do. Study the parables of Jesus from this perspective, and you'll begin to uncover much deeper levels of His ultimate wisdom and far more of His personal message to you and your potential through them.

Solomon, the wealthiest and wisest man who ever lived, cautioned us to be careful about how we interpret the Proverbs because they are "the words of the wise and their dark sayings" or "riddles." You must do your own due diligence, which includes intentional practice, in order for them to finally begin to distill in your soul. True principles contain the mysteries of the universe. They are based in deep truth learned only by personal experience and then clarified by grace and so can never be taught — only discovered one person at a time.

In one of my favorite movies, *Joe Versus the Volcano*, Meg Ryan's character says to Tom Hanks' character, "My father says that 'Almost the whole world is asleep, everyone you know, everyone you see, everyone you talk to. Only a few people are awake, and they live in a state of constant, total amazement'.

Supreme Court Justice Oliver Wendell Holmes, Jr., said, "I don't give a fig for the simplicity this side of complexity, but I would die for the simplicity on the other side." I often paraphrase his words by saying, "Lasting success can only be found within the simplicity beyond complexity, because the simplicity this side of complexity is naivety, but the simplicity beyond is wisdom!"

I believe it was Einstein who warned us that, "…to define the whole process before it is defined will only negate the birth and existence of new worlds. A student of science and life must first learn how not to conclude or define any process or potential until it defines itself and to know when that self-definition has occurred."

And to further clarify, I will add the warning to be aware of the 11th Commandment and not "fake thyself out" into believing that the definition has occurred before it actually has, because that is our natural human tendency.

As I often say, "Always be aware of and okay with not knowing, just never be content with it."

The pleas of great leaders are rife with the advice to hold off on creating definitions before they have defined themselves, and yet this incessant, devastating tendency to let our egos convince us that we know more than we do continues, unchecked, to trample individuals, communities, our country and even our world underfoot. Unchecked ego is so powerful that, if you do not intentionally, deliberately and wisely overcome it, it will forever be a boot on your neck, never letting you rise enough to see the truth — not even, and especially, in yourself.

All the money in the world cannot buy you wisdom. All the schooling in the world cannot impart it to you. It has nothing to do with how much information or knowledge you amass, how long you have lived, or what experiences you've had or haven't had. Although skills and talents are critical to success, without a firm grasp of principles to hold the integrity of those skills and talents intact, even these can never produce anything of intrinsic value for you or anyone else. Don't be deceived by the countless mansions built on the shifting sands of illusion. Regardless of how magnificent they seem or the pleasures they promise, in their own due time, they will fall, and great will be their fall.

Countless people, businesses, and organizations have created financial fortunes by preying on and exploiting others' weaknesses — slavery, drugs, pornography, alcohol, tobacco, media, food, war, and virtually every industry on Earth — anything that is addictive, coercive, controlling, or takes advantage of others. However, the universe never has and never will allow such preying behavior to continue for long. There is always a day of reckoning. My dad was fond of the old proverb, "If you're going to dance, sooner or later, you've got to pay the piper." I have come to realize he was unconditionally right.

The only way to truly get ahead in life is to make sure that whatever you do empowers, encourages, and enables others to get ahead, to give more than you take. If you ever take more than you give, you become indebted, and the universe will balance the scales eventually. If you give more than you take, the universe will make sure you receive an increase. (That does NOT mean self-sacrifice but rather selfless-sacrifice. Beware the difference. The first is self-decay the second is self-evolution).

Now that we have laid a proper foundation of truth, let us build us a palace of wisdom upon it!

The Way To Wisdom and Enlightenment

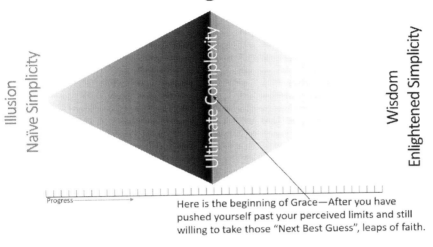

Here is the beginning of Grace—After you have pushed yourself past your perceived limits and still willing to take those "Next Best Guess", leaps of faith.

PART 2

Introduction:
The Most Talked About Secret that is Still A Secret

The Law of Attraction is real and many good things have come from it. However, today, the real *Secret* is still a secret. Why? Mostly because even the vast majority of so-called "experts" today still widely misunderstand and even more widely misapply it — even those who teach it on a daily basis. This Law of Attraction, as wonderful and powerful as it is, is only a small part of the laws of grace and the laws of grace are only a small part of the Laws of Creation. The Great Secret is not simply the Law of Attraction, but is a combination of principles that function perfectly together to make the whole greater than the sum of the parts. I have come to call them "The principles that lead to wisdom and harness the laws of creation" and "The Great Hidden Wisdoms."

Napoleon Hill talked about "The Great Carnegie secret". Earl Nightingale, "The Strangest Secret," and many, many wise people of the past and present have talked about it. Many of them did have reference to "The Law of Attraction." A few had reference to something far grander. Several of the people who teach about it are among my role models and mentors, and I have learned a lot and owe a great deal of my transformation to them. The interesting thing is that even now after so much publicity, so many books and trainings and broad stroke teaching about it, it is still a secret!

The Great Hidden Wisdoms must be seen and applied based on their context and purpose. Without understanding *why* these principles exist, it is impossible to really harness their true potential and power. The following 17 chapters are a few of these all-inclusive principles. Individually, they have impressive power for good. The more of them you integrate into the foundation from which you operate however, the more you will achieve, the happier you will be and the more power and freedom and real success you will enjoy — the kind of success that never ends, but compounds on itself forever.

My mission is to help paint and bring you that bigger picture that makes it all more logical and simple.

Again like I often say, "Real success can only be found within the simplicity beyond complexity, because the simplicity this side of complexity is naivety while the simplicity beyond is wisdom."

So, let's go beyond secrecy and naive simplicity into what I call the "The Great Hidden Wisdoms." These Great Hidden Wisdoms are simple and direct and comprehensive — they are the understanding of those principles that lead to wisdom and give us power to harness the laws of creation and create a life of abundance, fulfillment and happiness. A crucial key is to discover *why* these laws and the principles that support them exist. When you understand the why's beneath the what's and then mold them into your character, you will have the power to harness these laws and create your best future with them.

So, what are these Great Hidden Wisdoms? They are the intelligence and skills and character and insights about how you harness them to optimally work for you. That is what this book is all about. The chapters that follow will explain in greater detail, giving you a foundation that will enable you to build whatever your heart truly desires. Just remember that real understanding, that is the wisdom about these principles and exactly how you can optimally use them, will come to you through your own practical application and self-discovery. Like I mentioned in Part 1, principles cannot be taught, only discovered. In Chapter 3, you will discover the power of my statement, "What you remember can make you smart, but only what you discover has potential to make you wise." Through this book, you will discover how to not get trapped along your journey (within the simplicity this side of complexity that is naivety) and how to discover these Great Hidden Wisdoms within the simplicity beyond complexity; to create miracles and enjoy lasting happiness, fulfillment and success in every SPESIFC area of your life.

So we'll start with the one principle that brings into focus who you really are and will exponentially expand your potential.

Chapter 1
The Alpha and Omega Principle

This is the first secret ancient, hidden principle. It is a truth so simple, and yet so powerful, that just recognizing it will begin to loosen the shackles of limitation and present possibilities you never believed were available to you before. Who are you really?

You Are a Creator

I begin here because this principle is the foundation of *all* other principles; I call it the Alpha and Omega Principle because it is both cornerstone and capstone of this book because it is the beginning and the end of your identity.

Let us avoid any possible misunderstanding: You *are* a creator. You *are not* in training to become one; you were born one and you will be one on the day you die — and beyond. It doesn't matter if you believe it or not. It doesn't matter if you want to be one or not. It doesn't matter if you intentionally create or never try to create. You are creating every moment of every day, even when you are asleep. In fact, it is as impossible for you to not create as it is for you to not breathe.

The fact is, every single person creates all the time. You are living in the reality you created for yourself. The biggest problem most people face is a failure to recognize that their reality reflects their own conscious and unconscious behaviors. As the creator of your reality, you can also have significant influence over the behavior of those around you. As you make decisions, you control what the universe sends to you.

I've heard people — even many self- professed and so-called "educated" experts — state that only a select few people are creators; those who have what they call "creative" gifts and talents. Sadly, they have convinced the masses of their limited and false thinking. Their idea is simple: "If you aren't a 'creative thinker' or 'artsy' or good at coming up with 'out-of-the-box' ideas, an author, etc., then you aren't creative or a creator." Not true. This common, well-publicized fallacy is responsible for as many people failing to achieve their potential as any idea in the world today.

Thoughts: The Building Blocks of Reality

Now that you acknowledge yourself as a creator, a first powerful question would be: If I am constantly creating and have created my current reality, how do I create something better? The answer is simple — consistently think bigger and better thoughts and your actions (and, hence, your reality) will begin to re-shape into bigger and better results. Then a next best question would be: How do I think bigger and better thoughts? Read on, because we will get to that soon. First understand that your thoughts are the blueprints of your emotional intentions, your very character and these dictate your physical activities, which in turn create your reality. Your thoughts dictate every detail as you construct your own internal and external world. The more you entertain certain thoughts, the more you construct those physical, emotional and spiritual realities.

As James Allen, author of *As A Man Thinketh*, wrote:

> "Mind is the master power that molds and makes
> and man is mind, and evermore he takes
> the tools of thought and shaping what he wills,
> brings forth a thousand joys, a thousand ills.
> He thinks in secret and it comes to pass.
> Environment is but his looking-glass."

Allen also said:

> "men and women [must come] to the discovery and perception of the truth that — 'they themselves are makers of themselves' by virtue of the thoughts which they choose and encourage; that mind is the master weaver, both of the inner garment of character and of the outer garment of circumstance, and that, as they have hitherto woven in ignorance and pain they may now weave in enlightenment and happiness."

Your life really is exactly the quality and culmination of your previous thoughts. However, have you ever wondered how — and even more importantly, why — you have the thoughts you do when other people obviously have different thoughts and so created different things? How can you make sure you have bigger and better thoughts that will shape, tailor, and transform your current environment into the environment you dream of instead of more of what you already have? How do you create an environment that takes you forward instead of backwards?

There are lots of illusions around this issue, and in Part 2 Chapter 8, I will dispel those illusions and show you exactly how to guarantee that your thoughts take you where you want to go. The more you understand about what is between here and Chapter Eight, however, the greater value you will receive by the time you get there.

You certainly don't have to be perfect to live a fulfilled and happy life but a happier life will result if you are consistently discovering how to get closer to perfection than you were before. Learning how to accurately use the core building blocks of thought in your creation process is critical key to attaining true fulfillment and happiness.

Information vs. Principles

When I was young I remember hearing about a young man who, for the first time went to spend the summer with his uncle on the farm. Some of his chores included helping to milk the cows and feed the calves. Toward the end of the summer, the young man turned to his uncle one morning with an "a-ha!". "Oh, I get it Uncle! You put the milk into the calves when they are young and then take it back out of them when they get old!"

Public education, as I will discuss in detail in Chapter 4, is a failure, for the most part, following this same extreme naivety. Teachers spit out in lectures and students spit them back on tests. And then we have the audacity to call it "education." Our children are learning what happens but they are not taught why things happen. Poet William Blake saw this problem about 200 years ago. In "Auguries of Innocence" he demonstrates the difference between principles and information:

> To see a world in a grain of sand
> And a heaven in a wild flower.
> Hold infinity in the palm of your hand
> And eternity in an hour.
> We are led to believe a lie
> When we see not thro' the eye,
> Which was born in a night to perish in a night,
> When the soul slept in beams of light.

Can you hold infinity in the palm of your hand? Can you really find heaven in a wildflower? Even if you put a grain of sand under a microscope, can you really see a world? It depends, Blake draws an analogy — by studying parts of the universe, it is possible to begin to see the principles on which the universe operates. But, how likely is it that you are fooling yourself (remember the 11th Commandment from Part 1 Chapter 7)? Are you looking from an extremely limited, naive paradigm or through an extraordinary wisdom that you have cultivated through years of deliberate principle based study and practical application?

Throughout much of human history, people (including brilliant minds like Aristotle) believed there were only four elements — earth, water, air, fire — because that was all they could see. Despite the scientific advances that have expanded our horizons almost beyond comprehension, the great majority of people still choose to see the universe at face value. Even when dissected by the "best" minds of the 21st Century, there are few who really dig deep.

And therein lies the difference between information and principles: Information can be taught — anyone can share the facts with anyone else. Principles, however, must be discovered — you cannot give them to anyone else and no one can give them to you, you have to figure them out for yourself. Understanding, though, isn't enough. You have to internalize those principles, not just so you make them habitual but so that they become part of who you are at the deepest, core level (part of your DNA) and so they exude from you, as natural as breathing.

It's like learning a new language; you know you really understand it when you no longer have to interpret inside your head, but can think about it. When you really comprehend true principles, you naturally use them to harness the laws of the universe and create perpetual evolution within yourself and within the environment that you create around yourself.

Now, here comes a tricky part: This isn't just a mental or physical evolution. You aren't trying to develop better habits or a new way of thinking. There are unseen, foundational dimensions that can only be understood from spiritual perspectives. That statement isn't about religion, it's about connecting with the universe and obtaining all the control you want over your life and your future. Make no mistake about it, you can control far more than you do, but that kind of control comes only from this deeper understanding and paradigm. That has been unequivocally proven over the past 6,000 years.

Still much too limited, but a simplistic example from my cowboy youth:

One day, I was walking from the corral to the house when my older brother, Byron, drove up. I waited for him. As we walked and talked together, I haphazardly threw a loop with my lariat, over a nearby fence post. He stopped and looked at me funny for a few seconds and then said, "Do that again."

I looked at him in surprise and asked, "Do what?"

"Rope that post again," he said.

I coiled up my rope and threw it over the post a second time. Again he paused, looked at me strangely, and asked, "Who taught you to rope like that?" Now much more confused I responded "Rope like what? I caught it didn't I? What do you do, swing the rope with your teeth?"

He laughed and asked, "Do you want me to show you some things that will make you a much better roper? I responded, "Sure, I'd love to learn to rope like you." He said, "Okay," then he told me that he was going to show me a few things, but I'd have to promise to practice faithfully for least two months and not quit just because it is hard. He said I was going to wonder sometimes if his advice was just a trick to torment me. But promised that if I'd practice faithfully I'd get much better in a fairly short time. So I promised.

He proceeded to show me how to spin my loop differently, hold my hand on the rope differently, swing the loop over my head differently, throw it differently and then snap it back differently. I was blown away. I was amazed that there could be so much detail to something that had seemed such a straight forward and simple activity that I had never broken down and analyzed before.

His prediction came true. For the next couple of months, I was miserable. Everything was awkward. I had to force myself not to do things the old, easier way. I had spent so many years developing those old, bad, habits and it was hard to give them up. Besides, why should I do it differently, I could catch what I wanted most of the time. Was I frustrated? Extremely! Did I feel like giving up? I almost did several times but I remembered my promise to commit and his promise that it would be worth it, so I persisted.

One morning, as usual, I grabbed my rope and headed out to do chores. On my way across the back yard, I spun a loop and began swinging it over my head. I suddenly realized that I was swinging the rope exactly like he had shown me. It felt natural, not forced like before. I threw my loop over a fence post and snapped it back; wow, perfect! I felt that to the core of my soul and what a feeling! Time after time, it felt like magic. Seemingly overnight, I felt like that rope had become a part of my own body and completely under my control. It was amazing!

It was also, in retrospect, educational. As a roper, you must have absolute control over the rope to get the best results. If you want those results consistently, your form must be consistent and it must be optimal. That takes a mentor, someone who knows how to do it right. It takes practice, time to internalize the methodology. It takes perseverance — I was so close to giving up many times. I was tempted to just leave that rope in the house or to just do things the old way because it felt so much better and I could feel that instant gratification again. It was super hard to make myself keep practicing the new way. Though I never reached Byron's skill level, roping his way eventually became second nature to me, my body understood, without any conscious thought, how to do it right.

Another example, from my literary youth, (even though I was much older):

For several years, I had been telling people I was going to write this book and be speaking and training all over the world. I knew I would do it and I told lots of people I would do it because I thought that would motivate me to actually get it done.

However, every time I attempted to start, I was totally lost and didn't have a clue where to begin. I let myself get distracted with many, many other things that were more comfortable and that I convinced myself were just as important. Making a living for my family, doing honey-do's around the house, doing building projects, doing real estate investments, and on and on. One day, I was looking out my office window which overlooked my cabinet shop roof. It was full of branches and pine needles and looked terrible. I decided to pressure wash it off.

It happened to be early February 2006 but the weather was reasonable, so I broke out the pressure washer and began cleaning the roof. Just as I was finished and walking back to the ladder, the sun set and it instantly froze over. As you can imagine, walking on an icy metal roof doesn't work very well and down I came, crashed through the ladder and about 12 feet to the ground.

Sliding as if it were in slow motion I had a very vivid picture and a very strong impression that if I didn't get this book written that I was going to be in trouble.

After I crashed through the ladder and hit the ground, I didn't feel anything for a while and just lay there looking up into the sky with a funny smile on my face. It wasn't till I tried to stand up that I realized something was wrong. My right leg wouldn't move. My oldest son just happened to be visiting, heard the commotion and came running out of the house, he saw me trying to stand up and it wasn't working. He then yelled, "Just stay down Dad!"

Later, at the hospital, they discovered that I'd broken my hip, crushed my heel and severely damaged my ankle. I just couldn't shake this feeling that this would give me time to write this book. As uncomfortable as it was, I really did try to get this project going. I started going through hundreds of documents that I had written over the years. Also, over about the past 20 years, I had been an avid note taker and had about four and a half apple boxes full of notes that I particularly saved, to organize into different subjects that I thought should go into this book.

Many times I became so frustrated because this was such a huge task and I really didn't know what I was doing or how to begin. I had to take breaks once in a while just to keep from feeling like my brain would explode. But, time after time, I came to work on it again. For the first time in my life, I began regretting not paying attention in English class. I worked on and off, trying to organize these notes.

During this same time, one of my younger brothers bought an old home and commercial building he had started to completely remodel. Several times he called me with questions. Finally, after almost 3 months, when they were about to let me start walking again, my brother called again. I decided that, rather than talking over the phone, why didn't I just fly out there and spend a few weeks helping him. I may not be able to do a lot in the beginning but at least I could see things and know how to help better.

This opportunity was the perfect justification to put off writing one more time. Just as that remodel project was shaping up, my wife, Jackie came to visit, intending that we would drive home together. A couple of days before we were due to leave, my wife came to where we were working and with this funny little smile on her face, said, "Eldon, I just found a small apartment building that I'd like you to go check out with me." On our way back to my brother's house, we drove by to take a look. To make a very long story short, we didn't make it back home for about four years. Not only did we buy that building but, over the next couple of years, bought several more investment homes and properties.

Again, it was the perfect distraction. I justified not writing because there was so much work to do. About four years later, I awoke early one morning from a dreadfully troubling dream. Before I even got out of bed, I rolled over, kissed my wife good morning and said, "Jackie, I cannot do this any longer. I have to quit right now and write this book."

That very day, we began making arrangements to wrap up several projects we were completing. Within a couple of weeks, we had decided to move back to Washington, where we still owned a home. We figured that was the best place to go — where I would have the least distractions — and I vowed to finish this book before I did anything else again — at least for work.

Being that I didn't think I was a writer, I decided to hire a ghostwriter and figured I would have this book finished in one year. We packed up, moved, and immediately put out some ads for a ghostwriter.

Fourteen months passed; I was, again, extremely frustrated. Over that time, I had hired six different ghostwriters. Each one was fired or quit because they could not do what I asked of them. At least, I assume they quit, they stopped answering my calls and responding to my communication. Unfortunately, I was no closer than when I started and a lot of money gone for nothing.

Finally, out of frustration, I told Jackie that if this book was going to get written, I had to write it myself. So, I went to the office supply store, bought a big desk calendar, and wrote on that calendar five to six days every week, five to eight hours every day for the entire year that this is "writing time." Then I told her, "I am going to sit here in front of this computer until my brain discovers it is a writer and I'm going to write this book!" After a couple of weeks, I decided I still needed help so I looked on the Internet to see if I could find someone who could teach me how to write a book. I finally found Ann McIndoo, who has an amazing program. I took her course, finally got things laid out, reasonably organized and it started taking shape.

When I finally got all my topics listed out, I had almost 200 topics that I wanted to address. Over time, I condensed, discarded, combined, and organized them into a reasonable few to include in this first book. I also changed the title about twelve times and, finally, after another fourteen months, finished a first draft manuscript.

Then I started hunting for an editor. I actually talked with several different editors who wanted the job. I picked out a few I liked most and gave them each a small project. (I learned this from my writers' experience.) I explained very carefully and quite forcefully that much of this information would be different than they had ever heard before and so I was happy to take as much time as necessary to help them understand what I was trying to say. Not one of them took me up on my offer for further explanation and by the time I got their projects back, every one of them had so twisted and distorted what I was trying to say that none of them even came close. I tried to explain to each one of them how they had misunderstood and what I was trying to say but every one of them were offended and never talked to me again. I was willing to take whatever time possible to help them understand and even pay them for the time, but none of them could get past their egos.

There were a few more who expressed interest, and even raved about the manuscript and how profound it was, but still all talk and no results. Finally, again, out of utter frustration, through an acquaintance, I found an editor who took on the project. Cassandra was absolutely amazing. She immersed herself into the project, was careful to understand and was massively helpful in rearranging and putting this whole thing together in an understandable and meaningful way. I will always be grateful for that first huge relief. It was a much needed confirmation that I was absolutely on the right track, I could really see the edge of what seemed to be "that endless prairie."

Then out of the blue, she had to quit, for good reasons. One more time I hunted for an editor. After weeding out several who promised they could do the job I hired another editor. She was helpful but was having major health problems that I was unaware of in the beginning, she also struggled to "find my voice" but we worked for several months and finally I had to go on the hunt again because she just wasn't working out and I was wasting lots of time. I finally found my last editor who has been an absolute gift from heaven.

Now, I tell you both those stories because discovering principles is a process. At first, just like my brother told me about roping, "In the beginning, you may think that I gave you these instructions just to torment you." You, too, may feel like giving up and staying with your old status quo. Besides, what you have may not be that bad. At least, it is comfortable and you have some instantly gratifying rewards. In fact, you have spent many years and a lot of practice and sacrifice and struggle and learning to develop the habits and the belief systems that you have. You may even feel like you are doing pretty well. But are you even a little intrigued to discovering how things can be far better? A small glimpse into and taste of the thrill of living your life on your terms, the way you would have it if you could have everything you want? To have a life that will make even your grandest times pale by comparison? If so, don't let your ego stop you from going after what you really want.

Again, like Nelson Mandela said, "There is no passion to be found playing small, in settling for a life that is less than the one you are capable of living." So, it will take some deep thought and some time to really get a handle on the core of what principles are. Especially since there are very few places on earth you can go to learn them in a most empowering way. You will find many who will claim they can teach you but only a very tiny handful who actually can. If they are not creating miracles in the area you want to improve, run away from them as fast as you can — regardless of how convincing they sound. Just remember that, if you would like to improve any part of your life, it only takes discovering the beginning of one principle to drastically change your results forever.

Your apprenticeship may be scary or even painful to begin with — to let down your guard and entertain ideas may be new to you — but limiting your paradigms to face value will keep you from discovering the unexplainable freedom and passion that can be yours.

Again, King Solomon cautioned us about understanding the proverbs because they are "...words of the wise and their dark sayings" (Proverbs 1:6, King James Version). In other words, until we begin to grasp the principles from whence the wise speak and have insight into their paradigms, you cannot gain that wisdom for yourself. Their words can lead you to the path of discovery; understanding their intentions will lead you down it. If you travel the path long enough, you begin to discern how intentions and actions create their circumstances — another subject to be discussed in greater detail.

This understanding will lead you to comprehend principles which will lead to wisdom and enable you to harness the laws of the universe and focus their energy toward your own personal results. This, however, can never happen when you take the world at face value; "when you see with and not through the eye" as William Blake said. It only happens when you begin to really see things from deeper, spiritual perspectives.

All the vast stores of knowledge and the high technology we enjoy today are hardly a drip in the ocean compared to what there is to understand. Only fools believe they are learned. Then they blame others for their problems and live and die, lost deep within the shadows of their true potential.

It doesn't matter whether you believe this or not at present. You just have to ask yourself, do you have all the control that you want over your life and your future? If not and, if you wish to change it, you will have to understand that the beliefs systems that drive your behavior are faulty and be willing to trade those faulty beliefs for the truth. Only then will your behaviors (and your situation) change. If those changes create the results you want, you are on track. If they are not what you want, back to the drawing board and your next best guess.

You can control far more than you do, as long as you are willing to harness these principles and live closer to the truth, which is in harmony with the laws of the universe.

Faith and Miraculous Results

Regardless of where you came from, how you currently live, or where you will be in the future, the results you create will fall into one of four basic categories: poor, mediocre, extraordinary, or miraculous. I've never met anyone who didn't want extraordinary or miraculous results. I've met many who say they are satisfied with less but that is their fear talking, not their spirit or their heart. Tragically, almost all of the results people generally experience fall into the poor and mediocre categories.

The following statistics are from my own research and observations over more than two decades. These also represent the North American adult population only, not young children or teenagers.

Poor Results are the lot of approximately one-third of our population. Among these is a very small group who do not have the capacity to take care of themselves through no fault of their own. They are an integral part of our society and we are privileged to take care of them. In fact, talk to the parents, siblings, and friends of "special needs" individuals. You will rarely hear words like burden, affliction, or trial. You will almost always hear words like blessing, godsend, joy, and miracle. The rest of this group create poor results because they have poverty thinking. These people are not stupid (unable to learn), they are ignorant (uneducated and improperly trained). We have an obligation to educate them properly so they develop the incentive to take care of themselves; to stop being a drain on society and become productive members of society. Unfortunately, when we give the "poor and needy" hand-outs, we make the problem worse. We increase the burden on those who produce and we encourage those in need to become more and more dependent on those hand-outs.

Mediocre Results are achieved by just under two-thirds of our population. People create mediocre results because they live trapped by conventional thinking and ideas — what so many mistakenly call "conventional wisdom" which would more properly be termed "conventional stupidity". Regrettably, most college graduates and so-called "highly-educated" people are mediocre producers. The vast majority of those who follow conventional thinking are honest, hard-working, good-hearted people doing the best they think they can do. They are charitable and willing to help their neighbors in time of trouble. They are the heartbeat of our society. They are mostly, very good people. So, what's their problem? Why don't they achieve great things? The poor results crowd never comprehend the laws and principles; the mediocre results crowd has only a very surface level, partial comprehension of laws and principles. Some have a basic natural comprehension, others figure out some of it, which allows them greater success than the others. Sadly, for the most part, they still buy into the "conventional wisdom" trap. As Henry David Thoreau penned, "The mass of men lead lives of quiet desperation." Deep down, they want things better but don't know how and don't think they can. Also their egos won't allow them to take the risks to try.

Extraordinary Results have, historically, been achieved by approximately two percent of our population, though this number is quickly declining. People create extraordinary results because they think bigger and are willing to work harder and gather better information than the mediocre results crowd. These are the people with a "go-getter" mindset — over-achievers, outside-the-box thinkers, geniuses, and those who just flat-out work harder than the Average Joe (or Jane). These are typically business and community leaders who take deliberate and proactive roles to improve themselves and things around them consistently.

Miraculous Results are rare, consistently achieved by maybe one in 10,000 people, conservatively speaking — that's 1% of 1% of our population. They habitually and consistently create miraculous results because they have developed unlimited thinking. They have learned that miracles are part of the basic make-up of nature and the natural result of optimal performance toward goals and dreams that are far bigger than themselves. They have tapped into the grace that is built into the fabric of our existence. They also understand that, even when working with the best and brightest minds on Earth, there's somebody smarter than us all, and He wishes nothing more than to perform a little divine intervention to assist you in accomplishing your worthy plans.

Several years ago, I read an article by a gentleman who explained how he looks at creating miraculous results. He said that when he plans for the future, his goals are intentionally so much bigger than himself or his team that they require direct, divine intervention to be realized. Then he clarified, "If I set goals that I can accomplish myself, even if I have to stretch, what place have I left for God in my life?"

These people also know that, at the particular time they begin considering their plans, those plans are impossible without not just one miracle but a series of miracles. Most of the time, they have no idea how or where to begin. They just know that, if it is a worthy goal and if they are intelligent, persistent, and continue to ask the right questions of the right people — never question *if* it is possible but only *how* it is possible. Then they go to work, with absolute faith and put into practice their "next best guess" strategies, sooner or later, the universe provides the blueprints to make it possible. Mostly it comes in bits and pieces, a little at a time, but as they act intelligently, skillfully and with the right character, one way or another, it is impossible not to come.

Though he had his own problems, John F. Kennedy understood this principle of creating miracles. Many examples in his life proved that, one of several was the goal he gave America to put a man on the moon. At that time, we didn't have the technology and hadn't even discovered the natural resources we would have to discover in order to accomplish that goal. But true to the principle, again as James Allen taught, "…when spirit rises and commands, the Gods are ready to obey."

Grace and miracles are part of the universe, they were designed into it by a Creator who loves His creation and who wants us to succeed. Because we are inherently creators also (part of our divine heritage as His children), everyone has access to these resources but access comes at the significant up-front cost of conquering the trials of our faith. (We'll talk more about that later). As you become more familiar with this way of thinking, you will also be guided in how to measure your progress and achieve your dreams.

Consumer Mentality vs. Investor Mentality

Poor and Mediocre results are created with a consumer mentality. Instant gratification is an integral part of consumer mentality, an overriding desire to have your wants or needs handed to you immediately. Some call it "microwave mentality." It is a feel-good mentality, intentionally avoiding the pain of self-discipline. People trapped in the consumer mentality are those whose resources — time, money, energy, relationships, conversations, emotions, etc. — are used up so not enough left over and they don't have enough return on investment in the SPESIFC areas of their life to keep up with the time and energy flowing out of their lives..

They are consistently poorer tomorrow, next month, or next year as they are today. It is an illusion to believe that just because you have more money now than last year that you are better off. Now you are a year older, what has your life as a whole become over that year? Don't get discouraged though, it is just very important to recognize where you are before you can accurately draw a map and get where you want to be.

For the most part, consumer mentality is what we are taught in our families, communities, and our schools. Those with a consumer mentality come from all walks of life. They are employees and self-employed people; doctors, lawyers, teachers, carpenters, etc. some are poorly educated and many have college degrees. They are about 98 percent of American society.

Extraordinary and miraculous results are created by people who live with an investment mentality. Virtually everything they do is from an entirely different mindset than consumers — and most of the time completely opposite thinking. They realize that their capital — time, energy, money, relationships, spiritual and physical health, knowledge, and other resources — are extremely valuable, never spent but invested. Only used to make everyone richer and generate a healthy return on their investments. They are left richer than they started so now they can turn around and invest again with greater capital resources and reap compounded returns, over and over again into the future.

Most people believe that investments, by definition, are risky but that is a naïve and misguided notion. Gambling is risky because the odds operate outside the gambler's control, and the odds are always stacked in favor of the House. Also, gambling is a short-term, instant gratification activity. Those who think they are investing when, in fact, their activities are based on emotion or other intangibles are gamblers (like the majority of stock market transactions). Certainly, when you invest, you can lose your principle but real investments are based on research, mathematics and science; they include a minimum of speculation and a correspondingly low risk. In the long-term, you are guaranteed to win, even in times when things don't work according to plan. Real investors always profit —

either they gain financially or they gain knowledge that will better guide them to win with the next investments.

It must be clearly understood that wise investments are built on principles and don't always involve money. There are no end to examples, a business owner/manager can invest time and effort in philanthropic activities. We invest in our children and all manner of non-profit ventures. We invest in helping a neighbor mend their fence, baby sit for a friend, and the list goes on forever.

By the way, the consumer vs. investor mentality concept is a principle of the law of the harvest: "Be not deceived; God is not mocked: for whatsoever a man soweth, that shall he also reap" (Galatians 6:7, KJV), one of the universal laws and set of principles that give you access to it. The greater your understanding of this principle and its underlying law, the less likely you are to make consumer-based decisions which will cause you to lose you what you have.

Consumers spend their physical health and age earlier than necessary. They spend their relationships, that's why we have an epidemic of failed relationships and then blame others for their failure, spend their emotions, which creates stress, anxiety, anger, etc. and believe the world in unfair. Spend their spirituality, thus walk around lost in the world without purpose and real meaning and believe life has no purpose, spend their education by not staying on top of technological growth and thus become obsolete and complain when they lose their jobs and then expect severance pay, etc. Etc. Investors on the other hand understand and do the opposite. Everything they do today, sets them up to be more valuable and productive tomorrow.

Personal Accountability

Some years ago, I became acquainted with an extraordinary gentleman who, at a young age, started a business. He was born into a good family of means and received an Ivy League education. He discovered a significant need, applied some smart business practices, and created a very profitable international company. After several years of admirable success, he sold the business for an enormous profit.

A few years later, he decided to start another business. This time, things didn't work out as planned. Not only did he lose his new business, he lost all of his money, his home, and even many personal possessions.

Over the years, I have come to know several people with that same basic experience. It is amazingly common today and has been since the beginning of time. Some of those people have gone into major depression, withdrawn from society, a few even committed suicide. Some just take it in stride and change their life-style to fit their new circumstances. Others however, learned from the experience, jumped back into the game and made it all over again — sometimes,

58

they made it all back and a whole lot more! Not only did they make their money back, they also built character where it counts the most. Here is the basic difference between those who fall permanently and those who fall temporarily — those who take personal responsibility and learn from their mistakes are the ones who successfully rebuild. Those who don't, resign themselves to a life far below their potential, opportunities and privileges.

Now, you may be thinking, "I may have created some, but certainly not all the results in my life. I didn't create the schools I attended or governments I live under, the banking system or the economic situation, but I have to deal with them every day. Why are some born into abundance with loving families while others are born into abject poverty, abuse and lack? What about those who are victims of tragedies not of their own making?" Why does there seem to be such an extreme "unfairness?"

Everyone knows tragic stories, every community has people who have been through such hell that we all shudder and weep for them, especially those who are victims of abuse, illness or accident, natural disasters, terrorism and other "circumstances". Certainly, you cannot control what other people do or think. In fact, if you try, you'll just end up losing control of yourself and whatever good influence you could have had over others. So, what can you control? You can control how you respond to events and those actions create your circumstances.

This is a key point — and a specific definition of terms as we'll use them in this book: You create many, but not all, of the *events* of your life; others also create events and some of them are pushed on you. You create all the *circumstances* in your life; your response to voluntary and involuntary events. Your response is an act of creation. It is old (but still true) counsel, "When life hands you lemons, make lemonade." Otherwise you just end up a 'sour-puss'. The choice is yours.

Following are two great examples. The first person was my good friend in junior high school. He grew up on an Indian reservation in an abusive home with alcoholic parents. He was often in trouble in school, with other authorities and with the law. When my Native American friend was twenty-one years old, he was stabbed to death in a bar fight. I heard several people say things like, "You can't blame him. He really didn't have a choice. Look where he came from!" At that point in my life, I agreed and even repeated that to others.

The second person I met just a few years ago, was born in super high-crime ghetto. By the time he reached high school, virtually all of his family and close friends were either addicts, convicts or both. He decided to make a change. With tremendous effort, he become the first person in his family to graduate from high school then go to college and graduate with honors. Today, he inspires audiences and helps people around the country reach their potential. Today, he says, "When I was young I decided that I didn't really have a choice. Look where I came from!"

Taking personal responsibility for your life and exercising free will does set you free. But is it simple? To quote the wonderful movie *What If*, starring Kevin Sorbo as Ben, a materialistic rich man who gets a second chance to make the right choices, "Yeah, it is. It's just hard."

A Bold Statement

I now need to say something very bold. When you fully grasp what I am about to tell you, you will be catapulted to a new level of awareness and unbelievable influence for good among all you meet. This awareness will turn you into a wiser and more compassionate human being because of a much deeper, broader, more insightful and meaningful understanding about how life works but also — even more importantly — why life works.

I initially thought to not mention this here and wait to address it in a coming book because, first of all, it is an advanced principle that is difficult at best to understand. (Sort of like the laws of aerodynamics before the Wright brothers.) Second, you don't need to believe it in order to make good progress toward solving your problems. In addition, because it is a harder principle to grasp, it often elicits undue objections and, when people reject any truthful idea, it becomes a stumbling block to further progress.

However, the freedom, peace of mind and tremendous power, that you will gain from understanding it is so powerful, I had to take the risk. If it begins to get in the way of your progress, just set it aside for a while. You can always come back to it later. If you continue to study and evolve, you will, sooner or later have an "ah-ha!" moment where you will clearly see it as self-evident with no other possibility.

So here it is: Although you did not create all of the events of and around your life, you attracted them to you and placed yourself in them. Even the ones that have brought you the most pain and suffering! If you are willing to look at your life with complete objectivity, you will discover that those experiences came prepackaged with opportunities to help you grow in far greater ways than any of the other experiences in your life! If they have not been already, they have potential to bring you unimagined miracles. Not just in your life but so you can be a blessing in the lives of many others around you.

Through the past several years, I have come to understand that every unique situation and circumstance in every person's life is there for very specific reasons. I'm not talking about predestination; that is the opposite of what I mean. I am talking about an ultimate and optimal opportunity to exponentially evolve, your "… best-case scenario".

You have a spirit inside of you that is in touch with the spiritual realm. That spirit is continually guiding and urging you toward certain things and experiences.

Many people refer to this as your conscience. It knows your potential and knows you can overcome anything you put your mind to. It knows that when you overcome these ultimate challenges, you will become more powerful than from any other thing you could have gone through.

As German philosopher Friedrich Nietzsche said, "That which doesn't kill us makes us stronger." (I'm also fond of the Viking variation on Nietzsche, "That which doesn't kill me had better run!") Again, it isn't the events themselves but the way you deal with them that determines whether you become closer to death or more alive.

Now, we must also remember that other people are constantly having events and creating circumstances. Their circumstances are events in your life. They do not control or dictate your life but are simply raw materials that you can choose to include or exclude from your own creations.

The fact that you create your own life is central to the purpose of your life, which is to evolve. Here again, I know many will call this controversial and will want to debate the concept. That wish to debate has nothing to do with whether the principles are true or false, the desire to debate is just a sign that they do not understand the principle.

There are those who would have us believe that life is life — we begin at birth and end at death. This "conventional wisdom", like all "conventional wisdom", simply isn't true; it is an illusion based on a very naïve and limited understanding or an unwillingness to look beyond their physical senses, typically a character trait they assumed from someone else or a personally-imposed boundary. I hope you will not jeopardize your unlimited potential by clinging to limiting illusions. Everyone has limiting illusions and lives by them and that is where many of our problems first sprout. Winning your freedom from those problems means seeking and finding the truth to replace those illusions. Only then will your behavior change. Obviously, again, this isn't as easy as it sounds, but it really is *that* simple.

Conclusion

I love the quote I learned from Mark Gorman several years ago, "If you don't like something, change it. If you can't change it, change the way you think about it."

From studying and practicing the principles in this book, you will not only solve every problem in your life but also have an unprecedented opportunity to leave a lasting legacy that will bless others that you care about for generations to come.

Completely contrary to public opinion, I finally discovered, that life is absolutely fair, in every detail.

If life was unfair, there could not be a God or a great intelligence or an organizer of the universe. There would be no such thing as good or bad, right or wrong.

There couldn't even be a rhyme or reason to life itself, we would be no more than an accident without purpose or objective. Human life would be utterly pointless. But, there is a God, there is right and wrong, there is order to the universe.

Likewise, God is all knowing, all powerful, perfectly just, perfectly merciful — and life is perfectly fair. If not so, God would cease to be God, for His judgments could never stand scrutiny because our circumstances would not have been fair to begin with. Any objection to life being absolutely and inherently fair is incompatible with a universe that operates on fixed and unchanging laws and principles

I am well aware that the vast majority of people everywhere will disagree — some violently — and I understand. I used to feel the same way and adamantly disagree myself. In fact, it took a few years of focused study into these core principles of life before it finally struck me like a bolt of lightning that I couldn't have been more wrong. The more I discovered, the more the truth became so unmistakably obvious, that I finally had to stop fighting against the inevitable and embrace the truth.

Like the miracle it was, my life almost immediately took on a much deeper meaning and purpose. It instantly gave me much more control over my life and every one of my circumstances began to improve. In many aspects, the changes were incredible, I was happier at a much deeper level than at any time before, the fear and uncertainty of the future gave way to freedom, excitement, and possibilities.

Is what you see (your life circumstances) the simple and total reality of life? Of course not. What we see is just the tip of the iceberg. A hint, a clue, a taste of the vast, invisible, yet-to-be-explored spiritual realms and the forces of nature you can tap into to create and recreated your circumstances to your best advantage. This great University of Life gives us all, every moment, the optimal opportunity to maximize our ultimate potential.

Summary

Here's the million-dollar question: What is the difference between those who fade quietly into the night and are all-too-soon forgotten and those great leaders who bequeath a lasting legacy to future generations? The difference is the lessons and other resources they chose to take away from their life's experiences and the circumstances they create with those resources.

I call this concept — that each of us was born and will always be a creator — the Alpha and Omega Principle because it really is the cornerstone and the capstone, the beginning and the end, of everything about life on Earth. It is the beginning and the end of everything you are and everything you are here to learn and to do and to become. Your potential is ultimately to learn to create perfectly.

The more perfect you become, the more perfect your creations will be, and the longer life span those creations will have. Ultimately, these perfect creations will take on a momentum and even a life of their own and have potential to increase themselves forever. Thus your returns become compounding and perpetual.

I love the poem (author unknown) which I heard from one of my favorite politicians, Bob McEwen.

> You cannot control the length of your life, But you can the width and the height,
> And the place you obtain in those quiet halls of fame, That position is yours to decide,
> And the trail that you blaze on life's rugged hills, Can be broad and easy to find,
> And the height you reach, inspire others to climb.
>
> You cannot steal back, from a day that is spent, Idle words or one single deed,
> They are posted at night on the bill boards of time, For others who follow to read,
> Nor can you dictate what history will write, Be it maim or be it sublime,
> But what's written of you will have an effect, On those generations yet unborn to time.
>
> Did the world get a bargain the day you were born, Or has your life to others brought shame?
> Do you ponder the fact how the folk will react, When descendants of yours speak your name?
> Will the ink of your life stand bold, or fade out, As history appraises the lines?
> Is their untarnished value in what you bequeath, To those generations yet unborn to time?

There are things over which you have control and things over which you do not. Whatever time you spend fretting about those things not directly under your control is time you will never have to explore and pursue the greatest opportunities into your path. If you concentrate on changing those things over which you have control — yourself, your thoughts, and your actions — then will you find true success and satisfaction.

I remember one day talking with a trucker friend on this subject. He began complaining about the increasing cost of diesel fuel and that he was afraid it was going to put him out of business and the major problems that would have on his family, his employees and their families. He then scoffed, as if there was no solution, "How am I going to change the cost of fuel?"

Once I established that he really wanted a solution and wasn't just complaining and not willing to change, I suggested, "First you need take inventory about what you can and cannot change. What you cannot change, you stop complaining about and accept with a grateful heart. Then take the list of things you can change and divide them into categories about what you can change quickly and what will take longer, including how you run your business.

Next, understand that the trucking business is **not** going away. I have no question that some companies will go out of business and blame it on fuel prices but that is **only** because they are focused on their problems. Others will stay in business because they've decide that going out of business is not an option, so they focus on usable solutions — no matter what.

My friend needed to properly utilize the resources over which he had control and put himself in a position where the cost of diesel has nothing to do with whether he succeeded or failed. The more he consciously created and controlled what he can — and that includes taking advice from others who understand his industry best — the more influence he will have over his future. If he chooses, he could also put himself in a position where he has much more influence over things in the future that he cannot control today, perhaps even the cost of fuel.

Let me now share a personal experience that pushed me to search for more real meaning in my own life, and another step on my ladder to discover the truth: One night I was suddenly jolted out of a sound night's sleep. "Eldon, wake up, I need your help."

I groggily opened my eyes to see my dad hovering over me. Hearing the urgency in his voice, I jumped up and pulled on my clothes. As I followed him out the back door, I was shocked awake in the frigid night air that almost instantly froze the moisture in my nose. We hurried through the back yard to a nearby barn.

He only slowed down slightly as he snatched a rope from a hook on the wall and then continued to the back corner. Back in that corner was one of our first-year heifers, about to give birth. She was clearly in trouble. The calf's front feet and the tip of his nose were showing, but he was stuck. I knew this heifer. She was typically quite frisky, and yet this night she lay on the barn floor in too much pain to move. Her life and the life of her unborn calf were in danger. Dad looped the rope around the calf's feet and instructed me to tie the other end to a nearby post.

I had helped "pull" calves and colts before, so this was not new for me. Tonight, however, I was in for an experience that I would always remember and would ultimately be a great blessing through my own most difficult experiences. I won't go into great detail, as it was quite traumatic, but I had never witnessed a birth so difficult.

I understood that both these lives were valuable to our small farm and that night I was afraid they both might die. I will always remember my dad's calm, soothing manner and words, which were as encouraging and comforting to me as to the animals.

I don't actually know how long we worked and struggled trying to get this calf born, but it seemed like hours. Finally, the head emerged, followed by the rest of a living, breathing, healthy bull calf. His mother groaned and shifted on the floor in relief. I sat down in the straw and leaned back, exhausted, against the rails of the stall.

Suddenly, a rush of emotions surged through my whole body. I trembled as tears trickled down my cheeks. I could only imagine the pain both those animals had suffered. I looked out of the partially open barn doors to see the night sky begin to lighten with the first rays of dawn. I looked toward heaven, frustrated and confused with unanswered questions: "How did my father know? What if we had been too late? Why is life so unfair? Why doesn't life just work like it's supposed to?" My feelings were all mixed up. I thought, "Thank goodness we saved them this time, but what about times we might not?"

It would turn out to be more than twenty-five years before I really began to discover the solutions to those questions. Now, when I look back at those kind of experiences, I do so with a far different perspective. What most people think of as "unfair" is an illusion. Everything we experience is specifically designed for our optimal personal growth, to take us places that we can't even dream now. Whether things are in or out of our control, such as the high cost of diesel fuel for truck drivers or the problems of a cow with a difficult delivery, life provides everyone involved with optimal opportunities to learn and grow so that we have more control in the future. I cannot express in words the thrill and passion that it brings to me to share at least a small portion of these core solutions with you and hear from you about how you are gaining more control over those things most important to you.

Chapter 2
The Omega & Alpha Principle

The second principle of the great hidden wisdom is, like the first, so simple and powerful that just recognizing it will begin to loosen the shackles of limitation and present possibilities you never believed were available to you before.

The Laws of Recreation

Throughout history, every time people have neglected or abused recreation, destructive consequences occur until they begin to honor it again. They rarely recognize the real cause of these problems and blame all kinds of other things. When people honor this principle, they instantly begin to see miraculous healing in themselves and the world around them.

I call creation the alpha and omega principle and recreation the omega and alpha principle. Creation is the first and the last because it is the entire purpose of the existence of life and time. Of course, every coin has two sides and recreation is the other side of that coin. Recreation is the last and the first principle because it is the great enabler of creation. It is impossible to have one without the other. They are the natural and continuous cycle of your life.

Like creation, it is impossible for you not to be involved in recreation. Are you working for your recreation so that your raw materials and resources for creation are being consumed or is your recreation working for you and enabling you to compound your increase of resources?

Activities: The Cement of Reality

Recreation, by literal translation, means "to create anew." If you ask any 1,000 people what they do for recreation, you'll get 1,000 different activities which relieve tension, gratify the senses, and other things which have nothing to do with what "recreation" really means. If you gave those same 1,000 people a paper with 'recreation' written on it and asked them to write a definition, simply by its spelling, they would come up with an entirely different definition which is far closer to reality than the first one they gave you verbally.

Like several other words we've talked about in this book, this word has almost completely lost its original intent and meaning. "Conventional wisdom" has so twisted its definition that it is almost unrecognizable, almost universally misunderstood, and thus rendered it almost useless for our purposes. Not to worry, I have a work-around for that. Because of this, it is virtually impossible for recreation to have the positive impact and intrinsic value to your life that it could and should. Regardless of what you currently think about recreation, even if you have studied it and understand its origins, there are things here that you have never recognized before.

Recreation can be spontaneous or planned; exhilarating or calming; cerebral or physical. When you learn to think about recreation as it was built into the universe, you can unleash the fullness of your potential. We often make the mistake of assuming that, because we are planning something, such as our life paths, recreation is a distraction — something to fill in hours/days when we have nothing more important to do. Exactly the opposite is true, recreation is absolutely necessary, it adds enjoyment to our existence and provides necessary distraction. Many will tell you that you shouldn't (and can't) be as passionate about recreation as you are about your work or family or other commitments.

On the other hand, as many of my mentors have expressed, "most people spend more time and often as much money planning their vacations than they do planning their lives." In either case, they never recognize what recreation actually is and thus never reap because they have never sown. Planning your recreation is as important as planning your creation. Recreation is the blueprint to creation. Without adequate recreation there cannot be adequate creation.

Information vs. Principles

Here again, it *is not* about information — the so-called recreational activities that relax and renew us — but the principle that is the priceless treasure. You are shortchanging yourself and everyone around you if recreational activities are not an integral part of your plan — you will not realize all the possible miracles that could benefit you and everyone around you.

Now, let me take a small diversion and shed a little light on what I'm really talking about. Contrary to "conventional wisdom", God's commandments were never designed to produce specific results for you. They were not actually even designed to teach you anything in and of themselves; they are not the great universal laws. They are designed to pull back the curtain and uncover core principles so that you can discover and live them by your own, deliberate choice. As I've mentioned before, understanding the principles to harness the laws is the only system in which we can thrive and progress forever.

Why mention this here? Excellent question — in Part 1, I said repentance is a universal law and defined it as the deliberate process of harmonizing yourself with universal laws. The commandments are gifts from God, they give you a "sneak-peak-preview" into the universal laws and principles. The commandments are exercises in cause and effect, designed to teach you much deeper, bigger, broader things. They require that you change both your actions and your attitudes, which is repentance. In terms of the great hidden wisdom, you might say that repentance is a way to re-create yourself. (Hold that thought, I will return to it.)

It is commonly thought that there are three motivations to action: Fear (of consequences by some higher authority), duty (to that higher authority), or love (for that higher authority). It's probable that we all abide certain laws for each of those motivations. Persons of good character obey because of love, or are striving toward that attitude. If you are obeying the commandments with the right motivation and paying close attention, you will discover that obeying the commandments begins to peel back the curtains and let you see into the great warehouse of the principles it represents.

People who obey the commandments are happier and more successful, simply because they are operating within the reality of cause and effect. This is just a small taste of what opportunities await you to create and live in your own world of abundance and privilege beyond comprehension — a world much bigger and immensely grander than your wildest imaginations. The commandments are such a tiny part of the great laws and principles that they really don't even measure by comparison, but that does not mean they are not useful. In fact, one of the most powerful ways to almost instantly tell if someone is speaking or writing from a perspective of information, knowledge or wisdom is the extent of which their words and perspectives are in harmony with universal laws and principles.

I find it extremely amusing that so many people take offense to biblical concepts because, without exception, none of them have done their homework. They haven't studied the Bible enough to figure out even a small portion of what the book really is. They just repeat things they've heard other people repeat, that other people have repeated for a very long time. Look through all of human history, every person, ancient or modern, who exudes true wisdom has taken to heart biblical concepts — without exception.

I have a standing offer to anyone who claims he or she doesn't believe in the Bible: If you have the courage to stand up for your beliefs then sit down with me for one or two hours in a reasonable conversation. I will prove that you not only believe in biblical principles, but that you'd fervently love to know how to better live by them because your life would be significantly improved by them. Every person who has ever had derogatory things to say about the Bible does so through abject ignorance — they simply know so little about the book that they should be embarrassed to say anything about it at all, especially anything negative.

Faith and Miraculous Results

The principle of recreation is only one of the many examples of how connected the biblical concepts are to the principles and how the principles themselves are the very fabric with which we must live in order to truly tap into the fulfilment and joys of living.

Ignoring this great hidden wisdom guarantees disorientation (a lack of balanced direction in life), illusion (a lack of clear understanding of life) and mental stress (a lack of calm necessary to touch spiritual realms). These challenges can be so severe one becomes unable to distinguish between reality, the universe as it is, and illusion, the universe as "conventional wisdom" tells you it is or even irrational hallucinations.

In the extreme, humans do lose their grip on reality, some even die, without reasonable attention to this principle — and that happens on every SPESIFC plane. The Bible references this principle as the fourth of the Ten Commandments. "Remember the Sabbath day to keep it holy. Six day shalt thou labour, and do all thy work; But the seventh day is the Sabbath of the Lord thy God: in it thou shalt not do any work, thou, nor thy son, nor thy daughter, thy manservant, nor thy maidservant, nor thy cattle, nor thy stranger that is within thy gates: For in six days the lord made heaven and earth, the sea and all that in them is, and rested the seventh day: wherefore the Lord blessed the Sabbath day, and hallowed it" (Exodus 20:8-11, KJV).

Like all of the commandments, this is not a great law of the universe. This is a tool, specifically and brilliantly designed to teach us about correct principles so that we recognize our own potential, discover and increase our own personal power to wield those principles wisely, harness the great laws of the universe and create what we want instead of what we don't want. Think of it as following a recipe; the commandments are some of the ingredients needed in order to make a great meal come to life. Isaac Newton's Third Law states, "For every action there is an equal and opposite reaction." Therefore, as we actively participate in creation, there is not just a desire but a core-level need for recreation.

Recreation Mentality vs. Re-Creation Mentality

Now, let's have some fun with how we interpret this word "recreation". Even if you've studied the word, hang on, I'm going to try to expand that understanding and, if you take it to heart, it will bless your life in the form of direct positive and powerful results. For most purposes, "recreation" (/REK-ree-ay-shun/) is a familiar and adequate term. I propose a new term — "re-creation" (/ree-KREE-ay-shun/) — that we can use when we want to make a clear distinction between relaxation of the body and renewal of the soul.

As you know, the law of the Sabbath states that we are not to work one day each week. God didn't simply say, "Take the day off" — this is the "recreation mentality". To understand the divine intent, we have to view the whole context of what He said about the day. Notice that more words in the Ten Commandments are devoted to the Sabbath than any other commandment. That's a clue about how important and all-encompassing this one is. Unlike any other commandment, He reveals something about Himself: He worked for six days then, on the seventh day, He rested. We need to do the same. The law of the Sabbath is not just about rest; it is also about having six productive days. It is, truly, impossible to fully "keep the Sabbath day holy" if we have not completed six meaningful six days and we are not planning on following it with six more productive days — this is the "re-creation mentality".

Note that there are actually two completely different aspects of re-creation: First, fun and games, to laugh and spend time connecting with and enjoying family and friends — this is the limit of what most people define as "recreation". Second, diversion enables us to look at things with fresh eyes and new perspectives — this is the grander concept of re-creation.

A metaphor: You are building a road through a thick forest. For six days you are on the ground, clearing trees, pulling stumps, moving rocks, building bridges and fences, leveling and compacting the ground, and laying pavement. On the seventh day, you get above it all, make sure you're going in the right direction, and avoiding the major obstacles. If you don't take that time away from physical labor for some intellectual labor, you will lose your way, go in the wrong direction, encounter unexpected obstacles, or worse, fall off a cliff.

This is the key to the re-creation mentality. Now, take a step back, just for a moment, and keep this all in context. Everyone knows that God is the great Creator — even if they don't believe in Him, they know how the faithful view Him. Therefore, the time and energy of His life are invested in creating. That is what you and I do, we create things, smaller things. If God thinks recreation is vital, we must be equally invested in doing it right. In Chapter 1, I said it is impossible for you not to create. Re-creation is not the absence of creation; it is the complementary form of creation. Now, this begins to get very exciting because it starts to expand out so quickly that it's hard to keep track of. We start to see this in every facet of our lives.

We see this principle of re-creation in its most obvious state, as we sleep. Each day, we spend approximately 16 hours creating stuff intentionally and consciously. Sleeping is not just to refresh the body, it is also designed to give your brain an opportunity to file and organize the activities and experiences, even all of the inputs of our senses throughout the day so we have better access and understanding of today's new information and knowledge for tomorrow. Imagine a conveyor belt of mail being continually dropped through your front door all day. It takes several hours every day for your subconscious to open and sort all that mail; organize and file it in the most useful ways you can. You know what happens to sleep-deprived people. Granted, some people need less sleep than others but everyone needs sleep and, if deprived of it long enough, anyone will become psychologically and emotionally unstable. Sleep and other re-creation periods are vital if a human is to operate at the optimal level. Recall, please, my statement in Part 1 Chapter 5: "For the purposes of this discussion, I'm defining **perfection** as 'performing at the optimal level'. Not *your* optimal level, *the* optimal level, there's a difference — miracles help us make this happen."

Personal Holidays

Is this the bottom-line of the principle? Yes and no — not only is it applicable daily and weekly, it is the main purpose of holidays. Let's look more closely. If I ask you what the word holiday means, what would you say? If I then asked you to guess from its spelling where the word came from, you might eventually correctly guess that it actually came from the idea of a "holy day". Holidays were specifically designed so we would have a few extra Sabbaths to "rest" from our work or creations on a monthly basis and at the end of each season. To really get into the meat of why re-creation is such a crucial and powerful principle, let's expand that to the year. Here, we see a much more in depth process and purposeful application for recreation.

Each year is divided into four seasons — spring, summer, autumn and winter. For most of the 6,000 years of recorded history, humanity has been an agrarian society. Spring is for preparing the ground (to be an optimal state to nurture our crops) then planting our seeds. Summer is for cultivating, making sure the plants receive adequate sunlight, water, and nutrition as well as protecting our crops from weeds, bugs and other threats. Autumn is for harvesting and preserving crops. Winter is for resting; snows bring us (most of us) a new supply of water; decomposing leaves add nutrients to the soil; winds distribute wild seeds, and so on.

Why can't we go from autumn to spring, instead of separating them with winter? In addition to those reasons already mentioned, winter gives the ground itself an opportunity to "rest from its labor". It is as crucial for the land to rest as it is for you to rest, otherwise, the same things will happen to the land as happens to you without adequate rest, it literally becomes retarded and ceases to function properly. Other trees and vegetation also rest in the winter. Winter combines many elements to rejuvenate the Earth as it provides opportunities for people to rejuvenate.

Unfortunately, we have lost sight of this crucial part of our existence and, just as surely as we become unstable because of sleep deprivation, our society is becoming unstable because we are dishonoring this principle of re-creation. Anciently, it went even further than today — the Israelites celebrated every seventh year as a sabbatical. During that year, they left their fields fallow — they neither planted nor harvested. For six years, they would work and store part of their harvest, not only to get through each winter, but also to get through the seventh year. What an amazing commitment these folks made, not only to their existence but to their evolution.

A Not-So-Bold Statement

Let's revisit the core reason for the law of the Sabbath. Like all commandments, it is not to be taken simply at face-value. It was designed to help us discover the laws and apply this far more all-encompassing principle of re-creation:

Each night provides an opportunity to categorize and file the events of the day, so that we are wiser and better able to use the knowledge gained today to create miracles tomorrow.

Each Sabbath allows us to reflect on the previous week, evaluate what worked and what didn't work, gather with our mentors and other like-minded people and prepare to create new and better circumstances so the succeeding six days will be more productive than the previous.

Each month and season, holidays allow us to reflect on previous months and seasons and apply the re-creation principle in an even larger context.

Each year, winter is a time to reflect on the previous seasons and apply the re-creation principle in a still larger context and make sure next year's harvest is bigger and more abundant than last year.

Does that mean there's no room for fun and games? Absolutely not. Fun and games are all part of the great plan. It is important as a diversion and it is important for us to get out and laugh and have fun. Likewise, you have heard the old adage, "Find a trade you love and you'll never work a day in your life." Re-creation shouldn't be an escape from the drudgery of your employment — your employment shouldn't be drudgery. Your work should be enjoyable; it should be something for which you feel passion. If it isn't, you're in the wrong business. Find something that's more suited to your character and your personality. If you really enjoy your work, you'll do it better, be more effective, earn more and suffer less stress.

Also remember that recreation is intrinsically connected with this word "celebration". The word implies that you've done things worthy of celebration. Now be careful before you raise objections. I know we "celebrate" other people and the great things they have done. However, that's a significant clue. The only way to truly honor and celebrate what other people have done for you is to perpetuate their legacy by honoring, that is, pushing the limits of your own potential. Otherwise your celebration lacks integrity.

It is so important, in addition to other holidays, to celebrate when you reach certain mile stones. Especially sizable ones. The more you make it a priority to reward yourself and honor your own efforts by celebrating your wins, the more you are inspired, enabled and incentivized to make even better improvements in the future. That is a another ingenious design of built-in times for recreation. Let them push you to accomplish things worth celebrating.

Sometimes you may feel you haven't done anything to deserve celebrating, sometimes, perhaps you haven't. However, pay attention and celebrate your real victories. That obviously is never a license to justify not doing your best, but let it be a constant reminder and you will be amazed at how it holds your feet to the fire and makes you proud of yourself—not to mention the obvious gift of the better life you are constantly creating for yourself. That is a powerful place to live from.

Some Final, Miscellaneous Thoughts

The Omega and Alpha Principle is worth a book, even many books, on its own. I may write one in the future. For now, since I have more to teach you, we'll have to wrap this up. Before we do, I want to share a few more ideas that will be of use to you. The following paragraphs are not connected in sequence; they are included to provide additional insight into this principle:

The concept of the Sabbath can be invoked many times within every day as we transition among our daily tasks. As we set work aside for family or family aside for community service, we have a few moments to refocus and realign our thoughts. We should make a point to take a short diversion and start each new task with fresh eyes and spirit.

You may have heard/been part of conversations about what kind of activities we should be doing during the Sabbath as well as what kind of activities we should avoid. This question takes us back to what we talked about in an earlier chapter: "What is the answer to every question?" The answer is, "It depends." Is it really critical to do no work on the Sabbath? As you recall, I was born on a dairy farm. Do you really think it would be a good idea not to feed the animals and milk the cows on Sundays or holidays or through the winter or the entire year during the sabbatical? That would be cruelty on top of stupidity. Of course, there are things that need to be done if we want to survive and thrive. Remember, "The Sabbath was made for man, and not man for the Sabbath" (Mark 2:27, KJV).

Likewise, there is more to this principle than simply not working, and this, too, has been lost to much of modern culture. For instance, many people spend at least part of their Sabbath in study of God's word. Before you completely zone out on this concept, I remind you that when we talk of God's word, we are not talking about a specific religion. Our goal is to tap into the spiritual realms, to activate the gift of grace, and so on, as discussed in Part 1. God is the author of this concept, (check history, the first references to it are all attributed to God's words). as well as all the others. He knows exactly how things work best and why they work. Doesn't it make sense that one would devote part of this period He set aside to seek understanding of His way and why he created Earth and allowed us to be here like he did?

You are not just your physical body, you also have a spirit. If you don't continue to discover how to nourish and cultivate that spiritual part of yourself, nothing you ever do physically will make up for it and that will become a weak-link in your chain that will cause you extreme problems—even kill you if you don't change that habit. No different than any other SPESIFC of your life.

Part of setting strategy involves the criticality of getting together with your mentors and consultants; those people who are wiser than you are, so they can help you reflect and evaluate your past, by way of the amount of your harvest. These mentors can then coach you toward increasing the harvest tomorrow, next week, next month, next season, next year, next seven years. Who is the ultimate coach in this situation? Wouldn't it be the very author of the concept of Sabbath? Utilizing this principle allows us to begin to understand things on a bigger scale.

There are some myths that we should mention:

- The more effort we put into a project, the better results we'll have from it.
- If we stop working, we stop growing.
- Daydreaming is a waste of time.
- Keep your nose to the grindstone; your shoulder to the wheel, work hard, get a good education and you'll be fine!

These are all ½ truths, if we don't see the opposite, they are big lies. Can you spend too much time at work? Of course you can, but we've learned by sad experience that this mythical thinking and behavior produces major negative consequences. Many assume that, if we keep our "nose to the grindstone", we get more accomplished than if we take systematic breaks. The opposite is true. Like all principles, there is a balance that must be preserved in order to provide optimal return on investment.

There is part of the great hidden wisdom that will bring an entirely new perspective on how to accurately judge and measure which activities are worthy of your actual Sabbath and which are better suited for your Saturdays and other days. I call them "forgive and forget" activities. My responsibility to forgive others is never about the other person, it is only for myself. Getting back in touch with my spiritual roots, visiting the down-trodden, re-evaluating my goals and objectives, making sure I am headed in the right direction and for the right reasons, re-establishing my commitment to my own evolution, and so on. Paul encapsulated this idea when he said, "…but this one thing I do, forgetting those things which are behind, and reaching forth unto those things which are before, I press toward the mark for the prize" (Philippians 3:13-14, KJV).

Does that sound like *one* thing to you? That sounds more like *three* very major things, with a lot more all wrapped up together. What is he saying? Learn from the past and then leave it there. Then harness and laser-focus all those resources and energies that you have harvested from the past in your current moments into creating your optimal future. As you do, everything becomes one. You can only create something better in the future if you willingly let go of the past.

Conclusion

Now what actually happens when we make a habit of doing this in our lives? Let's go back to the actual words as rooted in the Bible. "Honor the Sabbath day to keep it holy." What does the word "holy" actually mean? It means "whole". Wholeness is also the definition of integrity and, having been a carpenter most of my working life, I understand, at least in part, what it means for a structure to have integrity. Any builder worth their salt will invest whatever it takes to insure that what they are building is mathematically, structurally sound. To be structurally sound is to be in harmony with universal laws, to reach optimal performance and create the best possible circumstances — that which is truly structurally sound can last forever.

Re-creation is a process to evolve ourselves so that we can continue to re-create ourselves and our circumstances to make us bigger, stronger, better and more fulfilled — to make ourselves structurally sound — to further our climb toward perfection. That requires wisdom — even the great hidden wisdoms.

The Great Native American Chief and spiritual leader Smohalla (of the Nez Perce, from Washington State where I currently live) counseled "Each one must learn for himself the highest wisdom. It cannot be taught in words. Men who work cannot dream, and wisdom comes to us in dreams." These dreams that Smohalla refers to, is a part of grace — a gift — that confirms to our soul, in recreation times, the truths we are discovering and provides additional guidance and directions to apply in our creation times.

Summary

To assist in your study of this principle of re-creation, I have devised an acronym, REST:

- **Reflection** on the past and remember what you did and did not do.
- **Evaluation** of what worked and what didn't work and what we learned.
- **Strategic** goal-setting with mentors — gathering new information, becoming more grounded in truth, and setting goals for the next week, month, season, year and seven years.
- **Tactical** planning — making definite plans with specific deadlines to best use those ideas in the future that will improve our lives.

And when do we do that?
- When ending a task (hourly even momentary).
- Each night (daily).
- Each Sabbath (weekly).
- On holidays (monthly).
- Each season holidays (quarterly)

- Each winter (yearly).
- Each sabbatical (every seventh year).

Hourly/Task Chunking	Daily/Nighttime	Weekly/Sabbath	Monthly/Holiday	Seasonally/Holiday	Yearly/Wintertime	Years/Sabbatical	Millennium
1	1	1	1	1	1	7	1000

Reflect on past and Prepare for next season—Brainstorm/Strategize for improvement
Dennis Waitley and richest man in China (500 yr. plan)—how long have you planned for?

live *Righteous, grow, evolve, increase, develop, magnify*

To be in the process of "living" means to be growing, to evolve, to increase.
What is opposite then?
The process of "dyeing" which means to be breaking down, to deteriorate, to decay.

evil *die, decay, deteriorate, decline, decompose, corrode*

In order to really "live" then, we MUST be realizing a "return on investment", create increase, (Investing vs. Consuming)

Lay up fruit against the season thereof... WHY? So you can focus on greater issues!

Adam & Eve "*dress* and *keep* this garden—Be fruitful, and multiply and *replenish the earth* and *subdue* it and have *dominion*". In other words, create increase (not just in children but) in every area of life. Learn to make the earth your profitable servant. Create harmony and synergy with all things. Teach the earth to produce a perpetual harvest...eternal yield. First & last lessons Jesus taught Apostles... *Reap an abundant harvest!* (fishes and grapes) IF you pay attention you will help transform this into Celestial kingdom.

Jesus gave us the formula AND THE STEWARDSHIP 1st to learn how and 2nd to produce, a rich and abundant life. Here are the raw materials and the directions to accomplish that.

Seed, soil, sunshine, rain, the seasons, the miracle of life, and human potential to improve processes and increase harvests.

RESULTS from **BEHAVIOR** from **ATTITUDES** from **INTENTIONS** from **CHARACTER** from **PARADIGMS** from **EDUCATION** from **ASSOCIATIONS**
Critical to keep in proper perspective and ALWAYS deal only with core issues NEVER symptoms.

Springtime =	Summertime =	Autumn =	Wintertime =	
Prepare ground	Cultivate	Harvest	Reflect to Roots	The wise man built
Plant seeds	Water	Preserve	Evaluate the past	his house upon a
Fertilize	Sunshine	Store up	Strategize/Brainstorm	rock...
Nurture	Protect	Prepare ground	Traject into future	Keeping on a foundation of universal laws and principles

Reflect & Evaluate *Strategize & Tactical*

(M T W T F S **S** M T W T F S)

Where there is no vision the people parish Seventh year sabbatical

Law of familiarity
Thoughts
Speech
Notes
(journal)

Act Upon

2 Opportunities for Learning
1) Others experience
2) Our own experience

Desire	Ask	Seek	Knock
Beliefs	Information	Knowledge	Wisdom

"Men and women... are makers of themselves, by virtue of the thoughts which they choose and encourage. That the mind is the master weaver both of the inner garment of character and of the outer garment of circumstance..." James Allen

RECREATION   NEXT
RE-CREATION   BEST GUESS

To spiritually 're-create' (tweak our recipes)

As Children of a Creator we are inherently creators

Laws of creation spiritual and physical

Earth is the ultimate Laboratory = Discovering correct formulas
Experience = Experiment

Sabbath = Holy Day
Holy = Whole
Whole = Integrity
Integrity = optimal strength/perfect

"Every person in life will pay one of two prices, they will either pay the price of discipline or they will pay the price of regret. If the price of discipline weight ounces, comparatively, the price of regret weighs tons..."!!! Dexter Yager

Chapter 3
The Owner's Manuals Principle

This principle remains part of the great hidden wisdom because most people don't believe it exists. Even most of those who do believe in it don't understand how prevalent it is. Explorers, entrepreneurs, and dreamers of all kinds have sacrificed, researched, and traveled to distant lands to discover it, mostly without success. Yet everyone who has found it has realized that it has been all around them all the time, hiding, just under the surface of what they believe they already know.

I'll bet, like me, you have heard people protest, "Life is hard! It doesn't come with an owner's manual." Of "I wish my kids would have come with an owner's manual." You may even know someone like that. Perhaps you know them intimately, like the person in the mirror. If it is, take comfort, I was that person for the majority of my life.

After a number of years of struggle and pain, I finally discovered that claiming ignorance about what to do because I didn't have an owner's manual was really nothing more than a terrible excuse not to push myself to think for myself. Plus, my excuse was absolutely not true. It is so common, and yet so disappointing, to hear ourselves consistently repeat so much of this kind of "conventional wisdom", which is in fact, just mindless repetition of things we've heard from others who never learned to think for themselves.

We all have access to the owner's manuals of life. We simply haven't been taught how to recognize or take advantage of them. Life's owner's manuals come from five basic sources:

One: The Spiritual Owner's Manual

Most people are aware — or, at least, suspect — there is something inside them from whence help comes. This is true — wonderfully, potentially miraculously, true! Each of us has access to a greater wisdom. Often, it's "just a feeling" — an emotion, an idea, a "gut reaction" — on occasion, there are actual words, what some have called "the still, small voice". Sadly, many people ignore this greater wisdom.

Why? From elementary school through college, our teachers taught us about our five senses — sight, smell, sound, taste, and touch. They omit (many times intentionally) the fact that you also have a sixth sense — one completely natural in every human being. This sense is far more powerful and crucial to your personal well-being than your other five physical senses combined.

For example, one of my all-time favorite heroines, Helen Keller, lost her physical senses of sight and hearing and thus her power to communicate. Through her amazing teacher and mentor, Anne Sullivan, Helen learned to rely heavily on this sixth sense and as a result, became a phenomenon and a powerful force for good all over the world. Strangely, for most of us, it takes what seems to be a catastrophe to open us up to much of what would have otherwise remained undiscovered insights and opportunities.

It is your spiritual sense. You may call it intuition, inspiration, guidance, discernment, or something else, but it is supernatural and providential in nature. Whatever you call it, many people have come to trust it implicitly, even more than their physical senses. Through experience, they have discovered that it is much wiser than themselves and more reliable than all their other senses. Most people develop some level of spiritual sensitivity without even realizing it and even unconsciously activate the gift of grace that we discussed in Part 1 Chapter 6.

In order to benefit most from this sixth sense, you must first realize it exists and then deliberately develop it through sensitivity, personal reflection, some form of meditation, or simply paying attention to it. Look back on those "ah-ha!" moments you've had. Most came to you by way of your sixth sense. Imagine how much better your creations will be when you conscientiously and steadily work on cultivating that sixth sense. It brings grace to sharpen, and enhance all your other senses. When "ah-ha!" moments cease to be miracles and become common events, you are evolved to new heights and are now capable of creating even bigger miracles.

Utilizing this spiritual sense will help you discover and interpret the wisdom of the universe that's hiding all around you in plain sight. Without acknowledging this unique and underutilized gift, you are left without the tools to control and guide your life towards a greater future. Without it, you are left to follow the path of least resistance, a path that never has and never can lead to greatness. Additionally, refusing to acknowledge this spiritual sense will only lead you into disasters of the most painful kind. This spiritual sense, properly utilized, enhances all your other senses. It is also a divine compass that leads you to the ultimate source of wisdom, peace and fulfillment by holding you accountable to the truth and shaping your integrity.

Important note: I am not speaking of religion but of the inner voice that we all possess. No matter what your religious beliefs, every person is born with a spiritual self. Also, I need to point out that there are, actually, three voices that speak to you and provide ideas about what to think and how to behave.

First, the voice from your own brain which constantly sends you ideas. Depending on your surroundings, these may be good ideas or bad ideas. This voice can only respond to the level of your desires and conscious and subconscious understanding you have of how the world works. These ideas may or may not be based on reality, they may be spot-on accurate or a simple guess as to how you should behave. They are always based on emotions and suggest behaviors that you believe will bring you pleasure and avoid pain.

Second, there is the spiritual voice that is your friend, an all-wise and caring mentor who has your best interest at heart. It will warn, encourage, and teach you to grow and become who you are best suited to be, if you let it.

Third, there is a voice that is your enemy. It prompts, encourages, and, in every way, tries to persuade you to think about and do things that may seem prudent or even wonderful or justified in the moment. Eventually, however, if you act on these prompts, your behavior will cause you decay, to lose track of your real purpose and potential, to lure and lead you down destructive paths in all the SPESIFCs of life.

A brief sidebar, as the judge would say: Those of you who are religious might have been wondering if I'd make a God-Satan analogy or reference of some sort. Oh, yes, and here it is: there are positive and negative spiritual forces in the universe — there are, actually, positive and negative forces (or influences, if you prefer) in everything. These three voices are one manifestation of those forces. The eternal war between good and evil, as some have called it. Be aware of these competing forces, learn which is which and make sure you are following the influences that have your best interest at their core.

Your own spirit naturally interacts with the spiritual forces outside yourself. Some will tempt you to indulge in actions that are bad for you — they dress-them-up with all kinds of instant gratification but will always end in painful circumstances. These are called temptations. Other spiritual forces urge you to act in ways that are good. Though many of these require a little longer-term thinking, they will, inevitably, help you create circumstances of success that no one can ever take from you. These we call inspiration. The more you pay attention to these temptations and inspirations, the better you'll learn to trust your sixth sense. Your conscience and other positive spiritual influences, will keep you on track to find and fulfill your ultimate destiny and potential.

Part of learning to trust your spiritual sense comes from asking yourself what long-term outcomes you are most likely to create by following this idea or that. Ask yourself what really is motivating your decisions. Are your decisions to choose a particular action based in selfishness or selflessness; toward servitude or service; in the indulgence of an appetite or in exercising reasonable self-discipline; in judging others unjustly or in honoring their goodness? In instant gratification which will rob you of resources to invest in the future or long-term, compounding success that will bring you rich returns?

You always attract the type of spiritual forces that are most like your current behavior. If you are actively pursuing the five crucial keys to prepare yourself for GRACE (Part 1 Chapter 6), you will attract positive, uplifting spiritual influences. You will also experience a growing sense of affinity with your spiritual sense, which will help you create circumstances of long-term satisfaction and inner peace. This will enable you to more fully tap into your spiritual powers even when you find yourself in the most difficult challenges.

Two: Your Historical Owner's Manual

History is a powerful owner's manual because history is nothing more or less than the results other people have created from their thinking and behaviors of the past. It is much easier to evaluate the long-term results of specific choices when you study the past than by trying to guess accurately what might happen in the future based on your own experience and today's choices alone.

What's the "conventional wisdom" (or, as I would prefer to call it, "conventional stupidity") on history? Mostly, it's memorizing names, dates, stories, geography, facts, and other data. That's not education, that's a foolish and pointless waste of priceless time and energy. If anyone ever tells you, "Oh, I study history to learn lessons," ask them, "In that case then, tell me *specifically* how your life is better today than yesterday — or even this month from last month — because of your history lessons?"

Now, strengthening your memory is obviously a good thing. It is also obvious, I hope, that the more valuable the things you memorize, the better off you are, if what you memorize is in pursuit of learning principles and understanding them more deeply. If you lose track of the core value of history — to discover and confirm principles that will improve your life — all that memorizing will be of no value to you. It will actually leave you poorer than before.

Can you show me how your life has deliberately and significantly improved because of your intentional history lessons over the last year? Show me that list of goals, how your history lessons enabled you to create miracles with them, and how the bottom-line results of your life have changed because of them. As I have asked audiences over the course of several years, I have only had a tiny handful of people out of thousands who could tell me specifically how their lives have directly and significantly improved because of their history lessons.

Every era of time has its wise men and women. They taught their own people and recorded their wisdom for generations to follow. Today, their teachings are more available than ever before. Anyone who rightly expects to improve their life must study them with a passion to grow. Just be aware that authors and self-proclaimed authorities are no different than any other occupation. You can find so-called experts everywhere — they are a dime a dozen — but good the ones are, still, very rare.

They are the sages who have proven what they teach by having produced miraculous results in their own lives and the lives of their students. They are the ones worthy of the time and energy required to study and understand their wisdom.

I have made a habit to study only those people who practiced, successfully, what they taught every day.

Beware also that just because someone creates miracles in one area of life, doesn't mean they understand other areas. There is a very devastating trend to take peoples advice outside their areas of expertise and even to assume people have expertise when they really don't. It is super-easy to get tipped over and mess up your life that way. Make sure the formulas they are teaching are in the same areas as the miraculous results they accomplished. Just study articles, books, videos, etc. where famous actors are asked about politics or sports figures about relationships or politicians about economics, etc., etc. where their answers were completely contrary to reality and yet the masses follow them in droves like mindless sheep and are lead to disaster.

Three: Your Role Models and Mentors Owner's Manual

Role models are great owner's manuals because, more than just their history, you can adopt them as part of your mastermind team and employ them as coaches. Even if your chosen role models or mentors are long dead, you can study their words, ideas, contributions, thought processes, and results.

Tony Robbins, another of my mentors that I encourage you to study, not only says that "success leaves clues," he also explains about "modeling" (following role models). To find someone who consistently produces the kind of results you want and then learn how they did it. If you do the same things, you will enjoy the same kinds of results. Likewise, we can learn powerful lessons about what not to do from people who create disasters.

Years ago, it dawned on me that Solomon, because of his true heart, was promised by God that he would become the richest and wisest of all men on Earth and, so, I began studying his life and words. I have received a fair amount of flak from several people who condemn Solomon for his later failures. Solomon's failures were real, but they don't negate his earlier wisdom. In fact, they confirm it — Solomon began to fail the day he stopped listening to his own wisdom. Anyone who condemns Solomon has only convicted himself or herself of not paying attention to the whole story in context, thereby missing a great opportunity to create miracles of his or her own.

When people criticize Solomon or anyone else who has accomplished phenomenal things, I am reminded of Theodore Roosevelt's comment:

> It is not the critic that counts; not the man who points out how the strong man stumbles, or where the doer of deeds could have done better. The credit belongs to the man who is actually in the arena, whose face is marred by dust and sweat and blood; who strives valiantly; who errs and comes up short again and again, because there is no effort without error

and shortcoming; but who does actually strive to do the deeds; who knows the great enthusiasms, the great devotions; who spends himself in a worthy cause; who at the best knows in the end the triumph of high achievement, and who at the worst, if he fails, at least fails while daring greatly, so that his place shall never be with those cold and timid souls who know neither victory nor defeat.

It also reminds me of what my father used to say, "We should be careful about judging others because more often than not, their mistakes and short-comings would have been our own if we'd had similar circumstances and occasions to make them."

When you do the research into the results produced by Solomon and his father, David (and so many others who are condemned by the ignorant and thoughtless), the evidence of their results is staggering. It's mind boggling! My life is richer in every way because of my own study of Solomon, David, and others. I often catch myself thinking, "What would Solomon do in this situation?"

Another common complaint from poor and conventional thinkers is that they have never had good role-models. But that argument is self-condemning. As soon as you get serious about finding the ideal role models for you, you will begin to find them, just like I did. If you can't be around them in person, you can certainly be around them from their writings, audios and videos. I have had many people complain "I don't have the money or the time or resources or youth or experience or" whatever. I have to remind them that there are these things called "libraries" and today there is more information on the Internet than you could study in many lifetimes. I also remind them they are the creators of their lives. If you don't carve out the time, you simply won't ever have the results. In addition, other peoples' bad examples can significantly shorten your own learning curve if you are insightful, conscientious and courageous enough to recognize and take them to heart.

Be aware that even many so-called "respected authorities" are despicable examples — merely riding a wave that will soon crash on the rocks of reality — while others now in dismal circumstances are in the process of rising from the poverty and wreckage around them to become some of the greatest leaders of the future. The trick, therefore, is to study and discover principles. The more you understand principles, the easier you will see through the face-value, facades and illusions of false success to the real winners who deserve your respect as role models. The sooner you learn about these principles, the sooner you will learn to discover how to find the role models who can and will lead you to your own unique and miraculous greatness.

God gave you two opportunities to learn; first, from your own experience, and second, from other peoples' experiences. If you refuse to learn from others, you are automatically relegated to learn only from your own experience and utterly waste your God-given potential for greatness. So you must use both to gain the maximum effect in the least amount of time with the least amount of pain.

Four: Your Personal Experience Owner's Manual

In Part 1 Chapter 4, we discussed principles. I stated that principles can never be learned from others, only discovered by yourself by way of your own deliberate experience. Your role models' and mentors' experiences will push you in the right direction, and, in many ways it's better to learn from other peoples' mistakes than your own. That said, it is equally true that you are going to make mistakes of your own. You need to learn from them. Somethings, such as the great hidden wisdom from principles, can only be comprehended from your own, personal experience. Therefore, your own experience is crucial and you must be proactive in creating your own owner's manual. The sooner you make this an intentional practice, the sooner you can leave naivety and mediocrity behind and venture into the world of the wise.

Remember, also, that you are unique. You need to learn from your life because it is *your life*, the best university you will ever attend. Your life is, in every detail, what you have created it to be and, therefore, includes optimal opportunities to gain the experience necessary for your own unique purposes and to maximize your own unique potential. You just need to recognize the opportunities that exist in your unique problems and exercise the courage to take those leaps of faith that enable you to solve those problems. Also, the better a student of life you become, the more you will learn from your own experiences, as well as from others, to discover the formulas that will get you what you want.

This is what my own personal journals are all about now. They are a record of the principles I have discovered through my own experience. The raw data of anyone's history may lend a good feeling or two as people reminisce about fond memories, or learn about others struggles and successes, but those journals will never do anyone else any good until future readers commit to and begin discovering the principles by which we lived and the results created by those principles.

Five: Your Nature and Environmental Owner's Manual

From my younger years on the farm, the lessons of the harvest have remained in my heart and mind and time and again bring understanding about why we reap the results we do, and how, if I want something different, I only need to follow a different formula. If you want things to be better, you must find and apply a better formula. The success of my mentors and my own real success have come about only as I pay attention to the lessons Mother Earth provides. As you pay attention to these lessons and correctly understand them and apply them in your life, you will also learn to reap the harvest you desire.

Many years ago, I heard a quote that hit me with such force that I immediately wrote it down and have kept in mind ever since. I have tried to find the author of this quote, without luck. I wrote, "Nature never reveals its secrets; it only responds to a method of questioning."

The laws of the harvest and principles of nature are all around you at every moment. All you need to do is pay attention to how nature works and you suddenly begin to perceive some of the most profound guidance and lessons of life. Unfortunately, as I stated earlier in this book, as a general society we are not close to the earth anymore. As a direct consequence, our senses are muted and dulled to the principles that are obvious to those people who do live close to the earth.

In any area of life, there are principles of cause and effect to discover. In discovering those causes and effects in nature and within your environment, you tap into a most powerful owner's manuals. When I was 20 years old, I first heard "Good Timber", a poem by Douglas Mallock. This poem instantly spoke to me, so much so that I later chased down the speaker and asked for a copy. Given my experience as a lumber jack living in the mountains, surrounded by the tall and slender lodge pole pines that were a huge contrast to the small, scrubby pinion pines and juniper cedars around our farm, I immediately recognized the poem's truths. Years later, its power even helped me to face my fear of living in a city. Currently, I live happily in a home close enough to the city for easy access but far enough away to appreciate and enjoy the open country spaces and clean, fresh air.

This poem is a powerful look into ourselves from the environment around us.

> The tree that never had to fight
> For sun and sky and air and light,
> But stood out in the open plain
> And always got its share of rain,
> Never became a forest king
> But lived and died a scrubby thing.
>
> The man who never had to toil
> To gain and farm his patch of soil,
> Who never had to win his share
> Of sun and sky and light and air,
> Never became a manly man
> But lived and died as he began.
>
> Good timber does not grow with ease:
> The stronger wind, the stronger trees;
> The further sky, the greater length;
> The more the storm, the more the strength.
> By sun and cold, by rain and snow,
> In trees and men good timbers grow.

Where thickest lies the forest growth,
We find the patriarchs of both.
And they hold counsel with the stars
Whose broken branches show the scars
Of many winds and much of strife.
This is the common law of life.

In her every space, crack, and corner, Mother Earth reaches out because she longs to teach you specific lessons and principles. Sadly, we are plagued today by a pandemic of "microwave mentality" — the desire for instant gratification and a plodding unawareness of those lessons from our Mother Earth. When you live out of balance with the law of the harvest, you are like the fabled grasshopper who failed to prepare for the long winter and ends up starving. Microwave mentality prevents anyone who adopts it from understanding and applying these laws and from ever achieving anything close to a happy life.

We see this lack of understanding all around us as society suffers from spiritual, physical, emotional, social, intellectual, financial, and chronological decay. The problem gets worse as we, in the arrogance of what we deem to be progress, fail to learn lessons from the past. The great poet Robert Frost wrote, "We all dance around in a ring and suppose, while the answer sits in the middle and knows."

"Conventional wisdom", in its arrogance, dances around claiming to increase and evolve while actually decaying from the inside out. While everyone around you is so busy supposing, do you ever sit still, calm your mind and listen long enough to recognize the guidance the environment has to offer? Do you then get up and take action to discover the natural wisdom which is inherent at the center of all reality? As Ralph Waldo Emerson wrote, "Let him learn a prudence of a higher strain. Let him learn that everything in nature, even dust and feathers, go by law and not by luck, and what he sows, he reaps."

Reaping rewards from the laws of the harvest requires intelligence, skills, character and insight but all these come naturally if you only begin and persist, while decay flows from idleness.

Conclusion

While you're at it, notice all of these formerly unnoticed nuances in your life. Begin to wonder not only what they are but *why* they are. Take to heart only what truly wise people say and recognize the colossal difference between being smart and being wise. Again, as I've said many times, "what you memorize can make you smart, but only what you discover has the potential to make you wise." As Jesus taught, "Wherefore, by their fruits ye shall know them" (Matthew 7:20, KJV).

The laws of nature are the laws of success. What makes things grow and what makes things die? What draws people closer to you and what pushes them away? What tantalizes your senses with momentary but fleeting pleasure in contrast to those things that bring you powerful and lasting happiness that compounds forever?

The following are the five basic steps you used to create the life you now live including all your current successes, habits and failures. The owner's manuals listed above will enable you to use these same steps to create a new life of whatever you want most.

1. You collected ideas from others around you and combined them with your own imagination and research to determine what you believe is possible.

2. You decided which of these perceived options are most valuable to you in any given moment.

3. You devised a recipe, a plan or formula to achieve those things.

4. You followed that recipe, which typically included lots of changes along the way as you gain additional insights from your experiences.

5. You received the only results possible from the ingredients and processes of the recipes you chose to apply.

Summary

Your *spiritual* sense — intuition, inspiration, guidance, discernment, or whatever you want to call it — is the gift of grace. There are unseen spiritual realms in the universe and God rules over them in the hope you will let Him help you. Those "ah-ha!" moments you've had can be better and more numerous. They can better your creations when you conscientiously and steadily work on cultivating the grace that ripens, sharpens, and enhances your spiritual sense. Such "ah-ha!" moments can cease to be miracles; they can become common events that help you create miracles.

All of *history* is at your disposal. Other people have created circumstances, based on their thoughts, the events of their lives and how they reacted to those events. With that as background, they set out to create circumstances by making specific choices. When you study the past, by reviewing what the wise men and women that lived in every era did, and, more importantly, why they did and what resulted, you'll come to comprehend principles that will enhance your ability to create positive circumstances.

We choose role models because their *success* leaves clues. Success comes from harnessing and then harmonizing with these universal laws. You can find healthy shortcuts by finding someone consistently producing the kind of results you want, copy their behavior and repeat their success.

Your *personal experience* is unique. History and role models can take you so far, but you need to learn from your life because it is your life, the best classroom you will ever have. Your life is what you have created it to be and, therefore, will include optimal opportunities to gain experience necessary for your own unique purposes and to maximize your own unique potential.

Mother Earth's *natural and environmental world* never reveals its secrets but it responds to proper questioning. Everything in the world operates by strict adherence to universal law. The farmer reaps his inevitable result based on what and how he sows and so do you. Nature's laws and the formulae control our environment; they are set. If you want something different, you only need to follow a different formula. If you want things to be better, you must find and apply a better formula.

Chapter 4
The Apprenticeship Principle

The fourth secret, ancient principle is, perhaps, the most intriguing. Every person on Earth has expended huge resources to discover and understand this great hidden wisdom and most have failed. Most people believe they have far more education than they actually have, as verified by the poor to mediocre results they produce. It is evident that the true nature of education remains, for the most part, hidden from the masses. We've been taught from our youth to look for education in places it can't be found, and so we end up defining it in incorrect terms that preclude us from ever discovering it in the future.

What is Education?

When I speak of education, I am not talking about formal schooling, where the emphasis is usually on memorization and testing. I am talking about how you develop the perspectives that allow you to properly interpret your life's experiences, how those interpretations determine what you take away from your experiences and how you use those takeaways to create positive circumstances in your future.

Mark Twain said it well, "Don't let schooling get in the way of your education." Understand this from the outset: schooling is absolutely *not* the same as education. Education is *not* about what you memorize for a grade. Education *is* discovering your real self and your place in the real universe. Education *is* interpreting life's events and differentiating between reality and illusion. Education *is* determining what circumstance you need to create to move closer to perfection.

In the computer world, programmers use the acronym GIGO, "garbage in, garbage out." If a programmer inputs flawed code or erroneous data, the resulting program will produce nothing or, worse, useless and misleading results. Similarly, when you operate your life based on inaccurate or false information, you get results that are inaccurate or false. Real education exposes the illusions and reveals truth.

The results you currently realize in each SPESIFC area of your life are direct reflections of (and the only standard by which you can accurately measure) how correct or incorrect your education has been. A great education is all about developing good character, gaining wisdom, learning the difference between positive and negative thinking, getting your ego under control, learning to stop looking for easy answers and develop habits of asking the hardest questions. A great education prepares you to naturally continue learning and produce a life of genuine happiness, peace of mind, and fulfillment by better organizing and managing the SPESIFC areas of your life.

The Five Concepts of True Education

When you go back to the original meaning of the word "educate" it meant to "lead them out", "bring up" or "rear" (as in children). It gets even more interesting when you discover the real meaning of related words like "teach" which, throughout history, has meant "to show", meaning by example, and with results to prove it, not just to tell or explain or help memorize. Add to that the literal definition of the word "learn" which means "to gain experience by following a track", and it begins to paint an interesting picture. Much different than most refer to these words today.

Understand the Spiritual

I think most people understand that *you* are not just *you*. "There is more to you than meets the eye," as the old saying goes. That something more is your spirit, the part of you that existed before physical birth and will exist after physical death. We have spoken of the spiritual realms of the universe and your ability to tap into their power. This spiritual aspect to education connects you so you can tap into spiritual power.

Many people are able to recognize this (more or less unconsciously) as intuition, inspiration, guidance or discernment, it is "supernatural" and "providential" in nature. Whether or not they can verbalize it is irrelevant, the fact that they can make use of this principle is priceless. Sam Walton, founder of Wal-Mart, once explained that he and his son often didn't know exactly why some things worked better than others, "we just got up every morning and did what we felt God wanted us to do." I have experienced this same thing many times in my own endeavors. Without any certainty of why I knew what to do, I acted on impulse, a quiet "ah-ha!" moment, only later to discover why it made sense.

Where spiritual education is concerned, please remember that illusion is a constant danger. The spiritual realms are not all realms of light, as I have previously mentioned. Whether you believe the God-Satan scenario is unimportant (at present), the fact that you understand there is good and evil in the world is absolutely essential. The "conventional wisdom" I've repeatedly denounced is an illusion the world pushes on us to distract us from the truth, and a lot of people are falling into that trap. Illusions seem very real until you climb to a higher plane and in a position to see what is creating the illusion. As your thinking processes expand and improve, as you tap into the spiritual realms of light, the truth becomes so simple and so clear you will wonder, "Why wasn't it always this obvious?" It was, you simply hadn't learned how to recognize it.

In my younger days, I heard about a monk who discovered a great concept for keeping his own life in check. He said that he performed every activity throughout his day with one eye turned toward heaven. He wasn't boasting about how good he was, he was teaching a concept to discover higher truths, better solutions, keeping his intentions straight and clear and which, as a result, produced miraculous results.

Develop Character

You adopted the majority of your character traits from others without even thinking about it. As a child, you naturally did what others (family and friends) around you did. Why shouldn't you? This was normal to you; it was what you saw every day. You used this initial education to produce the results of your life to the point where you had enough experience in life to see other lifestyles and, possibly, adopt them. This is one of the serious problems with modern collegiate life: A large group of new "adults" (most of whom aren't very adult) are running around with very little oversight, enjoying a level of freedom they've mostly never known previously. Naturally, most of us made a few bad choices in those years and some of us adopted improper character traits that we later regretted. Equally natural, a few small mistakes by a few people can feed on each other, draw more people in and grow into real tragedies. The more weak concepts of character children learn in early life, the more they will take part in bad plans later.

Like any other truth, good character is an absolute and unchanging standard. We may use a variety of terms — charitable, courteous, fair, honest, gentlemanly/ladylike, kind, respectful, socially adept, trustworthy, and so on — but those are just details, parts of what we now call the Golden Rule, "Do unto others as you would have them do unto you."

This concept doesn't seem like a secret. It is so necessary to a properly functioning society that it is found in almost every culture that exists or has existed in known human history. Variations are found in Egypt, Persia, India and China over 2,000 years ago; in all the major religions of today and even in atheistic, humanist and secular sources. In spite of this, we find so many people who have very poor character and, so, we realize that it is still part of the great hidden wisdom.

Character is a key concept because it is a solid predictor of action. It is also a powerful tool to change your future because character is greater than habit — habit is the *what* you do, character is the *why* you have your habits, and even why you override them at times. If I may put it so, habit is the path you travel; character is the reason you are traveling that path.

Here is some of the greatness of character education. Jim Rohn reminds us, "your character should be as educated as your intellect." The sages of the past, including America's Founding Fathers, understood and intentionally held that character was the utmost important education for any human being. In fact, they understood that, without character training, all the intellectual knowledge of the world was not just worthless, it was counterproductive and even destructive! And, yet, few colleges or universities have anything that resembles courses in good character. Hmm.

The core character trait that will open up all learning to you is charity — the purest form of personal selflessness. Charity stems from genuine love and love is literally the life-blood that keeps people evolving, individually and collectively. If we don't have enough, our life is cut short. That means cultivating a deep love for yourself before all else because you can only give to others what you first possess within yourself.

Suppose you don't really feel much charity for your family or your community or whomever. That's not good but selfishness is the trait that the world now encourages, so it's not surprising. If you want to develop charity, you need to develop love. If you want to develop love, you need to serve. "Service" is any act of kindness or assistance, without reference to the motivation behind the act. Service can be an act of fear or duty; it is always an act of "knocking" (which I'll define very shortly). Love, as you have often heard, must be nurtured or it dies. In fact, it must often be nurtured before it begins. As Admiral James T. Kirk reminded Lieutenant Saavik in *Star Trek II: The Wrath of Khan*, "We learn by doing." Serve others and you'll develop love for them. When you love others, you will desire, in fact, you will feel impelled, to give more service. Those desires are the first indications of charity. Of course, the right character on both sides is also important.

My dad and brothers specifically taught me, from words and example, that cruelty to animals is never tolerated — that I should treat animals similar to people with feelings and needs and desires who want be accepted and appreciated, like me. One day in Jr. High School, I overheard some kids laughing about tying fire crackers to a dog's tail and how funny that was. I never knew if that was just "macho talk" or if they actually had done it but I was shocked and had the hardest time believing that anyone could think anything of the sort was funny. I remember thinking, One day you will know how it feels to be bullied and I hope it comes sooner than later.

Michael Nolan said, "There are many things in life that will catch your eye, but only a few will catch your heart, pursue those." These few things should be the focus of your education. That direction of travel will save you untold pain and bring you untold joy. It will also help to put the pain that comes into your life into a context where it becomes your ally and never your enemy.

Also when you focus on these most precious things to you, you become powerfully driven to share them with others. This is where real charity comes from. This is also where you can give back in ways that mean the most, from deepest parts of your heart and your talents. Where you can be that light on a hill so all within your influence are better off because you have lived.

Gain Wisdom

How does one learn true principles? How does one tune into the spiritual realm? How does one become a person of good character?

When I was about 18 years old, I remember my mother telling me a story she'd read about a gentleman who worked as a counterfeit expert for a major bank. He was so good that he could pick out any counterfeit bill almost immediately, regardless of how new, sophisticated or how close to perfect the counterfeit was. He was in very high demand for his expertise.

The writer asked the expert about how he could have possibly developed such an extraordinary skill. There are so many new technologies and so many people getting better and better at counterfeiting. How was he able to keep up with all of that? The counterfeiters certainly don't share their latest and greatest techniques and secrets with you, do they, he was asked.

The expert responded that he never studied counterfeit bills. In fact, he said that he stayed as far away from anything counterfeit as he possibly could. Even when he saw clever counterfeits he would make an extra effort to forget them as quickly as possible. He said, "I only study the real thing and now I understand it so thoroughly, I instantly recognize anything different."

Real education, as noted, isn't the names, dates, places, and events of history. These are all trivia that have zero intrinsic value to improve your life, It was, most famously, Pontius Pilate who asked, "What is truth?" (John 18:38, KJV) but his question tells us a great deal about the "conventional wisdom" of the day that first questioned whether there is a universal truth, second, had never been taught to recognize principles and third because of that, had no standard to measure what is truth and what is illusion. Truth is simply what is real. Truth is the opposite of illusion. Truth is recognized when you see it is possible for one person to send a recipe to another person across the world and that recipe can be identically duplicated when followed precisely; to shoe a horse, build a computer, grow wheat, raise children, erect a high-rise, etc.

The counterfeit expert had the key: He studied the real thing until he knew it so well that any deviation from that standard was glaringly obvious to him. Likewise, you and I can study and discern many truths. Look at history — not the raw data of names, dates, and places, but the people, their paradigms, character, intentions, behaviors, and results. Ask yourself, "What worked that I can duplicate and what didn't work so I can avoid it?" In other words:

- What circumstances did people in past and present generations create, based on the events around them and the decisions they made concerning them?

- Did those decisions improve or worsen their condition?

This book was written to help you develop the ability to view events, discern applicable principles then create circumstances which improve your condition.

It was written to help you discover principles which allow you to harness and harmonize with the laws of the universe to your best advantage.

It was written to help you tap into the spiritual realm and become empowered to create miracles.

It was written to help you influence others so they are empowered to create miracles.

This is the wisdom you and I seek. Does it not follow that examining how others have acted and what results they achieved is the simplest way to begin comprehending these principles?

You may have noticed that, although gaining wisdom is the core objective of our lives, wisdom can never be attained by directly seeking it. Wisdom is not something we discover at the end of the journey; it is something we gradually acquire during the journey. It is deliberate experience coupled with inspiration.

Like me, you have probably heard plenty of times that "wisdom is the correct application of knowledge." Again, like all "conventional wisdom", this definition is so diluted that it hardly resembles truth. Still, it is readily passed on by those who have never discovered real wisdom for themselves. Obviously, when true wisdom is exercised, it is the correct application of knowledge, but it is far more than just that. The massive majority of correctly applied knowledge has nothing to do with wisdom.

So, what is this wisdom we hope to gain? At this point, I hope it's becoming more clear — the universal laws by which all existence operates and the principles that allow you to harness and harmonize the laws to your best advantage. I will give you no more specific definition; to fully internalize and make use of wisdom, you need to discover it for yourself. And just for verification, it is impossible not to if you persist.

Ask — Seek — Knock

Here is a piece of advice that may surprise you: Don't ever believe anything anyone tells you — not me, not your most cherished mentors, no one! You must do your own due diligence. As you build a foundation of the Gain Wisdom concept, you will naturally develop a vital skill — **Ask, Seek, Knock**. This concept comes from the Sermon on the Mount, where Jesus instructs His disciples, "Ask and ye shall receive. Seek and ye shall find. Knock and it shall be opened unto you" (Matthew 7:7, KJV). For many years I quoted that scripture, believing I understood it, until one day I discovered what it really meant and then through the years continued to discover more and more about it.

Ask.

You must not simply ask questions; you must ask the right questions, those that lead you to better questions. Several years ago, I decided that I never wanted another answer for anything again. That is, until I discovered the *one answer* that brings understanding and enlightenment to everything. I remember watching a movie about Steven Hawking when he said that since he was young, his great ambition has been to discover that one equation that explains every other equation. I was excited about that because several years before, I realized that I never again would allow myself to accept anything I ever heard or learned or discovered as an "answer." The fact is that answers stop progression, no matter what, every time. Actually, anything you ever accept as an answer is only an illusion, anyway, because whatever "answer" you think you have is lacking unless it answers everything about everything.

Jim Rohn often reminded us that "everything effects everything else." I remember learning and am often reminded that, if we are diligent to continue increasing in enlightenment and wisdom, we will one day reach a point where all truth becomes one great whole. That is called perfect understanding — when we see the relevance and interdependence between everything. Now, whether you believe you can ever reach that point or not is irrelevant. Until you get there, there will always be hidden parts of everything you understand. So any answer you believe you have, is, obviously, not complete and believing you have an answer stops you from looking deeper.

Why would you ever look for something that you don't know or even believe exists? The only way to look deeper is to recognize that there is or at least might be something we don't know. If that is or might be, then you obviously don't actually have "the answer." Until you know everything there is to know about any one thing (which means you would have to know everything about everything) there are hidden things that you do not yet understand so in order to find those hidden things, you must first come up with a question to focus your search.

The very moment you stop asking questions is the moment you stop living and begin to die.

That is one clue about why it is so crucial to discover principles, instead of simply acquiring more information and knowledge. Eternity is not long enough to memorize all the information, but as you begin to discover even one principle, as long as you are true to it, it will teach you an eternity of information. Principles enable you to be aware of and OK with not knowing, but never satisfied with not knowing.

Everything about how we have been taught to view the universe is either wrong or at least lacking because everything else always has a bearing on, context to, and new perspective about it that we do not currently see. Therefore, in order to make the most of our experience, we must keep an open mind. Answers close off your mind because they always falsely assume a lie.

Here's an odd analogy: It is like saying that 5x5=10. Mathematically, this is partly true because 10 is part of 25, but you'll never get partial credit on your math quiz with that answer. It certainly isn't all true, therefore, it is wrong (just like the 6 blind men and the elephant). Even if you say 5x5=25, that is correct but it's only part of the multiplication table. If you know that 5x5=25 and stop there, you settle for a very mediocre life. I'll cover that in Chapter 14, so stay tuned.

Questions bring uneasiness and irritation to your soul and your mind; they motivate you to look for answers. But only better questions will bring you deeper understanding — the better questions the better understanding and better solutions! This is by design; by the time you do get that ultimate answer you will not cease growing but in fact be finally ready to embark on a life of truly unlimited returns. You will be perfect. If life does continue after death (which it does) and you can learn one more thing (which you can), then it is possible.

Understand that asking is a critical first step but asking is essentially a passive activity on your part. You didn't have to put out any great effort to ask a question and you certainly didn't put out any great effort to listen to an answer that some wise mentor invested a life-time to acquire.

Seek.

Seek is, of course, an action verb. I started this part of the discussion by paraphrasing the first rule of journalism, which is, "Trust but verify." This concept goes hand-in-hand with what I explained in Gain Wisdom. (Everything in this section does.) In dealing with any problem, you have to do your own research. Crack open the books, get into the field, get opinions and perspectives from those who are authorities on the subject — whatever the subject is. Seek for *why* the information you received is correct or not, applicable to your situation or not. As you begin to see patterns and evidences, you can make more intelligent decisions whether or not this information is worthy of your precious time and energy to pursue, that is, whether the investment of additional pieces of your life are worthy of what you hope to receive in return. Seeking is actually just an advanced, more proactive form of asking that brings much clearer understanding.

Knock.

Knocking is when you take this knowledge and practice it in real life situations. Practical application is the experiment — does what you think you ought to do actually get you where you want to be? Remember the great declaration, "faith without works is dead," (James 2:20, KJV). You must be willing to follow through with what you learn. Otherwise you will stop receiving and finding.

When we take significant action (when we experiment) in pursuit of a worthy goal, knowing that success is possible and never willing to quit until we succeed, we have combined James' two great counsels, "ask in faith, nothing wavering" and "I will shew thee my faith by my works" (James 1:6, 2:18, KJV). This was my point in the earlier discussion of service. If you want to develop love for something, serve it! Don't go grudgingly, don't just put in time so you can mark a scorecard — there isn't one — get into the idea that you are helping people. Take an interest in them, let them express their gratitude and accept it graciously — another good character trait you'll develop on the way. By the end of the experience, you'll be eager to return for another round.

If you will pardon a misquoted cliché, "You'll get out of every knock what you put into it."

The promise is that if you ask, you will "receive", but Jesus did not suggest you should simply ask for answers. Taken in context with "finding" and "opening", it is clear that Jesus wanted you to discover truth for yourself, He didn't want it handed to you. (Notice that I am following His lead throughout this book!)

There will be many levels of improvement on this journey of experiments which you should cherish and celebrate. But how much do you want to improve ultimately? Do you really think you will be satisfied with poor or mediocre results? What about extraordinary results? There is always one more step you can take to improve, if you look for it and if the desire to improve is so engrained into your thought processes that it is automatic. If you have the courage to follow through with that desire (and, at times, this really does require great courage), you will eventually discover that perfect way. Additionally, as you Ask, Seek and Knock, you will realize a lifestyle with such a greater joy, peace of mind, and freedom that you'll do anything to help those you love also discover for themselves.

After a lot of "hard knocks", I still want that one answer which explains everything, the answer that causes all truth to be encompassed as one great whole. May not happen in this life, but I would never be one to entirely discount the idea. At the same point however, that is a silly thing to say because it's like saying, I probably won't reach all my goals by bed time tonight. Tomorrow is a new day, just like the next life is a simple extension to this one. If you don't plan for it, it won't work adequately for you. So, I will continue to search for that one answer and in the process, never accept anything less than discovering better questions, different perspectives, deeper issues and more whys. As I mentioned before, questions bring uneasiness and irritation to your soul and mind; they are motivation to go to work for yourself and this cognitive dissonance forces us to get off our butts and ease the pain by unearthing these great hidden wisdoms — that wisdoms which enables us to live to our fullest potential.

In a conference with Denis Waitley I attended several years ago, he spoke of a recent visit to the Orient. He had occasion to visit the richest man in China. During that conversation, he asked the man, "What do you feel is the greatest attribute to your success?" The gentleman replied something like, "I believe that a man can only be as successful as the distance into the future that he plans for."

Denis then asked, "Well, how far into the future have you planned for?" The man opened to the back page in his planner and folded out a long page. There he had a time line with goals and plans for the next 500 years. Denis then asked, as he looked at the page in awe, "How are you going to accomplish all that?" The man gave him a strange look and then replied, "I'm going to accomplish that, just like I have accomplished everything else in my life...one day at a time."

I now have a plan of my own for the next 150 years, and growing, that I continue to work on and fully expect to accomplish.

Learning through Pain

We all hate pain and do pretty much everything we can to avoid it. Although, contrary (again) to "conventional wisdom", pain is *not* bad, pain is *not* your enemy. In fact, it is one of your most powerful and beneficial allies.

Pain is the messenger that risks its own life to let you know about the real enemy lurking nearby. I look at pain as my own personal spy who infiltrates the enemy's camp and then risks everything to warn me of his plan. Pain is a symptom, not a problem. The problem is your lack understanding of principles and that problem will destroy you if you do not eradicate it. Another lie of "conventional wisdom" is "What you don't know can't hurt you." How stupid do you have to be to think that not knowing you having cancer will save your life?! What you don't know *can* and *will* kill you unless you change it. In fact, almost every death is at least in part caused by things that are unknown. Discover the power of real education and you are on your way to discovering how to Solve Every Problem in Your Life. If you "shoot the messenger" (just kill the pain) without regard to the real enemy, that enemy is left to grow stronger and more capable of killing you.

T. Harv Eker, an author, businessman, and trainer known for his theories on wealth creation and abundant living was the first person I heard say that, "A headache is not caused by the lack of aspirin in your bloodstream." Most people believe that their headache is their problem so they take an aspirin and when the pain is gone, they mistakenly believe that the problem is gone. But the headache was only a symptom, something created it and, if you don't discover the cause and fix it, it will return.

Now, it is important to understand that, even if we do the right things but do them for the wrong reason, that will inevitably produce negative results instead of positive ones and those negative results will be painful. In these situations — and don't sweat it, we've all made this mistake — hopefully, we remember pain as our ally, not our enemy and learn from it and change.

The Mentor/Apprentice Relationship

Classical vs. Modern Learning

You will probably recognize that throughout the 6,000 years of recorded history, the primary form of education was the mentor/apprentice format and it remains the most effective system of education devised. The very words education, teach, learn, and study come from this system, which is, in every way, far superior to the classroom lecture/test method so frequently employed today.

Why did society change the definitions of educate, teach, learn, study, and others? It may or may not have been intentional but it is because of our un-checked egos. We want to justify our current lack of wisdom and now our inadequate public school systems and cover up the fact that a few people decided to commercialize and control the system so they could make money and control people. Our current education system is based on the Prussian model. It was adopted by Victorian England because of their need to mold workers who could move from place to place and produce adequate results, which was necessary (in their eyes) to move the Industrial Revolution forward in the United Kingdom. This type of education did not seek to raise up critical thinkers, it intentionally dropped the classics from the education paradigm. It was a method of mass-producing workers with just enough knowledge to follow orders and produce adequate results in their small sphere.

Now, I have to preface this part by saying that I have many friends who are teachers and professors. Many of them I admire tremendously and appreciate the good they do within a corrupt system. That said, the fact remains most people today in teaching and leadership roles would better be called "tellers" instead of "teachers" and "repeaters" instead of "leaders". Likewise, most of those today called "students" would better be called "memorizers instead of "students" and "duplicators" instead of "creators". In the mentor/apprentice system, they would never qualify as teachers — they have little to no actual success in the subjects they instruct — or students — they leave college and go straight to work with little to no practical skills or real-world experience.

Mentors are distinguished by four circumstances:

- A proven track record as a master of the knowledge and skills of their trade or profession; they understand the concepts and principles behind the processes they are teaching you.

- A steady and consistent, self-initiated, self-directed program to increase their own knowledge and skills. They understand that the moment they stop learning from their mentors is the moment they lose the ability to be a mentor.

- An understanding of teaching by example — they are personally involved and committed to show you how and why things work and their own lifelong study shows their apprentices how to be great students.

- Mike Murdock wisely counseled that a real mentor is one who cares more about your spiritual growth than about your affection. Mentors hold you accountable, make sure you develop good character, inspire you to work and live to the optimal, and inspire you to continually improve.

Likewise, an apprentice is not just one who memorizes answers and acquires information or skills, an apprentice is someone who deliberately seeks wisdom through self-evolution. His or her objective is to become a master in his or her own right.

Today's retirement mentality is a great example of what's wrong with modern education. Classically, there was no retirement as we know it today. Quite the opposite, the wiser a master became, the more in-demand that master would be as a mentor. When a farrier, for example, couldn't physical craft a horseshoe or handle a skittish colt, he could still watch, advise and critique or stand with a horse and speak calming words to show the horse he and others were there to help.

Only the truly wise understand and teach, by example, the art of continual self-growth toward the optimal level. Here again, study the origins of the word "student" in contrast to the definitions in our typical dictionaries of today. It brings much needed enlightenment to your own stewardship and accountability to your own life.

The root of "student" means much more than we have been led to believe. It's meaning includes "eagerness" and "intense application" hence "application to learning." As close as has been discovered, the idea of "study" also produced "shove, hit" with the underlying notion of "application of extreme effort." So, then, "application of extreme effort" to "learn" is active, real-world experience on the road to discern truth from error and reality from illusion by way of practical application. It is interesting to note that one dictionary states it derives from a Latin word meaning, "to take pains". In other words, to intentionally and willingly go through the pain of learning in order to discover how to live pain-free.

Apprentices must complete five basic phases:

- The mentor explains, in detail, the end result and the process to produce it and shows the apprentice what to do. (This includes all aspects of the trade/profession — keeping records, marketing, interacting with customers and more.)

- The mentor leads the apprentice to understand why things work the way they do; they relate the tasks to the principles and laws that support and overlay them.

- The mentor then works with the apprentice and helps them accomplish each task.

- Then the mentor steps back and requires the apprentice to complete tasks on their own; lets them make mistakes and requires them to fix those mistakes, giving appropriate feedback correction and encouragement.

- Only when the apprentice has proven his/her ability to perform at premium levels does the mentor certify the apprentice as a journeyman; one ready to begin the solo journey of persistent application of skills and knowledge coupled with continued study to, if diligent enough, earn the status of master. The very word, "journeyman" meant one who traveled — in former centuries, travel was essential to acquiring the skills and experience that might someday earn the journeyman a mastery. (Today, it still denotes movement, intellectual as well as physical.)

Ask anyone who produces extraordinary to miraculous results and they will tell you that ninety percent or more of what was actually required to make them super-successful isn't offered in any school. They achieved it because they had the good fortune and/or foresight to find the right master to mentor them.

Finding the Right Mentor

In my story, at the end of this book, you'll read about my wrestling coach Joe Wolfe Davis. It was glaringly evident that Coach Davis was different kind of coach or teacher than I'd ever encountered. He developed a powerful rapport with all of us right from the beginning. He believed in and cared about us enough to never let us get away with second rate effort — never — that's real positive, not some pathetic tip-toe around hard issues. He held us accountable or we didn't need to be part of the team — regardless of our talent. He demanded respect from us all and we took it to heart. That was a significant key to our extreme success. As a team, we won every single dual meet we participated in that season, had two complete shut-outs where we won every single match. We took first place in every tournament, we won first place at region and every member of the varsity team qualified to wrestle at state, where we took first place there also.

As I said earlier, I did not learn the significance of many of those lessons until years later. I seemed to always be a slow learner. However, looking back at the four years previous and the year after, when I wrestled under different coaches, some very powerful insights began to emerge. Many of the wrestlers on my other teams had every bit as much potential as my junior-year team with Coach Davis, but all my other teams were only average at best. So, what made the difference?

Coach Davis taught us mostly the same basic moves as other coaches taught their wrestlers. Obviously we put in more time and we were in better shape, which made a big difference, but what made the biggest difference? He genuinely cared about us and made sure we knew that he believed in us. He held us to a much higher standard — "perfect form" — whether at practice or in a meet, even when we were goofing off. We could always improve, no matter how good we were, and he let us know that, no matter how well we performed in our matches. The biggest difference, however, was that he treated us like champions and expected us to be champions and, so, we became champions. Actually, not just champions, he expected miracles from us and, as a result, we created them. (And by the way, he held us accountable to extraordinary character as well as our intellect and skills).

Other than my father and older brothers who taught me to work the farm and the cabinet shop, Coach Davis was the only teacher in my life who was a true mentor to me. I understand that I didn't make it easy for any of my teachers and I don't blame them for my lack of success. Others would have treated me better if I had been more accommodating and treated them better. But that is precisely my point. Virtually everyone will treat you nice if you treat them nice first; that's no judgement of character. Even idiots do that. There are only a tiny few who just come in and take control and keep it by treating you right, regardless of how you treat them and who are wise enough to hold you lovingly and absolutely accountable to the highest standards. Coach Davis was the only teacher who ever created an environment in which I was committed to grow for myself.

Now, it also went much deeper than just that he was a great wrestling coach. He was a true mentor. He practiced *with* us, not just told us what to do. He exuded high standards of honesty and integrity and he held us accountable for those also. He never asked anything of us that he didn't exemplify himself.

I can point the way, but I cannot find the right masters/mentors for you. The ideas shared here are the best initial guide I can give you. Your situation is unique, your life is a unique combination of talents and trials. I can show you the truths I have learned but you must be willing to follow them. I echo Jesus' invitation, "[G]o, and do thou likewise" (Luke 10:37, KJV).

Conclusion

I share the feelings of Alfred, Lord Tennyson's "Ulysses", in which he writes, "and this grey spirit yearning in desire to follow knowledge [wisdom] like a sinking star, beyond the utmost bound of human thought."

I have made peace with the fact that nothing I ever do in my entire life will ever be "good enough." Not only have I made peace with it, but that very understanding has completely liberated me to such a refreshing perspective of life and opened the doors wide to accomplish my true heart's desires. Don't get me wrong, I am extremely grateful for every experience, result, situation, and circumstance in my life, but I am, simultaneously, completely unsatisfied with all of it. I have learned that anything I want is possible, as long as I simply find the right mentors and follow them. The secret, simple and ancient principle of real education is the key. The reward for understanding that key will open any door that you ever want to walk through.

Since I have begun to discover the secrets to real education, I also have begun to understand that the results I experience in my life are nothing more or less than feedback to the validity of the principles I follow. That has been the most eye-opening, exhilarating and liberating experience of my entire life. Since that time two extremely significant things have happened.

First, the negative stress in my life has virtually disappeared — stress from failure, from not measuring up, from rejection, from worrying about other people and their performance, from worry about taking risks and even from worry about dying.

Second, my own personal growth has so accelerated that it boggles my mind. I notice it, in significant, tangible and measurable ways almost every day. The relationships with the significant people in my life have skyrocketed. A few I chose to invest more time with and some I chose to spend less time with, depending on their own trajectory. My own feelings of self-worth, as well as my understanding about my own unique potential to make valuable contributions to the world has grown by leaps and bounds and continues, and so can yours.

So as my spirit yearns for adventure, my brain and body is discovering that real security lies in the same adventure my spirit yearns for and I am beginning to truly understand and echo Tennyson's words (again from "Ulysses"), "How dull it is to pause, to make and end, to rust unburnish'd, not to shine in use, as though to breathe were life!"

Summary

Education is discovering your real self and your place in the real universe and determining what circumstance you need to create to move closer to perfection. Education that is truly life-changing includes four fundamental levels of understanding and three fundamental admonitions:

First, information comes from asking but, this means receiving answers without any personal effort, so it produces poor results. Even so, one must always question everything and one must always be in search of better questions.

Second, knowledge comes from seeking and obtaining information through research; it produces mediocre results. Results can boarder on extraordinary, but never quite get you there.

Third, wisdom begins with knocking and experimentation in real life situations so as to discover right concepts; it produces extraordinary results. This is where you begin to tune-in to truth — your creativity becomes focused; your circumstances become joyful; and you find yourself on the cutting edge of personal evolution.

Fourth, character is the great key that enables you to discover correct principles; it produces miraculous results. When you are in-tune with principles, your wisdom develops exponentially and your character yields right behavior. You become empowered and highly skilled at harnessing and harmonizing universal laws and you find yourself on the cutting edge of global evolution.

Pain can be a valuable teaching tool. Pain is only a symptom, but it will lead you to the real problems you need to solve in order to progress. But you have to be willing to learn from it and not just try to diminish it.

Mentors are priceless. Any journeyman can teach you what to do, but only a true master can teach you how to live by what you do. The Chinese say, "When the student is ready, the teacher appears". How will you know which is the right mentor? The true mentor puts more effort into developing your character than into developing your skill set. The right skill sets will never evolve into great character but with the right character, you will develop the right skills no matter what.

Never retire — that is, never quit growing, improving, contributing and mentoring. Always move toward a more perfect life or you will by default move toward decay and death. That reality is true in your spiritual essence as well as your body and mind.

The Learning Process

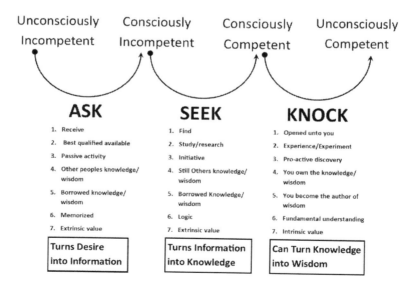

Chapter 5
The Joy-in-the-Journey Principle

This next secret ancient principle is another that most are aware of, but only at face value. With a little deeper understanding, you can immediately begin to shift your life's direction from chaos, frustration and being overwhelmed to an organized, laser focus. The more you understand it, the more leverage is added to guarantee the future you desire.

Maintenance is a Myth

Would you say that your life gets stressful, nerve-racking or overwhelming at times? Does that happen far too often? How would you like to learn how to never again be overwhelmed — to even completely eliminate negative stress from your life?

A large part of the stress in your life is attributed to the consistent upgrade it requires. How many times have you had someone tell you that you should maintain your cars, home, yard, and other possessions in order to keep things tidy, in working order, and organized? It takes a huge amount of time and effort to keep your body, mind and spirit healthy, let alone all the other things you possess.

It dawned on me several years ago that there is no such thing as "maintenance" — at least in the way we interpret it today. Nothing anywhere, anytime, stays the same. Life — and everything it entails — is dynamic, which means that it is either getting stronger or weaker, evolving or dying, becoming more agitated and stressed or more peaceful and calm and increasing or decreasing. There is no static state for anything. Nothing in life exists in a vacuum and so every single thing is changing constantly.

For about three years, I was the maintenance supervisor for a couple of large apartment complexes. After a few months on the job, I started thinking, "What kind of stupid word is 'maintenance' anyway?" The apartments are either in a state of intentional upgrade and renovation, or they are in process of decaying and falling apart. Human beings are exactly the same. There is no such thing as maintenance. The only possibility we have to evolve is by a consistent, deliberate and intentional improvement program. You have to make sure that you are following an improvement program that actually produces improvement, designed by someone wiser than yourself, and not just someone who thinks they are. It must be designed by someone who has already produced what you want.

We use the term in so many ways, for example we say that our police force and justice system "maintains the peace." But do they really maintain it? Of course not! I am personally grateful for them but we must recognize that not addressing the real problem and just cutting out the symptom after it has already disrupted society will only guarantee that the problem never goes away. That is not keeping or maintaining the peace. They've even re-named jails and prisons "correctional facilities." The term is at least a little closer but just changing the name to something more politically correct doesn't fix the problem. It only metaphorically puts a fresh coat of paint over a rotting structure. It blows my mind at how many parts of our society is trapped in that kind of foolish "conventional wisdom."

Most of our current governmental processes today have shifted drastically from where they were in 1776, and most of those changes are not improvements. Only if we entirely shift our paradigms away from focusing on symptoms and back to focusing on principles will we ever have the potential to correct our problems.

The only way to avoid decay is to intentionally and deliberately participate in a consistent process of upgrading, remodeling, rebuilding, and growth.

I was teaching this idea in a class years ago when a participant said, "Life is really simple. I know that as long as I am improving, I will eventually make it." At that moment, an inspiration hit me hard. I responded, "It isn't enough just to be on the right track. It isn't even enough if you're making what you think may be good progress. I went to the chalk board and drew the following diagram.

If you are not making enough progress to keep up with the time flowing out of your life, you are falling behind not getting ahead. You only have so much time and energy in your life and once you have squandered any unreplaceable resource, it is impossible to get it back. I remember my dad's oft-repeating saying, "Lost, somewhere between sunrise and sunset, five golden minutes, each set with 60 diamond seconds. No reward is offered; they are gone forever."

That is one reason there is no such thing as maintenance. In fact, maintenance is impossible, because the moment you stop growing, you start to die. If you're not advancing forward, you are, by default, falling backwards. Are you feeling stressed just contemplating trying to find answers to how to prioritize your time and energy, especially with seemingly so many things to do and so little time?

The New Testament records people frequently coming to Jesus for help. They came because they were stressed-out and confused. Why do you, personally, go to anyone for help? For the same reason. One way or the other, you have problems that you don't know how to solve. Every time Jesus responded to those who came to him for help, he first offered comfort. He used words and phrases such as:

- Fear not
- Peace be unto you
- Lay your burdens at my feet
- Let not your heart be troubled, neither let it be afraid
- Be not afraid
- Why are ye so fearful?

- As ye believe, so shall it be done unto you
- Be of good cheer
- Be not dismayed
- Let your heart be comforted
- Come unto me all ye that labor and are heavy laden and I will give you rest.

Why would he say such things? Because He understands things that we do not. He wants you to realize that your problems are not as big as you think they are. He knows that, with a little better understanding, you will learn to let go of your maintenance paradigm and find comfort in a new (and better) growth paradigm. Jesus explained how to find that comfort when He said, "Take my yoke upon you, for my yoke is easy and my burden is light."

How do you find rest if you're putting on a yoke? How can a burden become light? If a burden is light (and no longer a burden), can you stop pulling at the yoke?

Even though I've personally never used a yoke, I have used lots of harnesses. In my younger days, I worked as a lumberjack. Because I was good with horses and harnesses, one of my first responsibilities was to harness our work-horse and skid (drag) the logs from where they had been cut and trimmed, to the road so they could be loaded onto the trucks. On a single harness, there is a big, padded leather collar that fits around the horse's neck and against his front shoulders. The rest of the harness connects to the collar which enables him to pull a load behind him.

A yoke, on the other hand, is a wooden beam that is carved out to fit over the necks of two animals, typically oxen, which fastens them together so they can both pull a single load. The analogy, I hope, is obvious. You can harness yourself to a problem and pull it alone or yoke yourself to someone and pull together.

After being frustrated with the declining ambition, trustworthiness, work ethic, accountability, and personal responsibility of the general employee pool — like my lumberjack experience using a single horse — I spent several years working and tackling problems all by myself using only a single collar. Several years later I learned that finding the right people to work with simply a process I could learn and it would drastically improve my results and make my life much easier by pulling with someone else, especially someone stronger and more capable than me.

Another important point of the yoke analogy: Jesus never suggested He would take away your problems despite offering compassion and comfort. He said He would teach you how solve your own problems and as you work diligently to do so, He would be there to compound and maximize the process in the most effective and efficient ways. He also never said he would join you in your yoke to pull your burden. He invited you to leave your burden because you are doing things the hard way and join him with his burden because He's figured out the best ways to get things done. He cannot help you do things the wrong way. Your burden can be light when you leave your heavy burden (doing things the wrong way) and discover and follow correct principles (doing things the right way that creates the best results). All too often, we ask God to take away our problems because we have made a mess when we ought to be saying, "Thank you for this opportunity to discover how things don't work well. Please help me learn and grow and discover what does work so I not only increase my strength but pull a much lighter load. Please help me through this process to discover more optimal ways of doing things."

Enjoying the Journey, no Matter What

When my middle son was about 10 years old, he began having a recurring nightmare. After a few nights of this, it became troublesome for the whole family because he didn't want to go to bed by himself. When he did finally get to bed, he would have this terrible nightmare that sent him straight back to our bedroom, after which he'd keep us all awake for some time as we tried to help him calm down and get back to sleep.

During this time, while saying his nightly prayers he would beg "... and please help me not to have bad dreams tonight." One particular night as he spoke those words, his little voice quivered and his entire body trembled with fear. I felt so bad for him, and all of a sudden I had an inspiration.

I interrupted his prayer and explained, "Dallas, some prayers are never answered because we ask God for things that He would never give us because it would hurt us instead of help us. Then when He does answer us, it is usually not in the way we ask Him to. Far too many times we ask Him to take away our problems, but He is much smarter than that. He wants us to learn important principles so we can learn how to never have those problems again. If he just took them away, without any effort on our part, we would still be naïve and powerless the next time we faced a similar problem."

Dallas looked at me funny, and I said, "Say that again, just like you did in your prayer, and tell me how it makes you feel." He repeated, "Please help me not to have bad dreams tonight." Again he quivered and said, "It makes me afraid." I then asked him if he really believed God could help him with this problem and he said, "Yes."

"So," I said, "try asking in a different way and tell Him what you want instead of what you don't want. For example, 'Heavenly Father, please help me have good dreams tonight'."

He again folded his arms, closed his eyes and made the new plea, I watched and saw an instant calm come over him. When he finished, I asked him what kind of pictures were going through his mind and how he felt when he asked not to have bad dreams that night. He answered, "Pictures of bad people trying to hurt us, and it makes me feel scared." I then asked what kind of pictures he had in his mind and how he felt when he asked for help to have good dreams? He responded, "Nice pictures, and it made me feel good."

For the first night in several days, he jumped up with a smile on his face and said, "I know Heavenly Father will help me have good dreams tonight," and trotted off to bed all by himself. To this day, Dallas, who is now in his 30s, remembers this lesson he learned as a child and the joy he felt in grasping the new knowledge of one of the principles of prayer and seeing a miracle work in his life.

When you begin to understand that the quality of your life changes with the quality of how you learn to intelligently ask questions and then design and create your own positive journey through life, you will instantly begin to experience more happiness and better results.

Many years ago, while I was in Scotland, I came across a poem by Ella Wheeler Wilcox that I felt an instant connection with. I memorized it and have remembered it ever since. Just a few years ago, I quoted it while talking with a friend, and during that moment, I had an inspiration. I went home, and wrote a second part to it:

> One ship sails east and another west by the selfsame winds that blow.
> Tis the set of the sails and not the gales that tells the way we go.
> Like the winds of the sea are the waves of time as we journey along through life.
> Tis the set of the soul that determines the goal and not the calm or the strife.
>
> In fact, you know, if the wind didn't blow and the waves of the sea stood still,
> It would be a lot harder to get where you're going; it's this paradox of good and ill.
> So be grateful for strife and the trials of life, for only through them can you grow
> Into all that you dream when you work, plan and scheme, and then limits you never will know.

I wrote the second verse only to clarify the principle that Ella was trying to portray. I noticed when I quoted it to people, they thought it was nice but missed the bigger picture. For the first 38 or so years of my life, I lived in a world where life was full of "good" and "bad" experiences. Because of my perspectives, life brought to me many "good" and "bad" results. Through this new course of study however I finally discovered that life is simply life. There is nothing "bad" about it. There are only poor, mediocre, extraordinary and miraculous results, created by the decisions we make and actions we take based on the external environment we encounter and attract to us.

Now, all those experiences that I used to label "bad" have entirely changed to where today, I have never had a "bad" experience. I have had lots of painful, sad and difficult ones, but those are the times that forced my brain and my spirit to discover how to expand my potential and become the far stronger and wiser person today than ever before and that I could have never been without them.

Know Your Resources

A few years ago, my wife brought home the DVD of an old television series called *The Shari Lewis Show*. Lewis, who was a ventriloquist, used puppets to teach children about good work ethics and character development.

In one episode, one of the girl puppets who worked with Shari at the television station, was assigned a project that she thought was too big for her to complete. She became discouraged and was about to give up. At that point, Shari invited the girl puppet to her home for dinner. When her friend arrived that evening, Shari asked if she would please do her a favor and move her sofa to the other side of the living room. Being the helpful and caring friend she was, she looked at the large piece of furniture and said, "It looks pretty heavy, but I'll try."

She walked over to the couch and pushed and pushed, but it wouldn't even budge. The friend said, "Shari, I am so sorry, but I cannot move your couch." Shari responded, "Oh, yes you can. If you use all your strength, I know you can move that couch." The friend looked puzzled and went back to the couch to try once more. Again, she pushed and pushed with all her might, but, again, the couch didn't even wiggle.

Again she returned to Shari and said, "I pushed with all my strength and I just couldn't move the couch." Then Shari said something to the effect of, "You did not use all your strength! Aren't I your friend?" The girl responded, "Well, of course you are my friend." Then Shari said, "Well, if I am your friend, then I am part of your strength, and all you have to do is ask and you have more than enough strength to move the sofa."

Doing your best is actually using every resource you can muster for the benefit of your dream, idea, project or endeavor. This includes relying on family, friends, employees, investors, mastermind groups, mentors, other sources of knowledge, skills, talent or help and then far beyond that, activating the powers of heaven in your favor.

Moving Ever Forward

Life is nothing more than a continuous journey from point A to point B. Point A is where you are — the only place where you have the opportunity to decide what you want next and where you can go to get it. Point B is where you want to arrive — it gives you an opportunity to see if the formulae you chose to follow actually produced the results that you intended while you were at point A.

Of course, the moment you are at point B, it is no longer point B but your new point A. Now, you must decide whether to stay your current course and create more of what you've been creating or chose a different course and create something different. If you look at point B not as the final destination but as a mile marker and a new place to begin, you will never get "stuck in a rut." Point B is always your new point A; that is one of the beauties of life. It is a new opportunity to learn from the past and make a new, better and more intelligent start toward the future. Of course, each moment of our lives is actually a new point A.

This idea that this life is a journey brings about the awareness that you are not simply wandering aimlessly. Instead, you have the opportunity to find joy in deliberately going somewhere you have never been before. Every behavior comes from a specific intention; good behavior from the intention to improve your life. If there was no hope of any benefit, you wouldn't have had the incentive to begin the journey in the first place. If you pay close attention to what you are getting compared to what you want, it will help guide you in making decisions that you believe will get you there in the best way.

Although there are four basic kinds of results you can create (poor, mediocre, extraordinary, or miraculous), there are actually only two directions you can travel: towards your goal or away from it. Life is like a major freeway; each side is headed in the opposite direction of each other. People who are intentionally growing and self-evolving are the investors of life, making sure their efforts produce a healthy increase; they are traveling towards their goals.

Become as a Little Child

Jesus taught that if you want the best rewards available from your journey, you need to become as a little child. He meant "child-like" not "childish". At one point or another, all children are selfish, self-absorbed, short-sighted, and arrogant in their ignorance — some grow out of that behavior sooner than others, some never grow out of it, regardless of how long they live. So what did He mean? What is it about children that qualifies them for the best possible rewards?

The answer is in children's insatiable passion to evolve — a consistent willingness to take risks in order to expand their potential. It is their dogged persistence to learn, grow and change for the better as quickly as possible in order to create a better lifestyle that spurs their willingness to risk and learn from their mistakes. Children are never satisfied with where they are or with their current abilities, yet they love themselves unquestionably, unconditionally and can't wait to continue their unique journey. They believe in themselves, never question their abilities, and chase their dreams with passion and a wonder that is inspiring.

So why was Jesus telling this to adults? Aren't adults smarter and better off now than when they were children? Aren't we closer to where we'd like to go at this point than we were as children? Sadly, far too many are not because they've lost that insatiable appetite for learning and growing that is so natural to the young. They've lost what is the literal definition of living. The reason they have lost it is irrelevant. The moment anyone stops learning and growing with all their heart, is the moment they give up on living and begin to die. There is no maintenance level. Adults often feel as if they are living in a rut, and as Earl Nightingale, an American radio personality, writer, respected speaker and author, so graphically reminded us, "A rut is nothing more than a grave with the ends kicked out."

As you reach major milestones, you certainly have cause for rest and celebration (recreation is critical), but what is rest and celebration other than time to re-evaluate, re-charge, re-plan, collect incentive and motivation, to check and adjust our strategies and direction and then head out again on another adventure to pursue another point B? The enthusiasm and excitement, this dogged determination, whether by lack of fear or in spite of it, you feel as you set off on another adventure to a new point B is what it means to "become as a little child." This attitude allows you to look forward to learning and growing, to retain or regain that same joy and satisfaction that you treasured as a child.

Choosing Your Path

Now here is a little twist: Although you have complete agency (freedom) to choose whatever path you will, you cannot choose your results — only the path you believe will take you there. Point B is only a symptom, a natural result of the path you chose, and where that point B is right now for you is the *only* accurate feedback as to whether the formula you followed actually produced what you intended or not.

Every day, you are faced with countless options, each clamoring for your attention and promising its own unique rewards. Once you make a decision and choose your path, your results can be easily predicted. Of course, if you change your path, your future results will adjust automatically. Just because you do not know how to accurately predict those results yet is irrelevant. The path you chose, has a destination and if you stay on the path you will reach it. If you change to a different path, your destination changes with your new decision.

The more you understand about your creative nature and deliberately channel it toward your most sincere desires, the more you will realize that you created the reality you now live in by way of your past decisions. It is not luck or chance or a trick of fate or anything to do with what others have imposed upon you.

Every point B at which you arrive is because you specifically decided to take the road that led you there — some of those decisions, I should point out, you do make without much thinking or deliberation, and many are automatic responses because of habits (good or bad) you've developed. Regardless of how persuasive others may have been in influencing your choices or whether or not you correctly predicted where you will end up or what you would experience along the way, the choices were yours. Whether you accomplished what you wanted or surprised yourself with something different, it was your decision to take the road that brought you to where you are.

Even if others physically overpowered or coerced or manipulated you with false promises or frightening threats, you still decide your best choice under any given circumstance. You've all heard the expression, "a gun to my head". I sincerely hope that never occurs in your life but, remember, it has occurred many times in the past and, even then, it wasn't a situation of "I had no choice". Sometimes, a choice may be absolutely undesirable but, even with a literal gun to their heads, some have made *that* ultimate choice. Especially when you're in the midst of challenge, the more you decide to honor your core values, the better choices you will think of and be motivated to pursue, come what may.

Every time you give in to any kind of bullying, regardless of how severe the consequences seem, you give away your own agency and empower the bullies to continue and do worse to you and others. If you don't want to do something that others are trying to convince you to do, it is still you who has to decide whether to give in or to stand up for what you value.

If, instead, you chose to be a victim it is impossible to heal (and being a victim has nothing to do with the event but only about how you internalize why you do what you do about that event). Wanting revenge is an ever-decaying canker in your own soul and has zero effect on the other person. Forgiveness is a healing balm that brings peace and comfort and added power to your soul and, likewise, has zero effect on the other person. *Because it was never about them, only about you!*

Reality check: Right now, you are where you are and you cannot change that fact. You can complain and cry about how uncomfortable it is or you can learn the lessons your situation offers and, with that added knowledge, design and plan for what you want next. Though it will be difficult at times, the more you stay focused and persist, the more delighted you will become with your progress and the happier and more at peace you will become with yourself. Mostly because you have taken control of your own life instead of leaving it in the control of others. Another old quote is so true that "if you don't take control of your life, someone else will."

You are who you are and you have what you have today because that's what your past decisions created for you. Circumstances will change tomorrow to the exact degree that you make changes today. You cannot change today any more than you can change the ingredients of that peach pie after you've eaten it. If you want tomorrow's results to be better than today's, you are going to have to change today's recipe from yesterday's. We talked about this concept in Chapter 2, and now might be a great time to go back and refresh your memory of that chapter.

The speed of travel varies but the direction can only be toward dying or living. I love what Toby Hales, a successful business woman and speaker said (paraphrased), "as soon as you stop telling God how big your problems are and start telling your problems how big your God is, your life will dramatically improve."

Which Road Are You Travelling Now?

The closer your rewards get to those you promised yourself, the more you will know you are to the right road. If you are experiencing results you didn't want or even not as much reward as promised, you'll know that you either misjudged the length of the road (which is most common) or you need to change roads.

If you are on the wrong road, it is because you either have habits that are sabotaging your success, you got the wrong information from someone who wasn't qualified to give you the advice they gave, you believe you know something that you don't actually know, etc. Whatever the reason, a good mentor is the most important thing to help you understand and get on track. You may be in process of discovering and may even be going in the right general direction but somewhere, somehow you don't have it figured out yet. Results are the ultimate standard of measurement and they never lie.

Also there's no better time than the present to fix them. The hourglass of your life is running out of sand and there's nothing you can do to slow down or stop time. So, if you want something different from what you're currently getting, it's crucial that you schedule a change; today is far better than tomorrow. Develop an ever-increasing sense of urgency. Every time you catch yourself letting things slip, you ought to be consistently harder on yourself to change things — for the better. Again, a worthy mentor is invaluable here.

Contrary to what many psychologists say about loving yourself and to always be understanding and kind to yourself, I say hogwash! When you have let yourself down, wasted your time and missed your goals because you were not committed enough, or not set them to begin with, or even not high enough, one of the healthiest things you can do is to beat yourself up and make sure it is painful enough for you to learn the lesson to never repeat it! It is perfectly okay — even important at times — to beat yourself up, but, listen very carefully to this second part because it is crucial to your success, *it's never okay to leave yourself wounded*.

If you are acting immature, some "tough-love" is in order toward yourself. Just make sure it is really holding yourself lovingly accountable and not being abusive. That means allowing yourself to feel the pain you've created and not try to cover it up or blame someone else, so that you are motivated to change things appropriately. I love what Mike Murdock said (paraphrased), "A real mentor cares far more about your spiritual growth and development than about your affection."

Working hard and fast now will buy you more time and energy to do more of what you really want in the future and guarantee that you achieve compounded rewards. Otherwise, the only option you have left is being falsely contented with poor to mediocre results that will guarantee more struggle and for a longer period of time.

The most important advantage that you get from studying other peoples' experiences lies in learning to recognize the tell-tale signs along your own road, in order to better judge whether you're creating poor, mediocre, extraordinary or miraculous results for yourself. If you have the courage and ambition to consistently attain more and better information and consistently adjust your direction, the world will be yours. The wise throughout history have given us lots of clues about which roads lead to success and which ones lead to failure.

I know it seems silly, but more and more frequently I hear questions like these:

- "Who are they to know? They don't understand my unique situation or our time."
- "But their lives are irrelevant to mine, we are so advanced from them."

In fact, times change but people (human nature) never changes. Circumstances change but principles are exactly the same forever. Every problem today can easily solved by tracing them to similar problems in the past and the principles violated to create them. Again to quote Jim Rohn, "You can't hire someone else to do your pushups for you." The wise are the ones who have been down many of those roads and have carefully evaluated the results. They know others who have been down even more roads and have evaluated those results, as well. Why follow a path proven to be full of unhappy results?

Obviously, only God has a perfect perspective on all things. He perfectly understands where you will end up if you continue along the road you are on. God has inspired the wise, which is why they are wise, and God is the only place from which true wisdom comes. This is why we call it "granted wisdom." Only from godly-granted inspiration can you be assured you are on the right track. But again, while the inspired wise can point the way, their words and examples can only point the way. They cannot bequeath an understanding of principles. God and His wise inspired men and women of history have explained the landmarks and mile markers you will pass so that you will recognize when you are on the right path but they can't, as they say, walk the path for you.

Are your circumstances consistently changing for the better fast enough? Are you keeping a record of what didn't work well and how you changed things to work better — and then better again? Are you seeing an increase or decrease of miracles in your life or not recognizing many at all?

These results you get are the tell-tale signs and a perfect measuring standard by which to judge your performance and whether or not you are following and associating with the right kinds of people. Is it time to make a change? Again, Tony Robbins says, "Success leaves clues" so pay attention to the clues and apply what you learn. The miracles in your life will then consistently increase; it is impossible for them not to. The intrinsic value of studying your own and other people's personal histories is how your current life is directly affected and increased by them.

Do problems, frustration, struggles and pain mean that you are on the wrong road or that you simply lack understanding? The answer is "it depends." It could be one or both. If you try to avoid the uncomfortable emotions instead of discovering why you are feeling them and how to overcome them, your actions will only leave you more soft and vulnerable. A better way is to ask yourself are you willing and determined to learn from those feelings and where are you going to be in the future because of them. Everyone makes mistakes and lets themselves down on occasion. Also, no one knows enough. What matters is how you deal with it.

Jesus gave us the ultimate standard of measurement when He said, "By their fruits ye shall know them." What kinds of fruit are you producing? What quality and quantity of fruit are you producing and how much fruit do you have "...laid up in store against the season thereof"? It is only the wise who keep a detailed accounting of their resources — spiritual, physical, emotional, social, intellectual, financial and chronological (the SPESIFCs). Thus, they are the only ones adequately prepared for the future because they know where they are and are walking down the right path.

If you are gaining ground consistently, you do have license to rejoice even if you might still be in pain. If you keep it up no matter what, one day soon you will be free — as long as you are improving faster than 60 minutes per hour. If you are still discovering that you have been on the wrong road, don't be angry and miserable. Instead, get excited that you are finally recognizing the truth. It will bless your life forever if you only decide to use it well. At least you know where you are. Be grateful that you're discovering a surer track on which to run.

Taking Stock of Your Current Location

You see, life is about who you are becoming, not just about what you are getting. You can acquire possessions but nothing you acquire will bring you fulfillment unless it is accompanied by developing core character traits that allow you to keep things which are eternal.

What you really want is what one anonymous sage called "...happiness that does not fade with the lights and the crowds and the music" but exists in and of itself, regardless of your current circumstances. This happiness helps you during hard times because you know for a fact that when you are in uncomfortable or even painful situations, it is only temporary, and is one more experience to learn and grow from. The wisdom you gain will only increase your future happiness.

Several years ago, I discovered this interesting paradox — the secret to happiness is to forget about trying to collect it, even though you can only give it to yourself and concentrate on giving it to others, even though they can never get it from you.

Do possessions — a big, fancy house, expensive cars, a beautiful wardrobe and the like — measure how you are doing? Of course they do, at least financially, if they are actually paid for. But it doesn't mean anything about how you're doing in other areas. Over the years I have come to know quite a few financially wealthy people. Some of them are abject failures in other areas of life and I wouldn't waste a moment of my time with them unless they had a serious change of heart. But others of them are some of the most genuine people I have ever met and do all they can to bless other people's lives.

Does a totally fit and sculpted body measure how you are doing? It depends how you got it. If you followed a truly good plan, of course it does, in that SPESIFC area. But, how is the rest of your life? Here is a telling experiment for you: Look at your life and write down everything you see. What harvest have you stored up from your previous springs, summers and autumns of life? What is in your current garden of life that is ready to harvest? What are the things that are just taking root in your garden that, if you continue to nourish, will show up as your harvest? And what seeds are you harvesting that you now have to plant and harvest at a later date?

What do you want to harvest? Who can you find to learn from who has produced the most magnificent harvest ever in that area? One of the most common and heart-wrenching things I hear is, "Well, there are no guarantees to life." What a devastating thing to convince yourself of and, even worse, an excuse to be contented with poor or mediocre results when miracles could be closer than you think.

In this journey that you have chosen, are you headed for a cliff in the desert or to a mansion on a hill with all the luxuries of life? The only difference between the two results, or anywhere in-between, is the path you have chosen to follow and your daily decisions about whether to stay your course or make changes.

Here are some questions to answer for yourself that will help you measure the results you will receive at the end of your road:

1. What is the quality, quantity and substance of the inspiration you receive on a daily basis? It will always be a direct result of the road you are traveling.

2. What is better in your life this month from last month, this week from last week, today than yesterday — specifically because you intentionally designed and worked it out that way?

3. Are you following people who have actually already produced the same types of results that you want? Are these teachers and mentors giving you "conventional wisdom" or tried-and-true directions because they understand the principles and are a living example of them? Or have they simply stumbled onto those results accidentally or copied someone else and are on track for a crash because they don't understand those core principles? In other words, are they teaching you based on their own information, knowledge or wisdom? Are you memorizing information, gaining knowledge or understanding principles?

4. Can you identify the principles upon which the recipes you are following are built, and have those principles been proven over the course of history?

If you cannot answer the third and fourth questions with surety, what you're learning are, likely, not true principles. At the least, you need to continue to get better information, turn that information into knowledge by further research and practice, discover through revelation/inspiration that you are unquestionably on the right track and then discover through time and experience (experiment) how miracles are coming to you specifically from this journey you have chosen. Also how big are the miracles coming to you?

I cannot draw out a road map to exactly where you want to go. I am on my own path with my own intentions, dreams, objectives, plans, and goals. I can mentor you on how to draw out your own roadmap. Once you have drawn that roadmap, the mile markers, landmarks and sites you see along your way will tell you if you are on the right track or not. You will also be able to see if you are making good time and how you can consistently increase your efficiency within your time. Continue with a calm assurance that you are guaranteed success as long as you are committed to succeed no matter what.

The principles that guarantee your success are the same principles that guarantee mine. Though you and I will experience a different journey, the same principles are in play. During this time of discovery, you and I will each find greater joy in our journeys.

Always be Grateful for the Good in your Life but Never Lose the Committment to Make it Better

The motto that I live by every day — the one that has transformed and completely liberated me to find and continue to transform who I am — is "I am completely grateful for every single thing in my life and simultaneously entirely dissatisfied with it all. It has also brought more real happiness into every part of my life than anything else. It keeps me passionate to continually re-create who I am into who I'd rather be. All the while full of gratitude for who I am currently." That includes the problems and pain I've caused myself from wrong or even stupid thinking because they have been some of my most powerful influences to change.

Several years ago, it dawned on me that even though I was still not even close to where I wanted to be, for the first time that I could remember, I was genuinely happy clear to the core. I knew that I could and would accomplish what was most dear to my heart. Even during the hard times, I was so grateful to be me and to be in this exact moment because it was simply the best place for me to be in order to achieve what I wanted most — even if it was painful.

About 25 years ago, I was in one of my very first seminars with two of my first mentors, Don Wolfe and Doug Carter. They took us through a training that proved to be a major shift in my perspectives about life. If you had asked before that time about my "bad experiences," like most people, I could have given you a very long list.

When I went to bed on the third night of that training, I couldn't sleep. My brain was so full of ideas and epiphanies that I needed to write them all down, simply to clear out and calm down my brain. By the time I couldn't keep my eyes open any longer, I realized that I had started to write a poem. Though I never did finish it, it was a major paradigm shift that changed virtually everything about my past, present and future.

> As I look back through my past and all the problems I've had,
> I can see now much more clearly how they've all been good — not bad.
> For all those times I thought that I had failed in the past
> Have now become the triumphs that through time will always last
> As the greatest strengths and talents with which I have been blessed,
> And they magnify and maximize my life's purpose and quest.

Conclusion

I thank God I am where I am. Today, virtually everything has changed in my life. I have, metaphorically, traveled back to the day I was born, taken every experience that I ever labeled as "bad" and mentally changed them to be "good", powerful learning experiences. Now, when I look back on my life's experiences, I realize that I have never had a "bad" experience in my entire life. In addition, the negative stresses in my current life are almost nonexistent. My wife sometimes teases that, "Eldon doesn't have stress, but he is a carrier."

In some ways, I am a carrier because I never accept my own or anyone else's excuses. I'm not much fun for most people at parties because when they want to gossip or blame others for their problems, they quickly discover that I was the wrong person to start that conversation with. On the other hand, if they are willing to solve their problems and be accountable, I could be the best person to talk with.

So in retrospect, wherever you are currently is exactly where you belong. I have certainly found myself in lots of places and circumstances that I chose to leave, as quickly as possible, but I understand that I put myself there and in that moment, it was exactly where I needed to be. The good news is that if I put myself here, I can figure out how to put myself somewhere better. I will learn the lessons and move on. If my "next best guess" takes me further away, I can quickly recognize that and take a better guess. If it takes me closer, I can figure out how to make better guesses to move me along quicker and more efficiently.

Either way, I know for a fact I will reach my goals and that brings unbelievable joy to my journey.

Summary

A large part of your life's stress can be attributed to the consistent upgrade it requires. You know you have to service your cars, home, yard, and other possessions in order to keep them in optimal working order and organized. Likewise, it takes time and effort to keep your body, mind, and spirit healthy. This isn't "maintenance", there is no such thing. Nothing stays the same; everything in life is dynamic, it is getting stronger or weaker, increasing or decreasing. There is no static state for anything.

Most of us perceive the world as full of "good" or "bad" experiences. Life, however is simply life. It is neutral — until you make it one or the other, not according to what you wish for but according to cause and effect. Can it be hard, challenging, infuriating, of course. Can that be bad? Absolutely. Can that be good? Absolutely. It is up to you. Our experiences are actually the poor, mediocre, extraordinary, or miraculous results created by the decisions we make and actions we take.

Your challenging experiences, your tough times, force your brain and your spirit to discover how to expand your potential and become the stronger, wiser person that you are today or that you want to become tomorrow. You could never be what you are or your future as grand, without them.

Regardless of what you are today, if you choose to be something different tomorrow, and, for most of us, there's a lot of potential for improvement, doing your best means using every resource you can muster. This includes relying on family, friends, mentors and other sources of knowledge, skill, talent or help. Then how you activate grace on your behalf.

That new tomorrow is the point B that follows today's point A. When you reach point B, it becomes your new point A, time to decide whether to stay your course or chose a new course toward something different. Look at point B as a mile marker, not as a destination and you will never get "stuck in a rut," you'll always find new opportunities to learn from the past and make new, better and more intelligent plans for your future.

One powerful tool in this evolution of self is a child-like willingness to take risks in order to expand your potential. Children have a passion to learn, grow and change that spurs their willingness to risk and (most of the time) to learn from their mistakes. Children are never satisfied with where they are or with their current abilities, yet they love themselves unquestionably, unconditionally and can't wait to continue their unique journey. They truly enjoy their journey because they believe in themselves, never question their abilities, and chase their dreams with passion and a wonder that is inspiring.

But, remember this universal law — you have complete agency (freedom) to choose whatever path you will, however, you have no freedom to choose your results. Whatever path you choose, that is, whatever actions you take, will determine your consequences. Your point B is a symptom, a natural, unchangeable result of the path you chose. It is the *only* accurate feedback as to whether the formula you followed actually produced what you intended.

So, be realistic about where you are; choose carefully were you want to go and how you want to get there; go boldly down that path, accepting with maturity whatever happens. And, please, be grateful for whatever you have or experience. That gratitude will enable you to create miracles.

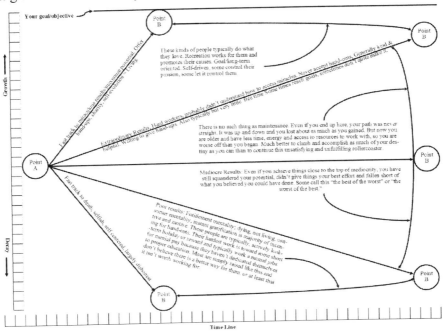

Chapter 6
The Next-Best-Guess Principle

The sixth secret, ancient principle is the beginning of every single success in history — bar none. It is the beginning and the crux of all your significant activities. Understanding the process of success is vital to every circumstance you will ever create. Why is this principle so hard? Because it begins with the utmost simplicity: It begins with a guess and, by the way, continues to the extent you are willing to keep guessing.

Application of the Apprenticeship Principle

When you begin to understand the universal laws and principles that pertain to any particular area of life, success for you in that area becomes as automatic and simple as walking or talking. In fact, being able to walk and talk is proof that you have applied some of these principles and brought under your control a few of these universal laws of creation.

When you learned to walk, for instance, you began to learn processes for standing, taking steps, and keeping your balance. In fact, when you decided to learn this new skill, you were completely incapable of walking. It wasn't just that you didn't know how, you literally had to force yourself to evolve; to become someone you had never been before, who was physically, intellectually and emotionally capable of walking before you could learn the skill.

Physically, you had to increase the strength, tone and agility of your muscles and to develop a sense of balance and maneuverability that you had never had before. Emotionally you had to force yourself to never give up, no matter what, even in the face of setbacks, pain, or embarrassment. (Granted, we're talking about a 15-month-old-child, but go with the metaphor.)

You had to keep the vision of walking in your brain — clear, bright, and bigger than any problem that could arise. You had to remain committed, regardless of how many times you fell down or hurt yourself. You had to decide that the reward of walking was worth more than whatever effort it took. Intellectually, you gained new knowledge by discovering and memorizing the right formulae and the more you practiced, the stronger your skills became.

In the process of developing this skill to walk, it was also necessary to discover some core principles about falling down, the opposite of what you were trying to learn. Even though that wasn't the result you desired, falling down taught you what to avoid so you could improve, avoiding future problems. Eventually, you even discovered that learning to fall correctly is a useful skill.

So, we all fell down plenty of times learning to walk. However, what did you actually learn when you fell? Did it teach you to walk better? Was falling a bad experience? What if you broke your arm or had some other more serious consequence, was it a bad experience then? If you repeat that formula exactly the same way, could you ever get different results? These are all good questions.

You, like everyone else in the world, are endowed with a conscious and a subconscious mind. The fundamental programming and functioning of these two minds keeps you safe by following a simple, basic concept — the only way to stay safe is to risk growing, no matter what. You are hardwired with this, not just a desire but the need, to improve. So much so that when you stop improving, you immediately begin to die.

Because of that wiring, in the process of falling, your subconscious mind logged every detail of what happened during your unplanned landing. It knows exactly how fast you were going, exactly how you lifted, moved and positioned your feet, how you leaned and the exact terrain you were on. It also knows that if you follow a similar formula again, you will experience similar results. Because its job is to keep you safe and the result of this experience was pain, your subconscious mind will never let you do the same thing again — unless it is the very best option it can come up with in order to keep you from suffering even greater pain.

Be careful, however, part of trying to keep you safe can trick you into refusing all risks or, at least, so many risks. I've heard said, and it's true that "The greatest risk in life is not being willing to take a risk." The same can be said of taking too few risks or limiting yourself to very small risks.

If you can walk today, you know that you didn't give up. You listened to your parents encouraging you to try one more time. Every time you fell down, your brain went back to the drawing board and said something like, "That didn't work like I wanted, I need to try something different." (Sounds weird to hear this said about a 15-month-old child but this is exactly what happens in that magnificent little mind and it started happening at birth, maybe earlier.)

Knowing that you will always get the same results from following the same formula is an important concept. To consciously and subconsciously recognize this keeps you growing and evolving and enables you to accept those experiences as powerful, important and valuable. If you learn that, you will, sooner or later, discover genuine happiness.

If you label experiences as bad or negative, that attitude will rob you of the opportunity to learn from them, creating destructive effects on your emotional, intellectual, and physical well-being. You will be worse off now than before because your negative attitude creates decaying circumstances.

If you label experiences as good or positive, that attitude will gift you with the opportunity to learn from them, creating constructive effects on your emotional, intellectual, and physical well-being. You will be better off now than before because your positive attitude creates growth circumstances. But those attitudes must be real, not fake.

"Spock, That's Extraordinary!"

Thomas Edison, according to legend, was asked how he felt about the thousand failures which preceded his successful incandescent light bulb. He replied, "I didn't have a thousand failures, I learned a thousand ways that didn't work." When you get back on your feet after falling down, you have an advantage, you know one more process to avoid. However, did that experience make you better at walking? Of course not. You still have no idea what works. The only choice you have, if you're going to figure out how to walk, is to take what I call your "Next Best Guess."

This might come as a surprise, whenever you attempt something you've never done before, you have to guess. In *Star Trek IV: The Voyage Home*, Admiral James T. Kirk asked Mr. Spock if his calculations for a very dangerous space flight were ready. Spock replied that he didn't have all the essential data so, "I shall make a guess." Kirk replied, smiling, "Spock, that's *extraordinary!*" A very surprised Spock then turns to Dr. Leonard McCoy to say, "I don't think he understood me." The Doctor replies, "Oh, he understood."

In fact, it was Spock who didn't understand the moment. As a Vulcan, Spock was devoted to logic, facts, and unassailable truths. He was warning his captain that he was acting on insufficient data, which set his ship and shipmates at deadly risk. Kirk already knew about the risk; it was an ever-present part of their profession. Kirk responded to a major leap forward in his friend's mental development. In their 20-plus year friendship, he had never known Spock to guess at anything.

Of course, the data was sufficient, the calculations were correct and the ship arrived exactly where it needed to be. It was Spock, after all — but, still, it was a guess. It was an "educated guess" — Spock used all the data he had and fudged the rest. You need to do the same. You need the best advice and research you can obtain. You should consider all possible alternatives. You **must** do your due diligence. This is the "Best" part of "Next Best Guess". Still, in most new situations, you won't have complete information so, it still is a guess. This is the "Guess" part of "Next Best Guess". By the way, I have already mentioned the need for constant questions. If you are serious about moving forward into new areas, you'll be asking a lot of questions. This is the "Next" part of "Next Best Guess".

Obviously, you will better understand the advice and research and make better guesses as you gain experience and wisdom. Paying close enough attention to real causes and effects will assist in gaining both. One caveat: Your brain is programmed to keep you safe and far as far away from pain as possible. This the great positive of fear — your brain is warning you of possible danger. Use that fear to stay clear of real danger, but don't let it control you. Risk is part of life and rewards rarely come without it.

Back to the learning-to-walk analogy: What do you believe will happen when you take your next step(s)? Almost invariably, your brain will overcompensate so that your second guess will cause you to fall in the opposite direction. Now most adults interpret mistakes like that as, "Wow, another embarrassing, painful experience. That was a bad experience." Subconsciously, they have a more reasonable fear, therefore, another reason to quit. Like most emotional responses, that subconscious fear can be very debilitating. It can keep us from success. Overcoming that fear is a conscious choice, made intellectually based on information and experience.

So, now you've fallen down again. But what have you actually learned? You've now discovered two perfect formulae — one that causes you to fall on your butt and one that causes you to fall on your face. (It's probably a good thing you were too young to understand the concept of embarrassment.)

Buddha was right when he said, "Enlightenment is in the middle way; it is the center between all opposite extremes." Jesus gave the same counsel when He taught, "Let your moderation be known unto all men" (Philippians 4:5, KJV). Like one of my great mentors Denis Waitley said "There never was a winner that wasn't first a beginner."

Wild guesses sometimes get positive results — we all get lucky — but never bet the farm on it! The center place is where all true success can be found. Likewise, all formulae are perfect, they produce the exact same results every time you apply them. Creating the best circumstances lies in figuring out which formulae produce the results you want and using them while learning which formulae produce the results you don't want and avoiding them.

Understanding the Difference between Needs and Wants

I'm sure you have thought about the difference between needs and wants before reading this book. I will set aside any discussion of physical needs — air, food, shelter, love — there's no choice involved in those and this discussion is about choices and circumstances. Other than the physical necessities of survival, some things you need, some things you want. Learn to distinguish between the two and you have learned one of the greatest lessons Earth life can provide. At face value, that seems pretty simple — the moment you really decide you need something; you are guaranteed to get it.

Obviously, you can choose to change your mind at any point, if you decide the cost is more than you're willing to pay. That shows you didn't really "need" it to begin with, you only thought you did. (This, in itself, is a useful lesson!) Deciding you need something is the first leap of faith, such as when you were a baby and decided that you needed to learn how to walk.

That doesn't mean we only get what we need. Most of the things we have were never "needs." We were able to get them because the price was acceptable. If the cost of certain things had been more than their perceived value, we wouldn't have parted with the resources it took to get them. The process of getting things begins with deciding what cost you are willing to pay. If no cost is too high, they are needs. If there is a limit to cost, they are wants.

So I cannot be misunderstood, I am *not* talking about being greedy and wanting a lot of stuff. Although "stuff" is included in it, I'm talking about wanting good physical health, making the most of your potential, a great education, long-lasting personal relationships, meaningful work, satisfying hobbies, being able to help others when the need arises, a nice home for yourself and your family, reliable vehicles and just about everything else.

First, make a list of what you want, everything you want. Don't resist writing things down because you think they may not be that important. Keep the list handy for a few days, lots of additional things will pop into your mind throughout your day's activities. You will even remember things that are super important to you and you'll be surprised you that you didn't think of them in the beginning. Your objective is to get everything onto your list.

I'm sure, like me, you've had teachers and other authority figures tell you to "quit daydreaming" and that your dreams are only "wishful thinking". More "conventional wisdom"; I'm telling you dreams are powerful motivators and tools that every successful person uses daily. The more you want something and the more you believe you can have it, the greater your motivation to create circumstances that help you approach your full potential, in place of wasting our life away doing things that don't really add intrinsic value to your life.

Second, you can categorize your wants into four categories:

- Things that you are absolutely not willing to live without — these are your needs.

- Things that are important because they will significantly improve your quality of life.

- Things that would be nice to have and fun for you, your family, friends, etc.

- Things that you would take if offered, but you really don't care that much.

Now, start with the list that is your absolute highest priority and order them from the very most crucial to the least crucial. Those things that you desire deepest — for which your desire burns hottest — are things that you are destined to have and for which you are uniquely suited. As long as they make you a better person and enable you to bless others, they are built into your destiny. Many years ago, I heard someone say "What you want also wants you just as badly." I've come to know this as a fact and that the universe is specifically designed to help you get them.

The flip side of this positive desire, by the way, is addiction. If something is dangerous — alcohol, drugs, pornography, almost anything could fit this category — you can still develop an overwhelming desire for it, to your destruction.

Notice, please, the careful phrasing:

- Those things that *you desire deepest* — for which your desire burns hottest — are things that you are destined to have and for which you are uniquely suited.

- If something is dangerous — alcohol, drugs, pornography — you can still *develop* an overwhelming desire for it, to your destruction.

Either way — toward your perfection or your destruction — you are the instigator. The universe won't just do it for you, neither will the universe do it to you.

Third, discover and then follow the processes that produce what you want while discarding processes that don't produce what you want. That may seem like an over-simplification but, truly, there are lots of people who already know how to get what you want and they can show you the way. (Also, as previously noted, many things in life really are very simple. That doesn't always mean easy, but very simple.)

If you asked random people on Main Street, Anytown, USA, what they really wanted, almost 100 percent would tell you about things they wish for but rarely mention things they want with all their heart and soul. Interestingly, that fear of being upfront about our deepest desires is a big reason why most people get so few of those important things.

If you find the processes that move you toward the desired result then fall down enough times to differentiate between what actually does work and what doesn't, you have a plan. Whether you recognize it or not, every time anyone actually obtains something, it is because of a plan. Unfortunately, most people's plans have not been thought through very well at all and, so, what they get is mostly by accident. Then, when what they get is not exactly what they wanted, they complain and believe the world isn't fair. But it is they themselves that have not deliberately taken control of their own plans so they are never really in control of their results.

Conclusion

The only way to discover how to do something right is to do it right before you knew how to do it right. You only have to be willing to guess enough times wrong until you finally guess right. In the process, you gained a priceless pearl of knowledge that you now have an opportunity to mold into wisdom.

Take the list "Things that are important because they will significantly improve my quality of life" and start writing down all the advantages and disadvantages of each one. Also, listen to your feelings — what seems right to you. You will soon begin to recognize which of them you should work on and in what order you want to accomplish them.

As you look over the advantages and disadvantages of each item on your list, you may decide that you "need" them, not just "want" them. If so, they will be yours much quicker. Once you actually make that transition in your mind from wants to needs, and you keep them as needs, it is impossible for you not to obtain them because your brain, habits, thinking processes, activities, and determinations, will prove beyond question that you will never stop. Once you have aced the trial of your faith, the universe will begin to turn over the plans to accomplish it.

Also, to your delight, you will see many of those less important things just naturally start showing up because you've trained your mind to obtain them. Like you, I'm often asked something to the effect "How is your day?" To which I typically respond "Just like I trained it." Whether that is poor, mediocre, extraordinary, or miraculous, that is true for us all.

Summary

Needs then are those things that you are no longer willing to live without and wants are negotiable.

First, if you want to accomplish something, there are some fundamental requirements:

- You must be aware of the options, Sometimes, this includes choosing among several possible options. Your choice becomes your objective.
- You must believe that you can accomplish the objective.
- You must believe that the risks involved in obtaining the objective are outweighed by the reward.
- You must have the physical ability to reach your objective. (however, just because you don't have it now, doesn't necessarily mean it is impossible).

Second, assign a priority to each objective:

- Things that you are absolutely not willing to live without — these are your needs. (They might also be your addictions, learn to tell the difference.)
- Things that are important because they will significantly improve your quality of life.

- Things that would be nice to have and fun for you, your family, friends, etc.

- Things that you would take if offered, but you really don't care that much.

Third, apply what my friend Phoenix Roberts calls The First Rule of Brainstorming: "There Are No Rules! Leave your ego at the door. Throw caution to the wind. Open a can of worms. Go for broke. Mix your metaphors. Bet the farm. Shoot the works. Try a little tenderness. Make magic. Have Fun!" Simply put, make as many guesses as you can, even those you may not think are very good.

Fourth, organize them by what you think are best to worst. Keep adding to them and trying best guess after best guess until you understand all the processes or formulae that will get you what you want and, then, as the old saying goes, "Work like it's all up to you and pray like it's all up to God."

Chapter 7
The Shortcut Principle

The seventh secret, ancient principle is interesting in that individuals, organizations, and communities, are hardwired to pursue it. It can be a tremendously profitable principle and, if you're getting better at applying the principles already discussed, you're already applying one magnificent concept of this principle. As your understanding grows, you'll achieve your objectives more quickly and efficiently — you might even change the world.

Sir Isaac Newton was one of those who discovered how to produce miraculous results, at least in some areas of his life. When questioned about how he accomplished so many seemingly impossible things, he gave us a miraculous formula, "If I have seen further than others, it is only because I have stood on the shoulders of giants." In other words, he used what others created but was never satisfied with those circumstances. Starting by understanding what others have accomplished saves you from "reinventing the wheel". It allows you to start from square two or square ten or it may allow you to jump directly from square 15 to square 25.

"Conventional wisdom" has many uncomplimentary things to say about shortcuts but most of the progress mankind enjoys has happened because somebody discovered a better way of doing something. Is that not exactly what a shortcut is? Beware however that if you just start where others left off, without learning from them how they got there, that is cutting corners, not taking short-cuts. I think you understand.

My Business was Cut Short

For many years, I was an extreme high-end cabinet maker and finish carpentry contractor. Even when so many contractors were going out of business though recessions and slumps, I had an ever-increasing customer base, mostly because of my reputation for never cutting corners and never allowing my employees or subcontractors to cut corners.

My customers recognized that and referred me to all their friends and associates. I made a point to let people know that I would never be the "lowest bid" precisely because I took more time and made sure things were done to a much higher standard than most other contractors.

I wouldn't want to even try to count how many times general or subcontractors (who advertised that they did "high-end work") tried to convince me to hire them. Sadly, when I went to see work they had done (even their best show-pieces) I wouldn't have allowed them on even my low-end jobs. Among those I allowed to audition, only about one out of 30 or 40 either did work of sufficient quality or were willing to learn and improve to that level of quality.

If all was going so well, why did I close that business? The real reason is because writing this book and launching this business, i.e., mentoring, training and speaking about solving problems began to call so loudly that I could no longer ignore it. However, it made the transition easier because of increasing difficulty to find people who were willing do the level of work my clients and I required. Harder than finding people who could do the work was finding anyone willing to develop the skill level for that work. Hardest of all was finding workers with the integrity and dignity to hold themselves to that level and never cut corners. Also, the tendency to be indignant when they needed to redo things that were done sub-standard was the norm. Even when I offered to show them how to improve their skills, they were more offended than teachable. As I mentioned before, it was also the case with writers and editors.

Shortcuts vs. Cutting Corners

"Do you like shortcuts?"

I love to ask questions like that to groups of all kinds because, when followed by a lively discussion, it forces people to think in new directions. I love shortcuts, I use them every time I can find them — all the time, in any area. As I mentioned, human beings are programmed to look for shortcuts. Sadly, like all principles, there is a corrupted version that has destructive instead of constructive results — cutting corners.

Let's be absolutely clear about these definitions: As I said, "conventional wisdom" says negative things about shortcuts but shortcuts are the positive. Discovering a shortcut will save you time and energy that you can use on something else that will bless your life. On the other hand, it is frustrating to me that the "conventional wisdom" is becoming more and more lenient all the time about cutting corners. The quick-and-easy, "microwave mentality" that our society has created enables many people to give-in to their egocentric and shallow-thinking urge to do it just good enough to get by. Their goal is to get out of work, avoid pain, and increase their personal pleasure, regardless of what happens to others. That is cutting corners. Then to top it off, they do everything they can to demand more wages for doing less.

Cutting corners means you weren't willing to put in the time, energy, or focus to do it right. Cutting corners means your work looks might look ok at first glance — if you don't have an eye for detail, but a closer examination quickly reveals many flaws. Cutting corners is being sloppy. Cutting corners is being lazy. In some circumstances, cutting corners is an invitation to a court appearance — if you don't do your job right and an accident or injury results, you can be held criminally or civilly liable. Ultimately, it is to sacrifice your integrity when something gets hard.

Coach Davis, my wrestling coach as a junior was a stickler about good form. He often reminded us that sloppy practice makes sloppy wrestlers and perfect practice makes champions, the more we were willing to continue to work toward perfect form, the more powerful we would be.

There is an old saying that "fatigue makes cowards of us all." For the corner-cutting crowd, that's true but history proves that fatigue (or opposition or ridicule or whatever) doesn't stop everyone. These are those few people who, even in the most trying circumstances, refuse to compromise their integrity, they never cut corners.

Discovering valuable shortcuts is a microcosm of my program. How do you find a shortcut? You educate yourself so you know what others have done, giving you your Point A; you make your best guess; you take some risks; you ask-seek-knock and work toward those perfect circumstances. That doesn't mean you have to be perfect, it means you can never live a double standard: You must demand of yourself the same high standards when you are tired and beat up as when you're feeling fine.

Another of my amazing role models is industrialist, philanthropist and creator of the Huntsman Cancer Center in Salt Lake City. Jon M. Huntsman, Sr., wrote one a powerful book that I also recommend to you. The title says it all; *Winners Never Cheat — Even in Difficult Times*. I encourage you to devour that book. The principles in it are priceless!

Losers cut corners and make excuses; winners discover shortcuts and make life better. Cutting corners shows a lack of integrity; it is dishonest and being a cheat — what they never realize is that it is far more damaging to themselves than to anybody else.

The Real World

Every human has flaws and, regardless of where you go, there will be people who are all too eager to point fingers and address those flaws. Again like Theodore Roosevelt so eloquently put them in their place:

> It is not the critic who counts; not the man who points out how the strong man stumbles, or where the doer of deeds could have done them better. The credit belongs to the man who is actually in the arena, whose face is marred by the dust and sweat and blood; who strives valiantly; who errs, who comes up short again and again, because there is no effort without error and shortcoming; but who does actually strive to do the deeds; who knows great enthusiasms, the great devotions; who spends himself in a worthy cause; who at the best knows in the end the triumph of high achievement, and who at the worst, if he fails, at least fails while daring

greatly, so that his place shall never be with those cold and timid souls who neither know victory or defeat.

Mistakes are unavoidable but as long as you learn from them, they will guide you to the right track. If you chose to deliberately not fix mistakes or for whatever reason, not put your heart into your work, and leave things worse than they should be, that is a problem. Especially if you then expect full payment. Any form of trying to get more than you have earned is cutting corners. In so doing, you may get away with it temporarily but, sooner or later, you will receive its horrible and degrading consequences. When you give in to the temptation to cut corners, you trade your integrity and dignity away and become a pathetic excuse for a human being. On the other hand, discovering and following worthy shortcuts will pay you back in exponential returns while bringing you respect and honor.

I cherish my role models — Joseph (who was sold into Egypt), David (who slew Goliath), Solomon (the wise), Buddha, Jesus, Viktor Frankl, Abraham Lincoln, Mahatma Gandhi, Martin Luther King, Mother Theresa, Ronald Reagan, and others — in part because their darkest times didn't push them to cut corners. Instead, they stood fast to their ideals and integrity. Obviously none of them were perfect and so you can point out mistakes and flaws but I think you are above that by now and can see the immense good examples they were. At least while they were at their best. As you develop a character that includes the integrity and the courage to take intelligent risks in order to discover shortcuts, you will dramatically improve your own life and leave a legacy that will bless many others' lives.

This doesn't mean every shortcut turns into a miracle. Humans often then adopt new practices before fully understanding them, only later to discover their downsides.

For example, farmers have been creating genetically modified organisms (GMOs) for millennia. The traditional method is called selective breeding and without it, we wouldn't have corn on the cob; 300 breeds of horses, 400 breeds of dogs; 4,000 varieties of potatoes; or 7,500 varieties of tomatoes. The downside, of course, is time — selective breeding takes generations, meaning decades or centuries are required to achieve the objective.

In the 20th Century, a miraculous shortcut (so we thought) was discovered — genetic engineering. Modern GMOs offered to increase crop yields by literally hundreds of times by splicing genes directly into seed cell DNA, instantly creating new plant varieties. In the beginning, it really did seem to be the answer to prayers. As research continued, problems were identified. Reduced food value and increases in health problems and disease. Our bodies have a difficult time trying to processing the new GMO's and we are seeing devastating effects.

In recent years we've begun to discover however that it was actually more a process of cutting corners than it was a short cut. The new GMO's were designed to produce major yield increases per acre of crops but how did they do that? By making the crops resistant against toxic pesticides. They even call them "Roundup Ready" crops. The incentive is not about providing more food as a service to humanity and certainly not about providing healthy food. It was all about greed and selfish interest.

Sadly, there is such a huge momentum it is difficult at best to turn it around. Obviously most people in these industries are honest, upstanding people who go home to their families every night and do not wish to hurt anyone. A few, many at the top of the corporate food chain, do not share those character traits. With trillions of dollars at stake, they find the temptations irresistible, so they buy leaders, doctors, falsify test results and cover up important findings, trying to hide the truth from the masses.

As awareness grows however, the public is demanding changes and parts of the industry are making good changes. Does this mean that what we thought was a shortcut is actually a cut corner? Like I mentioned earlier, some of it may well have started with good intent, simply as a "next best guess." Nothing wrong with that. When problems started to arise and a few at the top decided to hide those problems, it immediately turned to cutting corners.

Today, because of technology, new equipment and increased healthy farming practices, these GMO's have not proven any longer to adequately help us feed the world. We only need to stop accepting the propaganda, discover principles for ourselves, recognize when leaders have bad character and replace them with leaders who are willing to make the hard decisions and do whatever it takes to turn things around. We also need to stop patronizing companies who are willing to make a profit at someone else's expense, so that they either go out of business or change their character and practices from selfish hearted and dishonest leaders to servant hearted and honest leaders. If you want them honest, you have to hold them accountable, then everybody wins! That's what the Free Market is all about.

There is another aspect also to understand here, that brings us back to understanding principles. While the world is full and even over-flowing with opportunities to discover new resources and continue technological progress to use our resources more fully, God would never have created a world with an inadequate food supply. If we are going to try to improve on nature, it is insanity to let our greed run wild and/or our ego think that we are wise enough to make it better before we even understand the principles that support it. That is illogical thinking — actually not thinking at all.

Speaking of "win-win", in business and other areas, several scenarios are discussed — win-win, win-lose, lose-win, lose-lose, and so on. If one gets what they want, it's a "win"; if one doesn't, it's a "lose". They are entitled to their opinions. In reality, however, there is no such thing as win-lose, or lose-win. If both parties get real value from a principled transaction, it is a win-win. If neither profits cleanly or one party takes advantage of another, it is lose-lose. If any other person loses, we need to be willing to have the integrity to say, "no-deal" regardless of what it seems we may gain. If any person is willing to let someone else lose, especially because of what they might gain, they lose the most because they have sold their integrity. I have had several people say, "Well that's not true. What about war?" World War II is a perfect example. We won the war, at a tremendous cost. Our enemies lost the war at even greater cost, but what did we do immediately afterwards? We helped those who were our enemies to re-build and start a new with a much better foundation of principles. Today, they are our allies. That was a "win-win."

If they had been offended and refused our help to rebuild, that is perfectly OK. That would be their business and their loss. As long as we were ready and willing to help them win, then we have set the stage for win-win and that is all that is required for us to win. The ultimate choice to win is up to each individual side and even filters down to each individual belonging to each side. This brings us to an interesting perspective. Do you realize that every advancement in human history came about because someone had a problem and they were no longer willing to live with it? Many times, it wasn't so much that things were not working, or even working well, but that people wanted things to work better.

In the introduction, I stated that true success can only be found within the simplicity beyond complexity. Because the simplicity on the front side of complexity is naivety, while the simplicity on the back side of complexity is wisdom. As we discuss the shortcuts principle, keep in mind that most people have the wrong idea about what shortcuts are and why finding them is so important.

There's Nothing Wrong with a Good Shortcut

I've had opportunity to get feedback from lots of people over the past few years, and I've noticed that when I start talking about shortcuts, most people's reactions are quite negative. Upon further study, I've found failure is the biggest reason for negative reactions. At one time or another, many people attempt what they think is a shortcut only to find that it actually wasn't a shortcut after all and cost them more time and trouble than if they had stuck with the traditional route from the beginning. They label the unsatisfying result as a shortcut (instead of cutting corners) and a failure and decide that shortcuts don't work. Strangely, the pain of a failed shortcut is typically more powerful than the prospect of finding a useful shortcut. Virtually every time someone finds a real shortcut, it has come at the expense of discovering a lot of ways that were not shortcuts. (Recall Edison and his lightbulb! And chapter 7, The Next-Best-Guess Principle) These people are doing it right — they are experimenting — unfortunately, most give up before they discover success, so it looks like a failure to them.

The Exodus story is a powerful metaphor to teach us this principle:

Why did God want the Israelites to leave Egypt? He had something better in mind for them and He knew that if they stayed where they were, they would never reach their potential. Even though the Egyptians "did set over them taskmasters to afflict them with their burdens" (Exodus 1:11, KJV), their lives were good enough that it took very little time in the wilderness before they complained, "we sat by the flesh pots [in Egypt], and when we did eat bread to the full" (Exodus 16:3, KJV). Their life of bondage, in some respects, was simple. Other people told them how to live, and naive simplicity tends to settle for much of that.

Naive simplicity is sometimes perfectly normal; it's the lifestyle children live before they learn to be responsible for themselves. It is the same thing many do in finding and working a job. That said, it is always the hardest way to live because people are in bondage to their own ignorance. They usually do things the hard way. They don't understand the shortcuts to be free agents and discover real happiness. Such were the Israelites of Moses' generation.

God clearly understood that he could not just lead them directly to the Promised Land. The Israelites needed to learn a lot of lessons before they were capable of appreciating their independence and making their new land flourish. So, here's an interesting question: Did the Israelites actually take a shortcut to the Promised Land? The ones who made it did.

I can see some people's eyes rolling as they read those words. "You call 40 years in the wilderness a shortcut?" In fact, I do. What would've happened if the Israelites went directly to Canaan? As the account in Exodus makes clear, they were unprepared for freedom, for the responsibilities of adulthood. That would have been a shortcut to death — for themselves and their entire civilization.

The Israelites' lives in Egypt was the simplicity on the front side of complexity — naivety. They really were like children and had no idea how much they didn't know. That's the real reason they didn't have the freedom they claimed they wanted. The more naive a society is, the more vulnerable it is to oppression and abuse by others and the more vulnerable to mistakes from which they may not recover. Imagine leaving your five-year-old in the desert alone. Imagine you've left the child with adequate tools and supplies for an adult. The chances for survival are nil. Their naivety was so bad that the Israelites, even after all the miracles God showed them, were so afraid of the Canaanites they actually believed the Canaanites would win in a war against God. God was left with only one viable alternative — start over with a population untouched by the bad habits learned in Egypt.

During the 40 years of wandering, a generation grew up learning correct principles by precept and example. When the new generation entered Canaan, they understand the simplicity on the back side of complexity — wisdom. In fact, their lives were hugely simple — ignore the commandments and suffer, keep the commandments and prosper. Continue to keep the commandments, discover deeper insights and continue to increase

A worthy mentor will teach you how to avoid the pitfalls and find the shortcuts through the wilderness so that, when you reach your Promised Land, you are prepared to turn it into a paradise. That doesn't mean it will be easy, it means it will be easier if you made the most of your wilderness education. You still must discover the shortcuts to get to, and make the most of your Promised Land, but the moment you are ready, the universe will reveal their location and provide you access to the principles — just as it happened for the Israelites. By the way, if you didn't notice yet, the Promised Land is not a place where no work is required. It is only an opportunity for you to maximize your own potential and create your own paradise. No one can create it for you. That's your birthright as a creator, to create it exactly to your own specifications.

Like the Israelites in Egypt were in bondage to the Egyptians, the masses today are programmed with what to believe and what to do by most of the media, most educators, most government officials, most business leaders, that is, people who do not have the community's best interests at heart. As smart as these so-called community leaders may appear, one look at the results they are producing says it all — mediocre results at best and poor results the majority of the time. Our population is being taken advantage of — we are told what to buy, where to live, how to dress, who to trust, what is "cool", and what is right (well, what they are calling "right" this week) by people who are extremely naive themselves and not held accountable to anyone else.

Now don't get me wrong, this is not the problem of the media or politicians or CEOs, it is your problem and you are the only one who can fix it. You do that by understanding your options — what will create the win-win scenario — and then changing the way you do things to achieve that circumstance for you.

There are many wonderful employers who go the extra mile for their employees because they know treating their employees well means more profit. Many employees produce wonderful results and are great assets to their employers. The same is true of journalists, statesmen, and others but, as in virtually every area of modern life, they are the extreme minority.

Gandhi said, "Be the change you want to see." If you are willing, you can be the catalyst to push innovation and create healthy shortcuts in your family, where you work, and for your community.

Hand-outs vs. Hand-ups

One of the great tragedies of modern America (and many other places) is a corner cutting plan that masquerades as a shortcut plan. Hand-outs allow people to feel like they are helping when they actually damaging and making others more dependent.

Hand-ups are a great plan; they are temporary assistance that gets people through hard times. A hand-up enables and encourages people to discover what created their problems and how to evolve beyond them, in other words, hand-ups are shortcuts. They are part of the principle of giving and receiving grace that every human being must participate in to grow and evolve.

Hand-outs, by contrast, are freebies in both directions. They encourage recipients to become more dependent. They allow givers to just toss some money or food or clothing or housing, etc. at a problem. There's no accountability on either side: The recipients don't have to work for what they get. The givers don't have to care about the results of their gift. No one grows from such an experience. Hand-outs are usually given with good intentions — supposedly, they are a shortcut to improve others' circumstances. Without requiring any accountability for what has been given or received, hand-outs have the opposite effect. Far too many are given out of pity instead of charity, and that mindset by itself is a negative for everybody.

By the way, and most people will find this a hard saying to take, it is your duty and honor to accept hand-ups as well as give them. When you need them, hand-ups enable you to leap to greater levels of interdependence, which is the healthy give-and-take between people, and helps you create the circumstances you want.

Years ago, I met a single mother with two teenage children. Their only heat source during the winter was a wood-burning fire place. Many people before me had been bringing her family firewood every winter. My son and I decided we would also help. Many times we joined others from the neighborhood in a wood-cutting day, and several times we took wood by ourselves. We knew we'd been blessed and were happy to help. As time went on, however, we began to offer other kinds of help that would enable them to live in better circumstances. The resulting friction between the mother and me was fast and significant. One day, she became extremely angry and demanded that I never come again. What happened?

She had become so dependent on hand-outs — and she knew that others would continue to provide for her — that when I tried to give her a hand-up and be more accountable for her own improvements, she adamantly refused. We continued to help them with firewood until we moved to a different town but, before we left, we heard from others that she still almost never even said thank you, let alone tried to give back.

Every time someone gets something for nothing, someone else had to get nothing for something and, in the process, both become more of nothing than something. Growth takes effort. Without effort, there is only decay.

As I mentioned before, the biggest problems you will ever have stem from the lack of insight to recognize the principles you violated that created your problem. Everything in your life can improve, and a major part of being fulfilled in life is to continue to discover the shortcuts that are impatiently waiting for your diligence and commitment to discover them.

Success can only ever be achieved through shortcuts. The number of healthy, win-win shortcuts you discover, and consistently use to upgrade your life, is the real measurement of success.

Conclusion

Sir Isaac Newton said, "If I have seen further than others it is only because I have stood on the shoulders of giants." There are a lot of great things in the world, but things which need no improvement are rare as hen's teeth (that means there is no such thing). Be grateful for and use what others have created but never be satisfied with their creations. If you understand the foundations of what others have accomplished, you can stand on their solders and find shortcuts — you can make improvements — that can change your life and in so doing, change the world.

In today's world, lots of people want the optimal performance, but it is increasingly difficult to find people who do that level of work. Few are willing to spend the effort to learn it, fewer still have the integrity and dignity to hold themselves to that standard and refuse every opportunity to cut corners.

People love shortcuts but so many have tried a few shortcuts and not created the circumstances they want. Giving up on the idea before they achieve success often sours them on the whole principle.

Hand-ups are temporary assistance that gets people through hard times. They are shortcuts that enable and encourage people to discover root causes of their problems and evolve beyond them. They are part of the principle of giving and receiving grace that every human being must participate in to grow and evolve. Hand-outs, by contrast, are freebies requiring no accountability on the receiver or giver. They encourage recipients to become more dependent and givers to justify the easy way out and call it good, when it is actually bad for everyone.

Summary

Shortcuts are the positive — discovering a better way to do something will save you time and energy that you can use on something else that will bless your life.

Cutting corners are the negative — the quick-and-easy way, based on the lazy, shallow-thinking urge to do it just good enough to get by or to get out of work, avoid pain, increase personal pleasure, regardless of consequences.

Every human has flaws and there are always people eager to point fingers and address those flaws. Cherish role models who have overcome great challenges because those dark times didn't push them to cut corners. Instead, they stood fast to their ideals and integrity. As you develop a character that includes the courage to take intelligent risks and discover shortcuts, you will dramatically improve your life, even when your shortcut doesn't turn into a miracle.

Hand-ups are the positive — they are temporary assistance that gets people through hard times by enabling and encouraging people to discover what created their problems and to evolve beyond them.

Hand-outs are the negative — they're freebies in both directions. Recipients become more dependent and providers have no accountability for the results of their supposed good deed.

All of us will face tough times. All of us need hand-ups. To refuse aid when needed is a disservice to yourself and a disservice to the giver — people need opportunities for charity so they can grow.

Chapter 8
The Measurement Principle

The eighth secret, ancient principle cannot be avoided, if you want to succeed. If you follow it, you will know exactly where you are at all times and you will either have your next step or you'll know how to discover your next step toward miraculous success.

Having been a carpenter most of my working life, I can't imagine not always having a tape measure close by. Can you imagine trying to build anything without a way to measure? Or even more absurdly, beginning a project without any way to or giving thought to measure whether you are progressing, declining or at least have a reference of where you are compared to where you want to go?

How important is Measuring Results?

There is a common anonymous adage in business and other areas, "Performance measured is performance improved." The opposite is equally true — failure to measure makes improvement impossible and decay inevitable. How can you improve if you don't know how you're doing?

Everybody with any sense measures things constantly: We measure our incomes against our expenses. As employers, we measure employees' productivity; as employees, we measure our employers' generosity. We measure the electricity it takes to run an appliance, and the cost — just look at the little yellow stickers in any appliance store. We, the teachers, the school district, the federal government, everybody seems to be measuring how our kids are doing in school. Hopefully, you measure how much gas is in your car before you take a trip, because the alternative is just too embarrassing.

It seems pretty foolish not to measure personal progress doesn't it? Yet how many people actually go through the majority of their lives without standards and tools to measure their own personal progress in the SPESIFCs of life? They are disappointed, angry, frustrated, confused, etc., when their lives don't produce the happiness and results they have so desperately tried to collect but they can't explain why things aren't working out better.

Standards of Measure

Every bit as foolish as failing to measure progress is thoughtlessly using a standard that has been suggested by someone who is getting poor or mediocre results. Even more foolish is to make up a standard of your own without validation — will that standard accurately measure what you need measured? Flying-by-the-seat of your pants without any conscious and deliberate standard to reference along the way is the recipe for absolute, guaranteed, unconditional failure. (Not to mention actual death if you are, in fact, flying.)

For example, I'll bet that, like me, most of the financial advice you've received came from people who never actually had any significant amount of money. Most of the advice you got about relationships came from people who have never established long-term, powerful, growing relationships. Advice about business came from people who had never created a successful enterprise. Advice about emotional health came from people who might have seemed — but were really not — at the top of their emotional game. Advice about investments came from those who never controlled or fully understood their own investments and are not doing as well as they might pretend.

I've had a lot more exercise advice from people with little or no physical health education than from physical trainers. Most of the people who have offered me advice were not at the top of their game in the areas in which their advice was given. I know several people who are professional counselors, authors, or speakers who teach about marriage relationships but they've been divorced (sometimes repeatedly) or they've been married a lot less time than me and don't have nearly as strong of relationship I do with my wife. Who knows how long their current marriages will last or if they actually learned their lessons and are willing to keep their commitments this time around?

I once had a relationship coach get frustrated and hang up on me over a simple scheduling issue. There was never an apology or any indication that he had acted inappropriately. He accused me of not coming to appointments consistently. In reality, I'd missed only two weekly appointments over several months. They were due to family priorities and I always gave him adequate notice. All the other missed appointments were his cancellations. If he didn't have the skills to cultivate a respectful relationship with my wife or me, how could we trust his advice if he didn't follow it himself? I'm guessing that guy never had relationship coaching himself and, therefore, had difficulty measuring his own successes and failures. How, then, could he have integrity giving us advice?

Sadly, most of us were taught that there is no way to measure some things in our lives. I'll bet, like me, you have heard talks, sermons and lectures telling you how important it is to improve your life in some particular area but never explained how. Good advice? Sure but you already knew what you ought to do. What you need to know is how and even the how is lacking until you understand the principles that support it. Then if you are not taught how to track the progress in your SPESIFCs — that is to consistently measure them on a yearly, monthly, weekly, daily, or hourly basis — how are you going to know if you are improving? It's ironic to me that in the majority of divorce cases, one spouse, (usually the man) claims that he didn't think things were that bad. Why? Because he never measured how things really were.

If you cannot or do not measure, it is impossible to improve on a consistent basis!

Universal Law Governs All

I was teaching a class a few years ago about this principle, and I asked the question, "Is there anything in life that it is not important to measure?" As everyone was shaking their heads, agreeing that there was not, an older gentleman raised his hand and said, "I run the art department for our local college, and I know at least one place where measuring does not apply. Part of our curriculum is 'modern art'. The whole concept is that we never measure anything. In fact, it's important not to measure anything."

I then asked, "Would you explain to me how you could do a modern art painting without some kind of measuring"?

He replied, "You intentionally don't measure anything. For example, you may spread a canvas on the ground, climb up a ladder and splash the paint onto the canvas in a random manner."

"So," I said, "in that example, doesn't the student decide what position to put the canvas in, the specific amount of paint to use, where to set up the ladder, how many steps to climb up the ladder, the size of the canvas he uses and the movement he goes through in order to throw the paint? In essence, every part of that modern painting was decided upon and executed in order to create that specific and unique design. If one tiny measurement of any part had been different, wouldn't it have resulted in a different painting?" At first, he argued with me, contending that, yes, it would have been different, but the point he was making was that this modern art painting would be impossible to re-create.

I visited with him a few days later and he brought up the conversation again. I explained my point, which was that there was an exact formula that produced each exact painting. If by some miracle you could retrace every step exactly the same way (even though it may be impossible for us at this time), would you not get exactly the same picture because you would be dealing with an exact amount and viscosity of paint, the exact surface and texture of the canvas, the exact height from which the paint was strewn, the exact movements of the painter, the exact humidity in the air, the exact flow of air and all the other variables which caused the exact trajectories of the paint that would have produced the exact same picture?

The point is that universal laws are not abstract, they are uniform and constant. Besides, this is modern art. In and of itself, regardless of your perspective, it has no intrinsic value as far as success is concerned. Now, I certainly understand that some people spend lots of money on modern art. I also know that there are lots of artists who spend lots of time and energy learning it and a few who earn good money painting it. And it certainly can produce good feelings in those who like to create and view it. It would be a very rare instance where anyone would be interested in precisely reproducing any specific modern art work — especially given the need to recreate the exact circumstances that produced the original. In contrast, universal law is never subject to individual whims. It is the great constant behind every reality you see, whether in individuals or groups, both in natural and human creations.

The more you plan and calculate, by definition, the less "modern" art actually is. This is part of our interesting hand-out society. It is an obvious off-shoot of this destructive movement to promote that we are fine just the way we are, with limited or no need to improve, to conquer our weaknesses, to grow or evolve. What a tragedy.

The modern artist, even at his/her most avant-garde, still had to decide, even though it may have been on a whim, where to place the canvas, where to place the ladder, how high to climb the ladder, when to start and stop pouring paint, which color to pour, which motions to use throwing paint and every other detail, up to when to stop and call it finished. If the painter had chosen to do anything differently, the result would have been different.

I'm sure you've seen some of the amazing photos taken of the colors and patterns in space. Some of them are breathtaking, each is unique. Scientists, even with the extremely limited understanding we have of how the cosmos work, can explain, at least in general terms, why those colors and patterns exist in those exact places as a mixture of energy and matter. They can explain it because it all follows universal laws.

Most people live their lives like a modern art painter or sculptor, never deliberately investing the time and energy to create a plan and execute that plan for the life they want most. Plenty of people just make up measurements in the moment based on what feels good, what is within reason or what is socially acceptable. Even among college graduates — a group famous for choosing occupations and career paths — the vast majority have never actually planned their lives.

That aside, we are talking about *you* and the laws and principles that govern success in *your* personal and business life. Different formulae produce different results and you have your choice of many. Even if designed like modern art — made up on the spot — the results are always a matter of cause and effect. The general results of your lifestyle can easily be reproduced by virtually any person to achieve the same kinds of successes or failures that you experience. In order to reproduce them, you simply have to be able to accurately measure and reproduce the formula or recipe in use.

Finding the Standard for Measurement

We are all, obviously, better or worse at measuring some things than others. This is not because the things are intrinsically easier or harder to measure, it's because we have more understanding and expertise in some areas. The less experience and the fewer tools we have to measure with, the more difficult accurate measurement becomes. For this reason, I like talking about things that are easy for most people to measure because they have experience with them — money, farming, carpentry, and things like that. Spirituality and character are things that most people have not learned how to measure accurately. They've never been taught which tools and standards to use and how to use them most effectively.

For example, I remember when my father taught me to read a tape measure when I was 14 years old. In the beginning, it seemed a very complicated process. I would strain my eyes counting all the little marks between the inches and feeling nervous while cutting boards for fear I might have counted wrong, even if I'd measured five times. With more practice, however, my skill improved dramatically to the point where I could accurately measure within a 32nd or a 64th of an inch without even thinking much about it. Doing fine finish work, I learned to quickly measure to even to a hundredth or so of an inch with a quick glance — even with a tape measure marked only in 16ths of an inch. That skill doesn't take vast intelligence; it does take practice at being precise and accepting the fact that standards, in this case, inches and feet, never change.

This is the crux of a huge problem we see all around us — one continuously growing worse in modern society — people are trying to create their own standards of measurement. When that happens they, and everyone around them, are in *big* trouble. In order to see any progress, adherence to a universal standard is an absolute *must*. Universal standards are the reality, regardless of how much we might wish otherwise. Self-made standards are *delusional*; they always create massive decay. There never has been, nor will there ever be, any such thing as a self-made standard that produces anything of value. All self-made standards of measurement are illusions and will leave you broken and tattered with painful results.

First, no two people will ever make up the exact same standards. Then when their self-made standards collide, there can be no resolution other than one or both have to abandon or compromise their standards. That would be lose-lose.

A few chapters back, I told you a story about how one of my mentors, Dennis Waitley spent some time with the richest man in China. Again, in the course of conversation, Dr. Waitley asked this gentleman how he was able to accomplish so much in his life. Without a pause, the gentleman smiled and responded that he figured a person could only be as successful as the distance into the future that they planned for.

Dr. Waitley asked, "So how far into the future have you planned for?" The business man opened up his planner and folded out a page with a 500-year plan! Wide-eyed, Dr. Waitley then asked, "And how are you going to accomplish that?"

The gentleman a little a-miss, looked at Denis and again responded, "Just like I've accomplished everything else in my life: One day at a time."

The reality is that only when we recognize that there is in fact a universal standard that can never be broken or compromised, does it become simple to set long term goals that benefit everyone.

Keeping a journal with very long-term to short-term goals and commitments, being an avid note-taker of the "a-ha's" and lessons I learn and brainstorming with a pen and paper are a few of the best tools I have found to measure my spirituality and character.

As we discussed before, there are only two directions to travel in life. You are either in growth mode or decay mode. That is, you are either moving toward perfection or away from it.

If you don't Write it down, it didn't Happen

I kept a journal sporadically in younger years. Like most people, it was a history of my life's events. The journals I keep today are very different. First, I do keep a journal. I don't write in it every day, but consistently. Second, I no longer write much about what I did each day; 98 percent of my current journal entries are notes about critical principles, laws and the skills that I'm learning and "a-ha's" that improve my life.

This book is the product of my journals. I know I have more books to write because my notes and journals continue to grow with many deeper, additional concepts and principles. They are one of my standards of measurement in terms of how I made the journey from where I used to be to be to where I am at any given point in my life and for the rest of my life.

Who will benefit from my journals? I can guarantee one person will benefit — me! I write them primarily for myself, to record my plans and to track my progress. Other than making the ideas in them available for others (such as through this book), few, if any, will ever ready my journals, so I don't see that anyone else will benefit from them directly. Indirectly, those who take the initiative to learn and change based on what I have to share can profit tremendously. That choice, like everything else in this book, is up to you as an individual, not me.

Journals provide a reference to see where I was in the past, where I am today, and if I am on track for where I want to be. They are a set of powerful tape measures for me to see how I am doing.

For me, they are a process of setting goals (deciding on what new circumstances I wish to create); making sure I understand a realistic, universal standard to measure my success (what principles and concepts are required to achieve the desired circumstances); and tracking my progress toward those goals (my success at complying with the universal laws that govern this particular goal).

I have a specific process to keep my journals so they are of maximum benefit to me:

First, write down each SPESIFC area of life then go through one area at a time. I recommend you start in the area you most want to improve. Or even better, the one area you can improve that will create the greatest residual improvements in the most other areas.

Second, list the SPECIFCs in order of your need and desire to improve each area. Write down what you like most about yourself in each area, why you like those things and how they benefit you.

Third, list what you would most like to improve in each area and why not improving is hindering your success.

Fourth, write a paragraph (specific length is not important here) about how your life will improve as you get better and better at each individual area.

As you do this exercise, look around you to find people who are producing extraordinary and miraculous results in harmony with universal law. If you don't know anyone personally, do some research and discover who is succeeding and who has succeeded most in this way — the Internet is a great place to find authors, trainers, entrepreneurs, other successful people who truly walk their talk. Do your due diligence: Prove to yourself that they are men or women of character. Certainly, they won't be perfect; just make sure they are working their way toward perfection. Like all other areas, if you would like special help, you are welcome to contact me at www.SolveEveryProblem.com.

It's an oft-repeated theme of mine, because it is vital: Jesus said, "By their fruits ye shall know them" (Matthew 7:20, KJV). Far too often, what people say is not how they live and the results they produce are not what they claim they can teach you. But some people really are on the right track, even though they are not exactly where they want to be yet. Keep this in mind, when others have advice for you, find out where their advice came from and what they are personally doing about it. Find out who their role models are and then make sure those role models prove to be the kind of people who teach with integrity (which means that they live with integrity). Then study and follow them also, no matter what it takes. It's crucially important that you follow the people who are producing the results you want, not just hoping to do so sometime in the future and especially, not those who are just trying to get where they want to be, without a well thought out, deliberate plan that was approved by their mentors.

Don't Run Faster than You are Able

Although you need to focus on all seven core areas of SPECIFCs, you don't have to focus your plan on all of them at the same time. It is a great idea to record your strengths and weaknesses in each of the seven areas at the start. This is your Point A of the moment. Then, decide which one core area you think will have the greatest impact on your immediate future. Ask yourself, "Is there something that will help me in all areas?" Then ask yourself, "If I could only make one improvement today, this week, in the next month or season, which of all these improvements am I not willing to live without anymore?" Start there.

Depending on how crucial that improvement is and how it will impact your life for good, set a time frame to study and start this program, one to three months can be a good place to start. Before the end of that designated time frame, choose your next area of focus, your next improvement and commit to a time frame.

Develop this short-term planning into long-term planning. The more you take them one at a time and focus completely on one area while simultaneously rotating through those focus areas throughout each year, the faster you will begin to see exciting and significant changes. It will also be easier to pinpoint where you are now compared to where you want to be. You can begin to accurately measure your progress! From there, you'll see how each specific change (pun intended) relates to other specific changes (pun unavoidable) and you'll see how each change (pun evaded) can lead to other changes — initiating the compound interest concept that leads to exponential growth.

Take the Long View

In the 1970s television series, *Kung Fu*, Kwai Chang Caine, an American-Chinese Buddhist monk, travels the Old West looking for family. Raised in China, now in a totally new environment, he frequently flashes back to review past teachings as he tries to deal with present challenges. In one memory, Master Po, introduces himself, "You are the new student? Come closer."

Kwai Chang instantly notices Po is blind, "You cannot see," he says without thinking.

"You think I cannot see?"

"Of all things, to live in darkness must be the worst."

Po smiles, "Fear is the only darkness...Never assume that because a man has no eyes, he cannot see. Close your eyes. What do you hear?"

"I hear the water. I hear the birds."

"Do you hear your own heartbeat? Do you hear the grasshopper which is at your feet?"

Kwai Chang is shocked, "Old Man, how is it that you hear these things?"

Po replies quietly, "Young Man, how is it that you do not?"

Po and Kwai Chang develop a close bond, Po becoming the boy's principle mentor at the monastery. An excellent teacher, Po is constantly challenging Kwai Chang to grow, to the young man's occasional frustration.

At one point, Kwai Chang asks, "How long will it take me to learn these things?"

Po responds kindly, "Only a lifetime...and perhaps, a little longer."

Perfection will elude us in this life. Keeping a written record — such as a journal — will help you remember and organize your long-term and short goals. Some goals will occupy your attention over the course of years to come, others will come and go over the short term to help you in the process. Writing this book is evidence of how this has worked in my own life.

Conclusion

To remind us all, "When performance is measured, performance improves," to which another significant mentor of mine, Thomas Monson added, "When performance is measured and reported back, the rate of improvement accelerates." Again, it's that compounding concept that contributes to miraculous results!

Recently, I came across an article that made me smile. The author does misquote William Thomson, Lord Kelvin, an Irish-Scottish mathematician and physicist who is supposed to have said, "There is nothing new to be discovered in physics now. All that remains is more and more precise measurement." Clearly, in the 125 years since Lord Kelvin's passing, physics has discovered things never dreamed of by previous generations. It is interesting to notice, however, Kelvin's counsel to measure more and more carefully was actually the catalyst for many, if not most, of those discoveries.

So start measuring and reporting. Keeping a journal is a good way of reporting back to yourself. As you do you will discover that the more closely you measure any area of your life, the more precisely you will be able to measure that area in the future and the better results you will create for yourself.

Summary

Performance measured is performance improved. The opposite is equally, true — failure to measure makes improvement impossible and decay inevitable. Most of us were taught that there is no way to measure some things in our lives, despite hearing all our lives that it's important to improve your spirituality, physical, emotional, social, intellectual and financial well-being. If you are never taught how to track SPESIFCs — consistently measure them on a yearly, monthly, weekly, daily, or hourly basis — how are you going to know if you are improving?

Universal laws are not abstract, they are uniform and constant. It is these great constants that are behind every reality you see, whether in individuals or groups, both in natural and human creations. These are, therefore, the standards by which you can measure your own growth and improvement. We are all, obviously, better or worse at measuring some things than others. This is not because the things are intrinsically easier or harder to measure, we simply have more understanding and expertise in measuring some things over others. Money, crop yields, carpentry, many things are easy to measure because we know how. Spirituality and character are typically not as easy to measure, only because most people have never learned how to measure them. Once an individual learns standards and becomes comfortable with the tools, effective measurement becomes natural, almost second nature.

A key component to measurement is recording: Journals can be simple histories of events and circumstances or they can be tools of daily evaluation. If your journal entries are notes about critical principles, laws and the skills you're learning and the circumstances that result from your application of those principles, it will provide a reference to see where you have been, where you are today, and if you are on track for where you want to be.

Journal-keeping then becomes a process of setting goals, clarifying a standard of measurement, and tracking your progress toward the goals.

Take comfort in the concept that you need to focus on all seven SPECIFCs but not all on the same day. Start with one area, something that will help you in multiple areas, then pick one improvement to make over the next month or season and start there. Repeat this process, expand it to include other SPECIFCs and your growth will compound on itself, bringing you closer to the perfection you seek.

Of course, we know perfection will elude us in this life. We may be tempted, as Kwai Chang Caine was, to ask, "How long will it take me to learn these things?" Hopefully, there will be a Master Po to kindly remind you, "Only a lifetime...and perhaps, a little longer." But I add, fear not, for we can make the journey together.

Also remember: It will take as long as it takes but, if you persist, you will one day look up and realize you accomplished it and a new day has begun.

Chapter 9
The Association Principle

This ninth secret ancient principle reveals the *one* and *only* thing you have within your control to directly affect and change the results of your life. The decisions you make about this principle are the most crucial decisions of your entire life as they completely dictate your ultimate success or failure.

Now here is a piece of advice that may surprise you: Don't ever take any other person's advice about anything — not even mine — at face value! In order to create the life of *your* dreams, you will need to seek out and study several genuinely wise people. Only when you have a foundation of many wise thinkers on any given subject, can you begin to see the foundational principles that will intentionally produce what you want.

Here is a question for you: Do you know the quickest, easiest and most common way to get locked into poor to mediocre results? The answer may surprise you. In fact, in some form or fashion, we have all been encouraged and even counseled to follow this one colossal mistake by most of the leaders and authority figures in our lives and yet virtually nothing will keep you from success more assuredly. To compound the devastation of this, your ego delights in that because it doesn't have to work so hard to keep you feeling good about yourself. This colossal error is: To compare yourself to people worse off or with less ability than you.

Role Models

Everyone needs role models but beware of hypocritical people. For example, some people feel more guilt at doing something right that others feel at doing something wrong.

Anytime you are learning about principles, it is well to remember Solomon's warning about interpreting proverbs: "To understand a proverb, and the interpretation; the words of the wise, and their dark sayings." Huh? The dark sayings of the wise? Yes, every word you hear from the wise is a "dark saying." The core intent of their words are hidden from us because their words could never be understood by anyone who has not been through similar experiences from the similar, deep understanding of principles.

You must discover the truth for yourself, no one can give it to you. The wise learn from their wise peers and leaders but not to become wiser from their words. They never falsely assume it as their own knowledge, it is not their knowledge but only the knowledge of those from whom it came. They use it only as information, direction and guidance so they have greater opportunity to discover wisdom for themselves. If you want better results than you're currently getting in any area of your life, the only sane thing to do is to find wise mentors and learn from them.

When you discover someone who may be a role model, ask questions, listen intently, make sure you understand their perspectives as clearly as possible, practice exactly what they say as best you can, continue to ask clarifying questions, and, when things don't work out exactly right (which they never will in the beginning), figure out how and why you misunderstood something: Ask more questions, use your own imagination and creativity and tweak the formula until you get it right. Beyond that, with continued practice, you will become the master yourself and, likely, have the potential to improve upon their formulae. (Except Gods of course. Trying to improve on His will only result in cutting corners and cost you dearly.)

I have no idea who first came up with this, but I've heard many of my mentors talk about this concept: It is the concept of income probability. Over the years, I've learned that it is absolutely, unconditionally true, in every detail! It goes like this — if you take the six people you hang around with the most, total up their cumulative income then divide it by six, the result will be very close to your income. That may sound farfetched but it is virtually always the case.

Over the last few years, dealing with a lot of different problems from different people and groups, I began to discover that when you take those same six people you hang around with the most, add up their cumulative physical health and divide that by six, you will find your own physical health! You can do the exact same thing with your spiritual, emotional, social, intellectual, financial and chronological (SPESIFC) health. Not only that, I can predict, within very narrow parameters, at any given point in your future, where you will be, in every SPESIFC area of your life based on those you habitually surround yourself with.

The founder of Famous Amos Cookies, Wally Amos, used to say, "The only difference between where you are today and where you will be in five years or ten years will be determined by the people you associate with and the books you read." Well, today, we have to add the media that you watch and listen to as well. But what is the basis of this concept? It is simply that the people you've chosen to associate with will absolutely dictate how your life proceeds. Why? Because whomever you include in your circle of influence has a direct bearing on how you think, the state of your character, the extent to which you understand principles or not, and ultimately, the results you produce in your own life!

You've probably heard your parents and or others give you advice such as, "Be careful about the people you hang around with because you will end up just like them." The more you spend time with each other, the more alike you become — that is a scientifically-proven fact.

One of my most respected role models, Steven K. Scott, said it this way, "Every good thing in your life has come to you because of God and other people in your life."

It is interesting, almost seems a paradox at face value, that even though everything comes to you by way of others, none of those others can change you. Not even God can change you (without your permission). Only you can change you. The goals, strategies incentives, role models, and everything else you chose to make the changes is also entirely up to you.

Symptoms of Associations

It's interesting that almost everywhere you go to learn — school, church, seminars, conferences, business meetings, etc. — most of what people talk about are the results you can and ought to be creating. Yet, simply telling people how they ought to be is not only useless, it is counterproductive. Virtually everybody — on the order of over 99 percent of people — already know how they "ought to be"; they just don't know how to be that way. Ironically, most of the time, neither do the people who are preaching to them! Results are symptoms, not just decisions.

For many years, after I started learning about how the world really works, this became one of my pet peeves. Obviously, results come from behavior but simply preaching that you should do this and that and you should never do this or that, is not helpful either. Contrary to public opinion, we rarely actually *chose our behavior*. People need to understand that behaviors, like results are also symptoms, not a causes. Therefore, we need to understand how to effectively upgrade our behavior so that our results are naturally better.

Most people already have plenty of verification in their lives. They look in the mirror and are overweight and they realize, for the most part, this is because I eat too much. They climb up a flight of stairs or two and realize they're out of shape. They already know that they haven't been active enough or on a consistent exercise program for a while. They one day wake up and recognize that their spiritual life is in significant decline, that there are a lot of good things they could be learning that would improve their intellectual well-being. They already know that they treat people too harshly and that's why they have few or no friends or they don't discipline their kids adequately and that's why they are "spoiled brats" and so on.

Over the years, we've had a rash of authors and self-proclaimed authorities standing up and saying, "It's all about your attitude. Change your attitude and that will change your life." But let me ask you a question: How likely, or even possible, is it for someone to just decide to change their attitude and it instantly changes — let alone changes forever? Again, advice like that is not just foolish, it's counterproductive. All it does is make people feel bad that they haven't changed things or gives them a stick with which to beat each other when they don't recognize reality themselves. It certainly doesn't help them get where they want to be any quicker! Most of the time it is actually self-sabotage.

It's like the cartoon I saw a few years ago about a hijacker on an airplane who stands up with a bomb in his hand and says, "Now, everyone, just sit back and relax…"

Out of sheer frustration, I sat down one afternoon after coming home from a disappointing seminar and decided that if those people can travel around the country and make millions of dollars by standing up and telling people things that are not only worthless, but actually counter-productive, I needed to get out there and help people understand *how* to actually get up every day, have the character and drive and the right combination of correct formulae to enable them to go out and produce what they want forever more.

Most authors, trainers, and teachers tell people that they need to change the symptoms in their lives and never get to the core issues where change is possible. They are like doctors who have been trained to just cut out the symptom or prescribe drugs that only treat the symptoms but never actually solve the problems that created the symptoms. And thus the problems just keep returning, bigger and stronger.

One of the first modules I conceived was a simple cause-and-effect, logical look at what actually creates results and how to change them. Let's start with what you want, that would be a specific result. It is impossible to just create the results you want out of thin air, right? More specifically, as we've been learning, you will see specific results in your life only after you create them and never before. In other words, you can't just produce results because results are symptoms. They came from somewhere, but what creates results? That would be your behavior.

"Now then," you may ask, "I just change my behavior then I change my results, right?" Well, sure, *but*, how easy is it to just change your behavior? I understand behavior can certainly be forced at times, but there's something inside you that drives those behavior patterns. If you have to force your behavior, it is contrary to your character and, at best, will be very short-lived. You see, behavior is also a symptom and, in and of itself, can never change (consistently) just because you decide to change it. It is a symptom of your current attitude. However, your attitude is also a symptom. Have you ever heard someone say "you need to change your attitude…" or "you need an attitude adjustment"? How often does that work? Your right; virtually never — and yet we continue to say it!

But that, again, brings us to an interesting place. You can't just change your attitudes because they are symptoms of your current intentions. Likewise, you cannot just change your intentions because somebody tells you that you ought to. Intentions are symptoms of your character. What is character? Character is the crucial core set of traits that determines everything about your attitude at any given moment.

You've also heard things like, "that person has a really bad character." or "that person has a really wonderful character" but, humans are far too complex to fit into any such blanket statements. It reminds me of a plaque I saw hanging outside a lady's door one day. I liked it and asked her permission to write it down. It said, "There is so much good in the worst of us, and so much bad in the best of us, that it ill becomes any of us to talk about the rest of us."

In fact, in the right circumstances, virtually all of us are capable of things so horrible that we would terrify ourselves. On the other hand, we are also capable of things so extraordinarily selfless, that we would stand up and cheer for ourselves. The bottom line is, regardless of how good or how bad we think we are, or believe others to be, every behavior is chosen because it is rooted in our character. This is one of the reasons we talk about character so much in Chapter 3, on education — developing the right character is everything in producing what you really want in life. As core as character is, however, it is still a symptom that you cannot control in and of itself.

So where does your character come from? Character is a symptom of your paradigms. A lot of people ask me what is a paradigm? To keep it simple, a paradigm is a group of perspectives that give you a holistic view of something. You have a paradigm about yourself, about your spouse, your family, work, the government, the world itself, your life, and everything in your life.

Here again, there are no dials in your brain to turn and change your paradigms. They came from somewhere, thus they are also symptoms of something else. They are the symptoms of your education.

Again, when I talk about education, it has nothing to do with schooling. Each of us is unique, as is our education — the way you have been taught to interpret the events of the world you live in — but, then, since you cannot just change what, and the way you were taught to interpret your world and how to deal with it, your education is also a symptom! Now hold on, this really is not a never-ending chain of symptoms, like all things, there is a core principle and until you get to those core principles, you can never change your results.

So, even though you deliberately decided what you wanted and were willing to learn, at least in many instances, those things only represent an almost infinitesimal percentage of the things you've learned, inadvertently, from the people you have associated with throughout your life. Everything you see, hear, touch, taste, or smell; the emotions you feel; the people around you; where you live and work and what do to relax; the perspectives from which you view the world — everything you experience in life, even that invisible part of you we call the spiritual, are all symptoms. They came to you in one way or another because of the people you associate with.

Though he is a comedian, Mason Cooley was right when he said that "children pay little attention to their parents' teachings, but reproduce their characters faithfully."

The same is true with leaders and, if you have not learned this by now, learn it right now — you are a leader! That's why it is so crucial for you to make sure you have integrity in all that you do and say. At least one person is watching and following you every second of the day — that would be yourself. Others are also watching you most of the time. Lead them to greatness, not devastation. Also remember what I often say, "you don't have to *be* perfect to be a great leader, but you do have to be in pursuit of perfection."

As a kid, I was always right in the middle of things — including having five older and six younger siblings (plus 2 foster children who lived with us most of their youth — that was 14 kids). Growing up on a dairy farm, there was plenty of work for everyone and not much time for entertainment. Even when we had a few minutes here and there, we didn't have entertainment devices like computers and iPads — heck, we didn't even have a television for the majority of my childhood, so we created our own entertainment.

One of our favorite things to do was roping. That is, using a lariat to catch anything that moved and some things that didn't, like tree stumps and fence posts. We kept our ropes close by almost everywhere we went. After all, you never knew when you might need to catch something — like your little sister.

Byron, my older brother by eight years, was the best person with a rope I knew. He was a "real cowboy" and had a serious reputation as the "go-to guy" to catch that loose bull or to break a difficult horse — in fact, he still is today. For some reason, I was the one he usually asked to help him with his adventures and I loved it.

Although I never roped much with Byron, I watched him many times. Over the years, I practiced a lot on my own and with my friends. As far as my friends and I we concerned, none of us had any real training but we learned to catch almost anything we were after.

One day, I was on my way from the barnyard to the house when Byron drove up. I waited for him and as we walked and talked together I haphazardly threw a loop over a nearby fence post. He stopped and looked at me funny for a few seconds and then said, "Do that again". It took me by surprise and was so out of context with our conversation that I looked back at him a little surprised and asked, "Do what?" "Rope that post again," he said.

Feeling a little confused, I coiled up my rope and threw it over the post a second time. Again he paused, looked at me strange and said, "Who taught you how to rope like that?" Now much more confused I responded, "Rope like what? I caught it didn't I? Isn't that a good thing? What do you do, swing the rope with your teeth?"

He laughed and asked if I'd like him to show me a few things. I responded, "Sure, I'd love to learn to rope like you." He said, "I'm going to show you a few things, but I want you to promise that you'll practice faithfully for at least two months. During that time, you are going to wonder if this advice is just a trick to torment you. But I promise that if you practice faithfully, it will make you a much better roper". He then showed me several things extremely foreign to my habits.

He showed me how to "spin a loop" differently, to hold the rope in my hands differently, how to swing it over my head differently, let it go differently — so it was quicker, easier and safer to pick up again and dally around the saddle horn when I caught something. He showed me in a sequence where one thing built upon another, which made each step easy to remember. I was being amazed that there could be so much detail to something that had seemed such a no-brainer activity that I had never broken down and analyzed before.

His prediction came true. For the next couple of months, I was miserable. Everything was awkward. I had to force myself not to do things the old, easier way. I had spent years developing those habits and it was hard not to fall back on them. Besides, why should I do it different, if I could catch what I wanted — most of the time? Was I frustrated? *Extremely!* Did I feel like giving up? I *almost* did several times. But I remembered my promise to him and his promise to me and, so, I persisted.

One morning, as usual, I grabbed my rope and headed out to do chores. On my way across the back yard, I spun a loop and began swinging it over my head. I suddenly realized that I was swinging the rope exactly like he had shown me. It felt natural, not forced like before. I threw my loop over a fence post and snapped it back — Wow! — It felt perfect. I felt that to the core of my soul and what a feeling! Time after time, it felt like magic. Seemingly overnight, I felt like that rope had become a natural extension of my arm and completely under my control. It was amazing!

A few years later, my father sold the farm, we moved to another town and he focused on his cabinet business. It was the first time I didn't have farm chores to do and I greatly missed the farm and the open space. As my daily activities significantly changed, I didn't take time to rope much anymore. As a result, I never became a real expert like Byron and haven't really roped for quite a few years other than an occasional practice. Even though I've lost that "edge" it is still sort of like riding a bike. That rope feels comfortable in my hands and I still do pretty well.

It wasn't until I was almost 40 years old that it dawned on me how this experience was one more in a long list that proved how crucial it is to associate with and listen to the right people. With regard to my roping — I didn't even know I had a problem until someone, who knew a lot more than me, pointed out what I was doing wrong that was stopping me from accessing my full potential. In fact, I was quite satisfied with my roping until I began to compare it to someone who was really good.

Luckily he was also willing to give me advice and I was willing to take it. Compared to the friends that I hung around with the most, I was pretty good. Compared to Byron, I was terrible. Now I see how much more effective I became with a little wise counsel and a reasonably short time with the right kind of practice.

The message is so powerful, that I wanted to share it with you so you could also have, at least, a little benefit from my experience. It is a crucial key to discovering how to solve every problem in your life. Keep in mind that, in the beginning, I didn't believe I had any access to anyone who could show me how to live a miraculous life, but soon discovered I had all the access I needed through their books, videos, seminars, etc. A while later, I started to meet them in person. Today, even though they are still a tiny minority, they are more available than ever through libraries and the internet, etc.

Conclusion

In His Sermon on the Mount, Jesus taught, "Therefore whosoever hear these sayings of mine and doeth them, I will liken him to a wise man who built his house upon a rock... And everyone that hear these sayings of mine, and do with them not, shall be likened unto a foolish man, which built his house upon the sand" (Matthew 7:24, KJV). One key point is that both kinds of people built houses. This harkens back to the fact that we are all creators and we all put in the work to create things, like it or not, want to or not, it is just the way it is and you can't change it. Some have just learned to harness and use these principles more intelligently than others.

You've heard people say that you can learn something from anyone. That is true. One day, I was visiting my son's kindergarten classroom. I needed to use the bathroom and didn't know where it was. I asked him and he showed me. At that point, it was very important for me to learn and he proved a wonderful teacher. When it comes to things that will affect your perspectives and habits, which determine the results of your life, the best advice you will ever get is to learn from the very best you can find in the world. Otherwise, as you can already attest, you are going to waste a lot of time learning things that produce poor to mediocre results.

If you're ever going to improve, you have to unlearn your improper character traits and learn new and better traits — hopefully from someone wiser, this time. There will be plenty of mistakes along the way, so start by learn from the best possible mentors. You'll shorten your learning curve as much as possible and get better results quicker.

No single person can ever become great, and accomplish great things, on their own, that is an impossibility, and yet, it only takes *you* to make sure you get and accomplish everything you need and want.

You are the only person who has the capacity to make sure you succeed. I heard someone say it well this way: "The bad news is that it's *all* up to *you*, but the good news is that, it's *all* up to *you*."

Summary

If you want to Solve Every Problem in Your Life and in the process, create some phenomenal things for yourself and be the best example possible for those you love, you must:

Only ever compare your performance with the very best you can find in history.

Only listen to and take advice from the best you can find, in whatever SPESIFC areas you want to improve. Make sure those people actually practice what they preach. That they do in their own lives what they suggest that you do. That is the only way to judge and choose mentors worth following.

Make sure that you hang around with people who encourage and hold you accountable to push the envelope of your potential the majority of the time.

Be very careful of anyone else you spend significant time with because they will be pulling you in the opposite direction.

Remember that the only thing you can directly control and the most powerful influences in your life are your associations. Be careful who you hang around, because you will turn out just like them.

If you don't have or know the best people to learn from and spend time with, go find them. The added investment of making sure you get the best advice and the best influence will save you immeasurable amounts of pain and frustration from the poor to mediocre results you'll get in any other way.

Remember that good habits take time and practice to develop. So be grateful, patient and persistent.

Accept that bad habits also take time and practice to instill, and then take compounded time and pain to replace with good habits later on.

Process of Change
Symptoms vs. Core Issues
The one and only thing you have direct control over in your life

PS. Pain is NOT your enemy but a most loyal ally. Pain is only a messenger (a symptom), not a core issue. If you "shoot the messenger" without an intentional and correct solution to solve the real problem, you are only enabling and even nurturing the real enemy to grow, without restraint. The longer you ignore the real enemy, the more powerful it will become and the more harm and pain it will bring to you. Ignore it long enough and it will eventually destroy you.

RESULTS   BEHAVIOR   ATTITUDE   INTENTION   CHARACTER   PARADIGMS   EDUCATION   ASSOCIATIONS

When I speak of *education*, I do not speak of *schooling*, which today is becoming more and more only the *illusion of actual education*. I speak of something far grander, that represents the *true meaning and definition of education*. That is how you have *learned* to interpret your life's experiences and thus how you naturally direct the daily affairs, routines, habits and decisions of your life—either to your own demise or to your own profit. *Education* is only a symptom and like all other symptoms, can never be directly controlled, except by the deeper core issues that directly control them. Like children with their parents, we very quickly forget most of the words that other people speak, but we inadvertently adopt the paradigms & character traits of those we spend the most time with, even if we are not consciously aware of what they are. Best we learn to pay very close attention because they directly dictate all of our intentions, attitudes and behaviors, which inadvertently create the results of our lives. Your aura actively sees harmony and if it doesn't find it, demands separation. What is your aura repelling you from and compelling you toward? That is a clue about whether to keep or change your current associations.

Chapter 10
The Leadership Principle

This tenth secret stands unique among the ancient principles — everyone uses it all day, every day. Just as it is impossible to not create, it is impossible to not lead. No greater obstacle exists to Solving Every Problem in Your life than your lack of understanding of leadership.

As a college senior, Phoenix Roberts served as president of the Intercollegiate Knights, a service & honor society based on the King Arthur legends. In a leadership training conference, he proposed what he now calls the axioms of leadership. The first is, "Leadership is independent of anything, because leadership is inherent in everything."

Now, "conventional wisdom" says leadership is position, power, authority, office, or something similar. When they buy into this illusion, as most people do, they react by saying, "Well, nobody elected me or appointed me or anything — so I'm not a leader." The goal of this "conventional wisdom" is satanic in its evil genius — to get you to surrender your leadership power to some other so-called authority figure, resulting in decay, bondage, slavery, and, ultimately, death. In fact, you can no more cease to be a leader than you can cease to be a creator. If nothing else, and there rarely is nothing else, you are the leader of a group of one, with yourself as the sole member. Remember what we all said as a child, "You're not the boss of me!" We won't debate whether that was true or not but, even as that small child, you recognized this great hidden wisdom — *you* are the boss of you!

Think about it. If you cannot lead yourself, you cannot lead others. This is a major reason why few people go after "positions of leadership" and it's the major reason why 99-plus percent of those given opportunity for "leadership" fail.

We've already established that learning and creating are the fundamental purposes of life. This involves planning, decision-making, evaluating, and many other skills which are central to every attempt to define leadership. You are on Earth to learn to be a great creator and to share your creations with others synergistically, so you can both become more perfect than either could become on their own. That is leadership.

Leadership of Self

All the principles we wish to understand and the wisdom we hope to attain, all the success we strive to acquire, whether we recognize it or not, stems from an innate desire to be a leader. Phoenix' other axiom of leadership is, "Every group requires leadership. Every activity requires leadership. Whether the group is one or one million, whether the activity is planning dinner or ruling the world; the exact same principles apply — only the scale changes."

So, you're a leader, now what? (Good for you, that is asking the right questions!) Being a great leader is not dependent on knowledge and skills but on character and wisdom — it's not about *what* you do but *why* you choose do it. Remember the discussion about the "great commandments"? Jesus gave us "two" — love God and love your neighbor *as yourself.* Included in these is a not so subtle hint, that passes right by the vast majority. In order to obey these great commandments, you must first love yourself. It is impossible for any person to give anything to anyone else that they have not first acquired.

Just as parents want a better life for their children because they love their children, if you love yourself, do you want better for yourself? Of course, you do! Many people have a problem with these concepts. "Conventional wisdom" on one extreme says loving yourself is selfish, self-centered, or, somehow, self-righteous. Nonsense! If you want the best for yourself and others, you've already begun fulfilling the great commandments and you've already begun to understand leadership of self.

On the other extreme, "conventional wisdom" says that you are fine, just the way you are...with the connotation that you do not need to change. Hog-wash — that is called guaranteed decay. You *should* be absolutely, unconditionally grateful for exactly who you are, what you have and what you can do but the only way to truly love yourself is to simultaneously discard all contentment and constantly push yourself upward. That is the only way to find that sincere personal peace, self-esteem and intrinsic personal value that comes with knowing you are honoring your potential and winning the game of life. Again as The Buddha Explained, "Enlightenment is in the middle way. It is the center between all opposite extremes."

So, what, specifically, is leadership of self? You began with a choice — you chose to learn, a process we've already discussed: Find worthy mentors, listen to them, research them, do what they teach you, prove what works and discard the rest. In your early stages, your only capacity is to receive grace — to take, take, take because you are a child, (in reality or metaphorically, it doesn't matter). As you learn and grow, you naturally want to participate in this giving side. It is innately who we are. Unfortunately, those who produce poor to mediocre results, only have the capacity to give poor to mediocre advice and examples. As your leadership of self improves, your capacity to give excellent and then miraculous advice and examples also improves.

All this was covered in Part 1, so let me add a caution: Be extra careful how you measure extraordinary to miraculous results. Many years ago, I used to look at myself and say, "I'm not doing that bad, look at that guy, I am better off than him". That pacified me for a time but it was very poor leadership of self. Now, I know I still have a long way to go, I say "look where I am compared to my past self, compared to those who are creating the finest results ever created and compared to all the extreme possibilities for my own future!" It is an absolute liberating and exciting way to live. It is also, of course, a choice. You choose to look forward, not backward; you see your present and choose an infinitely different future — that is good leadership, of one, of the group or of a million.

As leaders, we need to trust others. In fact, I heard (I think it was Dave Thomas, founder of Wendy's Restaurants), say that one of the signs of a great leader is a person who trains the dickens out of people and then gets out of their way. The term is "delegation". Give those who follow you clear goals (or ratify the goals they choose, when appropriate), teach them the necessary skills, give them the necessary authority, then step back and let them do it. That doesn't mean you, as their leader, take things for granted. It means you give them their opportunity for leadership of self and others, you get regular reports, give useful feedback, help them solve problems (before they happen when possible) and continue to jointly improve systems and processes.

Allowing others to learn and grow is an act of love and confidence. Great leaders always act from love to serve those they lead and make it a priority to enable them with as much confidence as possible. Great leaders do their best to empower others toward their own perfection. As a result, those who follow such leaders willingly give whatever it takes to accomplish goals — then they give more — then they give their all. That's when miracles begin.

Leadership by Following

Long ago I heard someone say something like, "A real leader is not one who looks back to see who is following them but one who looks forward and makes sure about who they are following." We've all heard that leadership is all about leading people. But how do you lead people? Part of the answer is "by example" but the rest of the answer may surprise you: If you are leading people, it means people are following you. If you expect them to be great followers of you, the most crucial example you can set for them — one that gives you credibility — is to be the best follower you can be. Make no mistake, there are no real "top level" leaders. Everybody you can name has another level of leadership above them.

I often get a "Huh?" to that but, the fact is, the only way people can learn to be great followers is for someone to show them how (by example). People only earn credibility by exemplifying the characteristics they teach. The moment any person loses track of their leader is the moment they lose the ability to lead.

The word *lead* etymologically means "cause to go along one's way". My way lies in gaining the knowledge and developing the skills that allow me to lead others to miraculous results. Therefore, the only people I follow are the people who've already discovered how to consistently create miracles. The only way to create miracles is to be following someone who understands the miracles.

Let me point out two concepts in leadership by following:

Humility

The necessity of being a great follower was a lesson that first bubbled to the surface from my wrestling experience with Coach Davis. That season, I won every single match and took first place in every tournament except one — my second-to-last match on the last day of the state tournament. It was an ego blow to take home the third place trophy.

Five years later, a few of my friends and I traveled back to Monticello to participate in the rodeo. Coach Davis invited us to stay the night at his home. At one point during a conversation that evening, Coach Davis turned to my friends and said, "Eldon could have been the state champion if he had just listened to me." I'd always had a reasonably good character, my parents trained me well, but that season's success gave rise to arrogance — I decided that I was unbeatable. In the state tournament, I took third place because, the kid who beat me in the second-to-the-last-match went to the winner's bracket and took first place. His opponent took second. I won my last match and several people told me it was a far better display of my skills and talents. Still, I was awarded third.

We argued that it was only fair to have a "true second" match but our request was denied. It took several years before I took responsibility that I'd allowed my arrogance to lead me into in a false sense of security. That put me off my game. I didn't understand this concept at that time, but I had decided that I didn't need to be a follower because I was such a great leader, I needed no other. Without humility, my leadership of self was poor, meaning my leadership by following was poor and my results were far below my capability.

Respect

Humility is an inward-focused manifestation of this concept — it relates to how you view yourself in relation to others. Respect is outward-focused it relates to how you view others in relation to yourself. You have heard things like "respect your elders". Well, that is also another twisted truth of "conventional wisdom" — if we take it at face value or as a blanket obligation. Now, I'm not saying that you shouldn't be respectful to your elders — quite the contrary — but *being respectful* and *respecting* are different attitudes. Among the synonyms for being respectful are civil, considerate, gracious, and polite — all excellent character traits. Respect, however, entails more; its synonyms include awe, deference, honor, and testimonial. No one earns the right to our civility, they deserve it because we deserve it. That is the Golden Rule. However, as frequently noted in this book, respect must be earned. Give no one your loyalty, your followership, as it were, who hasn't earned that respect by the fruits of their leadership.

I'll take a short side trip here because there is a sweeping, left-wing, "politically correct" agenda all around us being forced down our throats. It demands we respect everything, regardless of worthiness — in many cases, specifically because it is unworthy. Those in this movement shouting the loudest for us to respect their choices haven't paid their dues nor earned respect. They don't have the foggiest clue about what respect actually means. Frankly, they are trampling on our rights and disrespecting us in a desperate attempt to attain some sort of justification and acceptance to ease their own conscience so they don't have to push themselves out of their own incompetence, like the rest of us had to do. Too many people, for fear of ridicule or for other reasons, are giving in to this extortion. If we give in to their microwave and entitlement mentality (that "spoiled-brat" teenage mentality that they never grew out of) we are only pouring gasoline on an already wild conflagration and lose our own integrity. Every day we are losing the vital traction we have so painstakingly gained over the past more than two centuries in our American culture. We ablolutely should be respectful but being respectful is a character trait we build into ourselves. On the other hand, you nor anyone else will ever obtain respect by demand, if you don't earn it, you will never have it, regardless of any ridiculous law or other attempt to demand it.

Law

I'll continue briefly on this side road long enough to remind you of Thomas Jefferson's world-altering assertion:

> [T]hat all men are created equal, that they are endowed by their Creator with certain Unalienable Rights, that among these are [1] Life, [2] Liberty and [3] the pursuit of Happiness" ... [4] the right of the people to establish "Governments ... deriving their just powers from the consent of the governed" and [5] "the Right of the People to alter or to abolish" their government.

Everybody knows the first three, but you need to remember that Jefferson named *five* inalienable rights, not three. (You should also remember that John Adams was wrong, "unalienable" isn't a word.) These rights are a universal law; an endowment of freedom, agency, independence, given by a loving God to His children so that they could pursue the perfection He enjoys and which He hopes to share with us. As Paul wrote, "we are the children of God: and if children, then heirs; heirs of God, and joint-heirs with Christ" (Roman 8:17, KJV).

The United States Constitution, in theory, guarantees those right and others, however, it really is just a piece of parchment. The true American Constitution resides in the minds and hearts of patriots. As long as people who love freedom are in the majority, every American will retain their freedom of opportunity. However, the day our government truly demands that every American receive equal results is the day the Grand Experiment of the American Republic has failed, because the people failed. When the people put in power those who champion "anti-rights" — demanding and forcing some to provide others with results those others have not earned for themselves — freedom dies because character has died.

We *follow the law* just like we follow other men and women, to assist us on our pathway to perfection. If a law does not lead us in the right direction, it's bad law and needs to be changed — and, while we're at it, we need to remove from office the incompetent people who passed that law.

Leadership of Others

Solomon

There are very few monarchs whose names have entered our language as iconic concepts and most of those are bad examples — Caesar, Genghis Khan, Napoleon, Hitler. In contrast, there are few praises higher than to be compared to Solomon. He is an example of the highest qualities of leadership. While many gain fame in history, the book of First Kings says Solomon achieved that fame in his own lifetime, "And there came of all people to hear the wisdom of Solomon, from all kings of the earth, which had heard of his wisdom" (1 Kings 4:34, KJV).

What made him so wise? Certainly, he kept his own counselors — the wisest people he could find — close at hand but his true wisdom came from following God as his ultimate leader. The greater leader and the more closely you follow them the more you will accomplish. Sadly, in later life, Solomon made the mistake of "believing his own press", he lost his humility and then lost the one most important thing that had made him the most powerful leader in history. He lost track of his leader. In this, he ended up being an example he did not want to be. A deep and careful study of the biblical accounts of Solomon gives insight into many, if not all aspects involved in leadership of others, including how not to be successful.

Any time I hear someone put down Solomon for his mistakes, I remind them, "when you have accomplished even a fraction of what Solomon accomplished, so much so that you become a world-wide house name, synonymous with wisdom, then I'd like to see how you change your story. Only a tiny handful of biblical authors have as many of their words in The Bible as Solomon. Why do you think that is the case?

My Son

Speaking of unsuccessful, I had an incident with my son one evening that opened to me a great principle. I was helping my youngest with his homework. It was one of those days where I was having a very hard time motivating him to get it done. He was extremely distracted and I was getting frustrated because he was almost finished and, despite trying everything I could think of to 'bribe him' to just focus for a few more minutes and get it done, nothing was working.

One of his distractions was a pencil that he'd sharpened almost to the eraser. It was so short he was having a hard time just holding on to it to write. In frustration, I snatched the tiny pencil from his fingers and said, in a gruff tone, "Go get a pencil that you can actually write with and finish this assignment," as I threw the tiny pencil in the garbage. He immediately jumped out of his chair with a horrified look on his face and shrieked, "No! Don't throw away my pencil" and ran to retrieve it.

I stopped short, smiled, gave him a hug and said "OK, I'll make you a deal. If you get these last three problems finished in less than ten minutes, you can keep it — if not, I get to keep it and do whatever I want with it, deal"? He stared defiantly at me for just a moment and then with a funny look said, "Okay". He sat back down and finished in less than five minutes. What changed?

When you have responsibility for someone else and try to deal with them on your terms, you're going to beat your head against the wall and be frustrated and get nowhere. Be willing to discover what is valuable to the other person, recognize that it can have value to you (even if you can't immediately see that value), use that shared value in a constructive way to build the results you both want. That is the essence of the win-win scenario, the easy way to deal effectively with others.

Leadership by Precept

Invite

Your responsibility as a leader is to exercise as much moral influence as you can over others without controlling them. It reminds me of the words of a song, "Know This That Every Soul is Free" (composer unknown), that I learned when I was young, that we are responsible to "… call, persuade, direct aright and bless with wisdom, love and light, in nameless ways be good and kind, but never force the human mind."

Teach

Now, here is another interesting, paradoxical idea. We've already established that the only person you have capacity to change is yourself, yet virtually everything you will ever do of significant value is about helping others. How do you do both — improve others as you improve yourself?

Teacher and religious leader, Yogi Bhajan is frequently quoted, "If you want to learn something, read about it, If you want to understand something, write about it. If you want to master something, teach it." While his basic idea has some truth to it, taken at face value, it is extremely misleading and even completely false. So I explain it this way "If you want to become aware of something, read about it (that is only information). If you want to better understand it, write about it (this can help to clarify, but only if you see it from true perspectives). If you want a better understanding of it, teach it (this process can help you decipher truths and errors about it, but again, only as long as your character and perspectives are right). However, the most critical part he left out because all of that (like the vast majority of our formal education system) is only based on memory and theory. If you truly want to master something, you have to live it—long enough to consistently reap the results and guarantee actual cause and effect from universal law (this is irrefutable practical application). Only then can you teach with credibility and integrity. Also, If you keep what you have worked hard to become to yourself, it will not benefit you, it will, ultimately, leave you miserable and a failure.

Joseph Smith was, as most of you know, founder of The Church of Jesus Christ of Latter-day Saints ("the Mormons"). Among his other accomplishments was the founder of Nauvoo, Illinois, in the early 1840s as a city of refuge against religious persecution. Converts to Mormonism arrived daily from all over the United States and several other countries, swelling the city's population past that of Chicago, for a time. A visiting state legislator once asked Mayor Smith how he maintained such perfect order when it seemed impossible in other cities. Smith replied, "I teach them correct principles and they govern themselves."

Deal in Reality

Some people, of course, are slower to learn than others. That's alright, there is a simple solution, one that worked well in our childhoods and can work in adulthood. As Michael McCleve of James Madison University, once said, "If you can't convince them that heaven is where they want to be, convince them that hell is where they don't want to be." Although the carrot-and-stick approach is not the optimal solution, it is, at times, necessary as a step toward a better system of education. Just as the Law of Moses (the law of ordinances and performances) was a schoolmaster to the Law of Christ (the perfect law of love), leaders can use the carrot-and-stick approach when needed. By the way, it's a tool we all need to use on ourselves now and then.

Leadership by Example

Many years ago, a very short, very clever story appeared in *Readers Digest*. To paraphrase: back in the 1970s — the height of the feminist movement — a businessman was walking up to the front doors of a large office building in New York City. Reflected in the doors' glass, he saw a woman approaching behind him. He grabbed the handle and pulled the door open, stepping side to hold the door for the woman.

Obviously a devout feminist, the woman was incensed, "You don't have to hold that door open for me because I'm a lady."

Unphased, the man replied instantly, "Quite true, madam, I have to hold it open for you because I am a gentleman."

What is the real tragedy of modern leadership? Most modern leaders (i.e., people in charge of something) block our way to greatness instead of leading us toward it. Those people do no good and a lot of harm with their poor examples. Did you hear about the federal judged who was impeached for corruption? A few years later, he was elected to Congress. Did you hear about the mayor who lost his re-election bid because he was busted for smoking crack? He got out, won re-election to the city council and was then re-elected mayor. Most people in positions of influence today are trying to be the ultimate leader but feel they should be accountable to no one. Those who follow such examples are doomed to poor results. Remember, nothing is stagnant, not even decay; it breeds new decay, creating a terrible cycle that is difficult (at best) to break. In fact, if you attach yourself to people who consistently produce poor to mediocre results and, if you try to do better, they will pull you down, back to their level. These peers are afraid that rising above their level will free and leave them in bondage and that isn't part of their plan. (No, it isn't an accident, it's a plan, but that is another book.)

The ultimate question of leadership by example has always been, "What do you want others to get from you?" If you want them to learn laws, principles and concepts that produce extraordinary or miraculous results for themselves, they need to see those laws, principles and concepts at work in you. You have to be the leader and mentor I have told you to follow. If you are not creating things that they want to create, they have no reason to follow you because you have nothing they want.

Since you have read this far, it's evident that you are in the small minority of people who are serious about leadership. Within certain reasonable limits, it isn't a matter of *if you can*; it is only a matter of *if you will*. It isn't about *if it's possible* but about *whatever it takes to make it happen*. That sounds like a strange caveat, "within reasonable limits", what does it mean?

It means be *realistic*. No human being will fly by flapping their arms, that is an anatomic impossibility and everybody knows it. Few people have the talent and skill level to be a successful professional singer or writer. The long lines at *American Idol* auditions and the rooms full of book manuscripts at publishers' offices demonstrate that many people haven't caught on to the fact that they don't have professional-level skills. This is not to say that they couldn't develop them, but will they? It also doesn't mean that none of those who don't face Simon Cowell and none of those in the "slush pile" will ever be successful. You, the aspiring artist, must weigh costs against rewards and your own willingness. Is this one goal so overpowering that it must be achieved no matter what?

A wise person — a good example — understands sacrifice and sets priorities on each of his/her goals. You could say it isn't about leadership, it's about character. Develop a superior character and the answers to questions about priorities become natural. Superior leadership — that is, superior results and superior example — become the natural, unavoidable, logical effect.

Conclusion

As people mature, there seems to be an increasing sense of responsibility to give back so that others are enabled to be better also. Human beings are naturally hard-wired for that. Age has nothing to do with maturity, it comes as we grow closer to perfection. As we discover great hidden wisdoms, we mature faster and our capacity for great leadership increases. Correct leadership qualities afford you the opportunity to be on the giving end of grace. Sharing that leadership will bring the return on investment you are looking for. It doesn't matter if those you try to help reject what you offer — again, many hand-ups, no hand-outs. Like forgiveness, leadership is never about others, they will either choose to follow or not to follow. You make the offer (your example), you make the offer as attractive as possible (you are the best example you can be) then you leave it to them to exercise their freedom of choice. As Jack Canfield, co-founder of Chicken Soup for the Soul series often reminds us sw, sw, sw, sw (some will, some won't, so what, someone's waiting).

Now, an important question: Are you growing for yourself or for others? Obviously for yourself and don't ever let anyone ever lead you to believe otherwise! You are the only person that can "save" or even "serve" you and you're first priority will always be to save yourself! However, if you go about it selfishly, it will only hurt you, not help you. Natural, selfish tendencies are, if unchecked, the thing that will keep you from the ultimate success you seek. So, where is the balance?

Wikipedia.org says, "Ethical egoism is the normative ethical position that moral agents ought to do what is in their own self-interest. It differs from psychological egoism, which claims that people can only act in their self-interest." An interesting third perspective comes from Joseph Smith, who said, "It is a correct principle and may be indulged upon only one rule or plan — and that is to elevate, benefit, and bless others first. If you will elevate others, the very work itself will exalt you." In describing what some might call *spiritual egoism*, Smith did no more than rephrase Jesus' guidance, "For whosoever will save his life shall lose it: and whosoever will lose his life for my sake shall find it" (Matthew 16:25, KJV).

I remember Robert Allen teaching that we can be successful only when we realize "No one can ever come to our rescue." Others can help you but you, ultimately, have to do it yourself. Likewise, trying to control anyone or anything other than yourself, you fail, twice: First, you lose control of yourself because your actions are dictated by what you think you need to do to get somebody else to act a certain way. Second, you really can't control someone else. The old saw, "Nobody's holding a gun to your head" is worth mentioning. Even if somebody is, you *can* choose to take the bullet — many people have. It is the ultimate extreme choice, but the fact is, you always have that choice.

Let me add another caveat: You should never even "control" yourself, not in the long term. For short bursts, to create healthier habits, strict discipline it is a positive but, in the long-term, it's more than a negative, it's an impossibility. If you want to change your habits or how you do things, exercise that leadership of self and develop the right character traits. You'll then naturally do the right things. Solomon's most fundamental downfall was that he lost the capacity to be a great leader the moment he lost track of his leader. Follow his earlier example and learn to avoid his later example.

Everywhere we look today — in families, organizations, businesses, communities, governments — we see the same exact things. Poor leadership resulting from poor understanding of principles which, in turn, results from poor character. As a result, they undermine the structural integrity of systems that were intentionally put into place by people much wiser than themselves and they put at risk the SPESIFC health of all those around them. You and I must be better than that; we must be willing to stand up, draw on our good character, our intellect and leadership skills to change us — work on core issues, never symptoms, that is wisdom!

Summary

A poem, author unknown:

> God said to build a better world and I said, "How?
> "The world is such a big and dark and lonely place and|
> "I am so small and useless and helpless, there is nothing I can do."
> But God in all His wisdom said, "Just build a better you."

Two axioms of leadership:

- Leadership is independent of anything, because leadership is inherent in everything.
- Every group requires leadership. Every activity requires leadership. Whether the group is one or one million, whether the activity is planning dinner or ruling the world; the exact same principles apply — only the scale changes.

I'll repeat Admiral Kirk's admonition, "We learn by doing." I add some dimensions that may surprise the Admiral, his advice was more profound than he knew:

- As I do, I am practicing — I am improving existing skills and adding new ones.

- Others involved emulate my example. I am responsible for their results. Best to make sure I am creating excellent and miraculous results for myself before I engage in teaching others.

- Whether I'm directly overseeing a project or observing a delegated project, I am responsible to do my best to see old concepts through new eyes and gaining deeper understanding of principles.

- Every person I lead knows something I don't know, so I can learn from them. My mentors however have already traveled this road so I am most obliged to follow their counsel above all else. That will assure I consistently grow as a leader.

- I must keep my own mentors and leaders close so I remain a better follower than my followers and thus remain a great leader by example.

One last thought. Greatness is not a place in which you can reside. The moment you try to "rest on your laurels" is the moment you lose it. Greatness is simply a beautiful and peaceful place to rest for the night until you leave in the morning and rediscover it tomorrow.

Chapter 11
The Communication Principle

This eleventh secret ancient principle stands as one of the most fundamental of the principles but, despite the fact that everyone uses it with everyone else, most people communicate quite poorly. Virtually every problem that exists between two or more people is due to misunderstanding of this principle. No greater obstacle exists to solving problems than believing it is the other person's fault. If you were involved, you must discover your part of creating the problem.

An unknown sage once said, "Never approach a bull from the front, a horse from the rear or a fool from any direction!" The phrase is entertainingly clever but the point, I hope, is obvious: Communications is not all about words. It's about respect for others and their nature. It's about never trying to make someone or something else what they or it is not.

If you approach a bull from the front, you have directly challenged his territory, his ego and his perceived authority. He will take offense and you have created a problem for yourself that is 100 percent your fault. By failing to understand his psychology, you directly communicated yourself as a threat to him. There will be consequences, without exception, because you will never change the bull. His brain is hardwired to protect his territory and herd; it is part of his survival imperative. He will do exactly what is in his nature and anyone who believes anything to the contrary is a fool.

If you approach a horse from the rear, his blind spot, you will likely startle him. When startled, horses tend to kick. It is a natural instinct. — as with the bull, it's a self-preservation imperative. If he kicks, he'll knock you for a loop. Believe me, I have firsthand experience — it doesn't matter how big and tough you think you are, that horse is bigger and tougher. You are smarter, generally, than a horse and, if you fail to use that brain to understand him and treat him right (as the horse defines right), you've lost before you've begun.

If you approach a fool from any direction, again, you have only caused yourself a problem. Why even approach a fool in the first place? Do you want to learn something from the fool? Of course not, if you did, you wouldn't think that person a fool. Do you want to teach something to the fool? Of course not, if you thought that person capable of learning, you wouldn't think that person a fool. Do you want to argue with that fool? "Never argue with a fool," the old saying goes, "people might not be able to tell the difference." Think of any reason that one person interacts with another. You'll find that, if a fool is in charge, you have no reason to get involved, except to remove them from being in charge.

Speak!

Marion Romney, a cousin of former Michigan Governor George Romney (Mitt Romney's father), is attributed to one of the great gems of human wisdom; a prime concept of the communication principle, "Do not speak so you can be understood, speak so you cannot be misunderstood." Failure here can have devastating results. An example from my own family:

In her senior year of high school (when I was a sophomore), my sister, Dixie, fell in love with Randy, a friend of our older brother. Both boys had long-standing reputations as fighters. Our parents and his were called to the school on many occasions. The principle admitted he didn't believe either boy ever started a fight but, somehow, always seemed to be available to finish them.

Concerned for Dixie's future, my parents insisted Randy was a bad influence and forbade her to see him. No surprise, this worked like unintended reverse psychology. I clearly remember several arguments and many tears of both sides. Finally, Dixie and Randy eloped to Nevada. I happened to be nearby when Dixie called home and told Mom what they had done because this just seemed the only option. I vividly remember the conversation because Mom was not one to take kindly to direct disobedience.

"Well don't come running back here crying if it doesn't work out," she said, in a stern tone.

It took several months for Dixie and Randy to finally feel welcome and integrated back into the family. I'm happy to report that they are still married. They are now happy grandparents and we are all truly honored to have Randy in the family. "And now, the rest of the story," as Paul Harvey so often said:

Over 20 years after they were married, we were together at a family reunion and Dixie, Mom and I found ourselves talking around the kitchen table. I don't remember how the subject came up but I remember Mom said something and Dixie turned to her with a puzzled look and said, "Oh, yes, you have." Mom looked up in surprise, "What do you mean?" Dixie replied, "When you disowned me the day Randy and I were married!" Mom's eyes widened, her mouth dropped open aghast and replied, "I did no such thing!"

Dixie continued that she was deeply hurt for so many years because she just couldn't believe that Mom would ever do such a thing and (to make it worse) never apologize to either of them. Mom couldn't believe what she was hearing or what Dixie had believed. As the conversation progressed, I actually became amused at the misunderstanding. I never realized till then that Dixie had taken Mom's words to mean that she was being disowned.

Finally, I spoke up and asked Mom if she remembered her actual words. She replied, "I certainly remember the time but not the exact words." I then asked

Dixie if she remembered Mom's exact words. She did not. Then I said to Dixie "I can see how you could have thought that. I remember that conversation very well because it is burned into my brain." I repeated, almost word for word what I heard mom say so many years earlier — "Well don't come running back here crying if it doesn't work out!"

I followed with an explanation that Mom wasn't saying that she didn't love you or never wanted to see you again. That was only her way of saying she'd tried everything she knew to try to keep you from the pain she felt this relationship would bring but, now that you had made the decision, you were accountable for it and she didn't want to hear any complaints. She didn't believe the marriage would work out but that was all on your head now. It was never about disowning you.

As Dixie and Mom realized the long struggle and pain that misunderstanding had caused, they both started to cry. Then tears welled up in my eyes as I watched them in a long embrace. It was a time of healing for them both. For me, it was a vivid "*A-ha!*" moment about how we interpret what we hear instead of what was intended.

Perception is Mostly Illusion

The old proverb, "Say what you mean and mean what you say," pertains directly to honesty but it also applies here and follows directly from the previous concept. When others speak, they always understand what they mean, we almost never understand completely. How could we? This came from their brain and their paradigms and their intentions, not ours. To be certain we understand, we need to ask lots of questions and get specific feedback to verify. We need to get inside their minds and perspectives and then speak to their way of thinking. We don't need to *accept* their point-of-view but we do need to be *aware* of it.

Several years ago, I realized that, although my wife and I had been married for about 15 years, I didn't think we had actually ever genuinely understood each other in any conversation, trivial or serious. I was interpreting what she said and what she did through my paradigms. She was interpreting what I said and did through her paradigms.

This began my road to comprehend this concept — misunderstandings happen every day, in almost every relationship. Arguments, fights, damaged relationships, harm to people we love, even feuds and wars occur, for the most part, because someone misunderstood someone else's intentions. I vowed that I would be extremely cautious — for the rest of my life — about how I interpret other people's words, perspectives and intentions and how I project my own. The lack of understanding and further unwillingness to understand is at the core of this ridiculous political correctness movement in America and now abroad.

Unfortunately, few people are ever taught how to get out of their own paradigm and experience life from another's paradigm. Most aren't even taught to recognize the need to do so and some aren't even taught that other people have different paradigms. Certainly, we all live in the exact same world but no two of us perceive reality in the same way. This has nothing to do with reality, I'm talking about our *perception* of reality, which is mostly illusion. No one person actually understands another until they intentionally get out of themselves and, with deliberately guided effort from the other, learn to "walk a mile in their moccasins" as the Native American proverb advises. If you want to understand another, you must, as best you can, see what they see, hear what they hear, and feel what they feel.

Statistics declare approximately 85 percent of marriages fail because of miscommunication. I put it at virtually 100 percent. The same for business partnerships, regardless of other factors like dishonesty or employee turn-over, failure of product or process, misaligned perspectives, or whatever; it always boils down to a lack of communication.

Miscommunication runs through the middle of almost every problem between people. I'm sure you've heard many ideas about the biggest causes of divorce: Money, infidelity, sexual incompatibility, lack of intimacy, addiction, abuse, child rearing challenges, religion or cultural differences, unmet expectations, priority clashes, growing apart, and so on.

Here's a mind-blowing concept: None of those things are marriage problems, each one is a symptom of a deeper problem. When you strip away all the symptoms, you'll find that miscommunication is the real problem behind every marriage on the rocks. I am always saddened when someone says their marriage broke up over money. Money is an inanimate object and money problems hit people in every socio-economic level from mega-rich to micro-poor. Likewise, many poor people and many rich people have successful, lifelong marriages. Having money and not having money simply aren't problems in and of themselves. Set a pile of cash (stocks, property, or any other *valuta*) on a table between two people and it will never cause a problem until the people get different ideas and priorities about how to deal with it. It's a people problem, not a money problem, and people problems are virtually always rooted in misunderstanding. Thus with a little wisdom, there is ALWAYS a win-win solution. (It's the same in business).

Listening vs. Hearing

There is a very big difference between listening and hearing. Another of my role models, Tony Alessandra, author and creator of the *Dynamics of Effective Listening* program made a comment that has stuck in my mind since I first heard it many years ago, "Most people believe that they can listen just because they can hear but that is as foolish as believing that just because you can see, you can read."

Listening is a skill. It is complicated and takes a lot of deliberate practice in order to develop it into a good skill.

I've heard people talk about "actively listening" and perhaps some people need that extra explanation. But in reality, real listening *is* active listening. If you are participating passively, you might be hearing but you definitely aren't listening. So, don't be deceived. The definition of listening has never changed and it means what it means — if you are not actively listening, you are not listening.

If I interpret something that someone else says through my own perceptions, I am hearing. If I am trying to see through the other person's eyes, that is still hearing. If I do everything I can to literally become them and see the world through their eyes, hear it through their ears, feel it through their heart, understand it through their experiences and sense it through their spirit and character traits, then I might be listening. In order to communicate properly, I need to actually understand far more about what is not said than about what is said because real communication is always about motives and intentions; it's never about the words.

When you are listening, the words that others speak mean very little, perhaps even nothing. Only their intent and context are important. When you are talking, your words combined with your tone, expressions, body language and underlying intentions are everything.

Non-verbal Communication

I think most people are well aware that only a very small percentage of communicating comes from words. The largest majority of communication comes through our body language, tone of voice, and underlying connotations from the way we pronounce our words, posture, i.e., the way we sit, the way we stand, eye contact, and so on. All of that is communication. Even our aura as it emanates from us in a combination of vibrations, frequencies, colors, and sounds are picked up and registered subconsciously by others. Some are better at picking up on "vibes" and correctly interpreting those than others but we are all affected by them to one degree or another.

More than a few times I've gotten myself into trouble because I didn't control the tone of my voice. Even when I don't mean it adversely, people can interpret it negatively. This quick, defensive reaction goes back to our self-preservation imperative. A threatening posture or tone will always elicit a defensive response. Our subconscious collects the data and, if we feel threatened, our ego jumps in to save us from as much pain as possible. Tone of voice is one of those things that you'll be mindful of if you want to be a better communicator.

Defining Our World

A short while after I started to recognize and study this major problem of communication, I was sitting in a restaurant with my wife. I couldn't help but over hear a conversation between another couple at a near table. They were laughing in the beginning but it soon turned into an argument. It was obvious they were singing from two completely different sheets of music. As Jackie and I were leaving, I walked to their table. After a friendly introduction, I mentioned that I wasn't trying to eavesdrop but couldn't help overhearing a misunderstanding and asked if they'd like a short explanation?

They invited us to sit down. I congratulated them for being out on a date and recognized it as an attempt to nurture their relationship. After a couple of questions, I asked the gentleman to explain to his wife what he meant by his comment that started the argument. Then I asked several follow-up questions to drill down and bring out his core intention for that comment. His wife was getting a different picture. Then I asked his wife to explain how she originally interpreted his comment and why she interpreted it that way. Then back to him and why he responded to her like he did. I intervened a couple of times reminding them that we were only trying to discover the truth, and that unbridled emotions don't help. It was fun to watch them so surprised and relieved with each other at resolving such a simple misunderstanding that would have otherwise spoiled their evening and perhaps more. About 30 minutes later, we all departed with lots of smiles and a little wiser. I am surprised at how often I overhear similar misunderstandings, just in my every day experience, at the store, the airport, church, etc.

One of the major challenges in communications is that individuals often define and use the same word differently. Even common words. Professionals call this *semantics*. The more I recognized how many problems are founded in misinterpreting words, the more I was intrigued about words real definitions, not just the way we use them today but the original intent of the words, the standard they used to hold us to and how they have changed through history and degraded that standard. As crazy as it might seem, one of my favorite books is now *The Dictionary of Word Origins*.

Despite our growth in some areas, almost without exception, the changes to word definitions have deteriorated, reflected back and forth in our declining society. In our language, it's like we accept tin from each other today, where we used to demand gold. It is not just that meanings have changed but they have significantly decayed.

For example, "ignorant" means lacking knowledge. That's not an insult, it's a simple fact. If you've never studied pre-Columbian archeology for example, you are ignorant on the history of the Americas before Europeans arrived. There's nothing wrong with ignorance; every one of us are ignorant about most things in the world. However, *call* just about anybody "ignorant" and you've stepped right in front of the bull — most people will assume you've challenged their ego and intelligence and insulted them deeply.

Sadly, our society does not even recognize how we have altered and deteriorated the definitions of so many words, principally because of that same ego-driven desire to make sure we feel enough value in ourselves to survive. We are driven by our own egos to accept information at face value, to accept the illusion that we are smarter than we are. We are afraid of failure and rejection and, therefore, unwilling to go through the hard work of learning because that would mean admitting we don't know something. Ignorance is a trait most define (incorrectly) as vulnerability. To many, an admission that we don't know is to feel (unjustly) that we are incompetent. That we are better off than we are. While we definitely need to develop much better character and treat others with dignity, the huge majority of this *political correctness* movement is simply an easily predicted cancer of unchecked egos and lack of personal responsibility and accountability.

So we avoid putting ourselves in positions where we may look foolish and, thus, don't get the practical education discussed in Chapter 3. Then, when we have to teach our children or others, we do it without a core understanding of basic principles. Instead of doing our due diligence about what we teach others, our out-of-control egos won't allow us to be vulnerable. We put on a facade (conscious or subconscious) that we do understand. When words come up and we do not comprehend their full definition, we compromise the definition to fit our illusion of understanding. Our followers, by the same method, pass those words along with an even less-correct definition. To justify our foolishness, we invent terms like "conventional wisdom", and we continue changing the definitions of words to justify our lack of education, experience, and wisdom. As more people begin to believe these diluted definitions, the decay of language compounds on itself. People become offended and defensive, even angry, believing false concepts and their own illusions and then blame others for the decay of our culture and society. Nothing is further from the truth.

Part of poor leadership of others is unconsciously passing on those same, stilted definitions and connotations to those over whom we have responsibility. In order to save face or remain *in control*, be accepted, or mostly, just out of "ignorance," we go with the errors we learned. The problem is that we don't even know that we have fallen far short of the mark ourselves, we, instinctively, don't want others to know the truth. That would mean we must change ourselves and that's too much work. We trick ourselves into a false contentment in the acceptance of the new, and incorrect, definitions (remember the 11th Commandment). Subconsciously, we have stripped the precious truths from the words we use, words which, only a short time ago, were so well-evidenced by those truths.

Humility is as vital to furthering your education as it is vital to all good character traits. "The only true wisdom is in knowing you know nothing," said Socrates, Constant learning, including constant improvement of our communication skills, are excellent avenues to personal advancement — in work, in community, in every part of our personal progress toward perfection.

We can improve our understanding of our language by listening to worthy mentors and leaders — that would include the authors of classical literature (those with the highest quality writing and whose principles transcend culture and even time itself) — by practicing what our mentors teach until we become truly literate and skilled communicators. Mastering the principle of communications is a major step in discerning reality from illusion.

Understanding

You've heard the phrase, "God gave you two ears and only one mouth so you should listen twice as much as you talk." I say, He truly gave you two ears but he also gave you two eyes, two arms, two legs, two nostrils, and several different parts of a brain — all of which serve completely different functions to facilitate your own learning and communication. Likewise, a sixth sense and even beyond that, a spirit to feel and transport yourself into others' shoes. All this helps you to sense what others are feeling, imagine their world, their experiences, their perspectives, their whole paradigms and reach a level of understanding that allows us all to be better human beings. Empathy is part of a character skill that leads to wisdom by helping your other senses put you in other people's lives. That one mouth? This shows a much closer perspective on how much your responsibility is in the communication process.

By the way, all the skills you put into understanding others can also be put to use understanding yourself. In fact, you might be getting the impression that, in order to really empathize with others, it takes a full and serious effort to first understand yourself, before you attempt to understand others enough to actually have meaningful communication with them. Like Steven Covey used to say, "Seek first to understand, then to be understood."

Another huge problem is believing we live in the same world as others do. Of course, we do, but, in this sense, the old political adage, "Perception is reality," (although being false in its actual context) does shed a little light on understanding others. Everyone perceives the world differently and everyone, therefore, mixes their own mostly-unique illusion with their reality (like the 5 blind men and the elephant). In order to really communicate with someone, you must understand the other persons' world. To do that, you must understand, as best you can, his/her perception and illusion — and you will if you can discern what fractions of reality are sprinkled in the mix. Combine this with your understanding of your own world — your perceptions, illusions and sprinkles of reality — and your commitment to continually learn and grow and evolve. Then you've put yourself in position to truly begin to understand others.

Now, you have a real opportunity to help them through their illusions and a chance to better understand your own illusions and discard them in favor of reality. That's a win-win.

Back to Romney's counsel about speaking so you cannot be misunderstood: You must accept full responsibility to set the stage and keep others' attention so they have the motivation, incentive, and interest to keep listening so they can begin to understand you. Do it well enough and people will think of you as a mentor they need to listen to and learn from.

Steven K. Scotts' program *Master Strategies of Super Achievers* contains a module that is the best I've ever seen on the art of communicating with others so they not only understand what you say but actually feel what you feel in the process. I highly recommend it to you.

Conclusion

One of the most powerful lessons I've ever learned about communication came from studying the life of King David. Nathan heard that David had committed adultery with Bathsheba and then, to cover up his sin, had her husband, Uriah, put in the front of a battle so he'd be killed. Nathan went to David and told him a story about a rich man who had great flocks of animals and a poor man who had only one sheep that he'd raised in his own house as a cherished pet. When a traveler came to visit the rich man, instead of preparing a meal with one of his own sheep, he took the sheep of the poor man for the meal. When David heard the story, he was so furious he declared that the rich man would repay the theft four-fold then be put to death.

Nathan then told David that this story was really a metaphor about him, Bathsheba and Uriah. David was stunned. The message was so powerful that it immediately shifted his behavior — he ceased covering up his misdeed and began a long repentance process which included making amends (as best he could) and living righteously, to the best of his ability, for the rest of his life.

Nathan's metaphor worked because Nathan knew David — a just man at heart, a shepherd who'd risked his life for his sheep, the boy who again risked his own life for his country in facing Goliath. When the prophet spoke to the King of value and justice against a seemingly all-powerful opponent, David had to respond the way he did, David *could not* misunderstand.

Summary

"Do not speak so you can be understood, speak so you cannot be misunderstood." If others misunderstand you, that is your problem and only you can fix it. If you misunderstand others, that is also your problem that only you can correct. If you are listening, the words others say to you are of little importance; you must discover intent. If you are talking, words are everything and must be chosen carefully, along with your body language and any other resources at your disposal.

Ask Questions

Nothing in life will pay you richer and more abundant rewards than the investment of consistently discovering how to ask better and better questions. You can only measure the quality of questions by the benefits you personally receive from them. In communication, what you receive in response to questions allows you to understand other people's point of view on a deeper level. That deeper level is how you measure the effectiveness of your questions. The right questions won't just put you in their shoes, it'll put you in their unique world — that will allow you to experience their paradigm.

Exercise Ultimate Courage

You have to be so willing and even eventually become so completely confident and comfortable with yourself, that you can get completely out of yourself. Don't fear what you might discover in others — not the paradigms that might vastly differ from yours, not the darkness they might carry from past experiences, nothing. Only by being willing to discover and truly understand another, can you truly communicate with them.

Love

You must connect to the other person — they have to know that you care about them as an individual, distinct person. "Nobody cares how much you know [or what you say] until they know how much you care." No one will open up to you if s/he believes you don't care. Without openness, you cannot comprehend his/her perspective. Without comprehension, miscommunication is certain and bigger problems are on their way.

On its most basic level, communication is a spiritual activity. You have to be willing to genuinely love the other person and have that win-win character. You must be willing to push that love to the limit, regardless of what you discover in the other person to not be judgmental but only have desire to improve yourself and help them improve themselves. Many times even so that they can and will excel beyond you.

Lead

Great leadership is not dependent on knowledge and skills but on character and wisdom. It is not about what you do but why you choose to do it. Communication is one of the cornerstones of leadership and understanding is its mortar.

Everything you do in every part of your day (and night) is all about communication. In fact, we are constantly communicating with spouse, children, coworkers, customers, supervisors, employees, neighbors, other drivers, and everyone else our lives touch, however minutely (and even with yourself). Other people's lives are events in your life.

Every attempt at communication with others is a circumstance we create in reaction to those events. Misunderstanding will regress us (and influence their regress) on our pathway to decay and ruin. Mutual understanding will progress us (and them) on our pathway to perfection.

Chapter 12
The Destiny Principle

The Highest Path

The twelfth secret, ancient principle is the beginning and continuation of every great success story in history. Without it, people wander all their lives, lost, lonely, looking for love in all the wrong places, and they die with their dreams unrealized. Apply this principle and you will live a life that you always dreamed about and more. It will show you a higher road — your mission, should you choose to accept it and doggedly pursue it, especially through those times when achieving your dreams seem impossible — will bring you a life of fulfillment and more genuine success that you imagined.

One of my role models, Nelson Mandela said, "There is no passion to be found playing small. In settling for a life that is less than the one you are capable of living." No truer words were ever spoken.

This requires a bit of explanation, so bear with me:

"Chapter One: I Am Born. Whether I shall turn out to be the hero of my own life, or whether that station will be held by anybody else, these pages must show." Like Charles Dickens' David Copperfield, every person is born into a unique set of spiritual, physical, emotional, social, intellectual, and financial circumstances that provides SPESIFC core programming. This programming determines how that growing child initially views the world, deals with themselves, deals with others, and deals with their environments. Most mental health professionals believe these birth SPESIFCs form the basis for our entire lives.

"Hear me, oh African, the flesh of thy flesh is free!" declared Chicken George to the spirit of his grandfather, Kunta Kinte in *Roots*. While the initial neural pathways certainly form the foundation of our character and may play a part throughout our lives, we are not slaves to our birth SPESIFC. We are intelligent life forms with a God-given agency. We have the potential to alter our initial programming and replace it with SPESIFCs so powerful that the original programming can be effectively overridden — almost as if they never existed. I've seen and taken part in several addiction, phobia, negative habit, and other recoveries in which people permanently change their lives for the better. I have also seen several people transform themselves in the opposite direction and become completely lost.

"Commanding a starship is your first, best destiny," said Mr. Spock to Admiral Kirk in *Star Trek II*. I'm redefining "destiny" in this usage, in spite of my harsh words for people who do this. The scripts of our lives are not unchangeably written but "destiny" comes closest to describing what I mean. It's similar to a military term, "best case scenario" and there's solid, scientific evidence that there are things you're uniquely suited to do, a contribution you can make that is superior to anyone else in some way.

Michael McCleve of James Madison University, in a TEDx lecture, noted the following:

> Through the development of the Clifton Strengths Finder assessment, which more than 7 million people have taken to date, Gallup [the famous pollster] has been able to demonstrate that the odds of another person having the exact same top five strengths, in the exact same sequence as you, is more than 1 in 33 million. Think about that! You have a set of strengths that are virtually unmatched by anyone else.

Discovering and achieving this personal destiny should be your prime directive.

A little over 20 years ago, I had to make an unexpected business trip from Washington State, where I lived, back to Utah, where most of my family still lives. Since it was just a quick trip, I thought I wouldn't stop to see anyone but just hurry back and forth. During the day I was there, however, I kept getting an impression that I should stop to see one of my brothers who lived nearby. So, early in the evening, I drove out and knocked on his door without notice.

We were having a nice visit when the conversation turned to a struggle he was currently going through that I was unaware of. He was a highly gifted cabinet/furniture maker and finish carpenter but was feeling torn in a few different directions for a life-long vocation. It quickly became evident this was no trivial struggle my brother faced, it was a major life crossroad. I invited him to sit down with me in a quiet space, with a notebook and pen. Over the course of a couple of hours, I took him through a series of processes which helped him decide exactly what he should do and, even though he didn't know all the details of how it could be made to happen, he felt assured this was the direction of his destiny.

Within a few weeks, he'd made arrangement for additional schooling and, after working through several challenges, he discovered some doors of opportunity — even miracles that no one could have guessed would have come his way. Today, he is very successful at this new vocation, passionately fulfilling his destiny.

Over the years, I've had the great pleasure of helping several people become more clarified about their own priorities and what things will bring ultimate fulfillment, meaning, and passion to their lives.

As I continue to study people's lives, I become more and more aware of how and why most people simply follow the path of least resistance through their lives. Whether they seem to achieve poor, mediocre or extraordinary results in any area, they are typically more reactive than creative in their plans for the future.. They rarely question and, even more rarely, step out, face their fears and exercise the courage to significantly expand what they do to take advantage of opportunities that would have provided them the most passionate and rewarding life.

To most, this path of least resistance seems like the path of destiny and, so, they just follow it by default. This generally includes complaining and whining about how hard they have it and in-equality in general. Taken at face value, this gives most people the illusion of predestination. Before you make this terrible mistake and shackle yourself to a fate that will never produce miracles, know that this is just another "conventional wisdom" lie.

Some are born into privilege and wealth, but that is only one among your SPESIFCs — one which can create as many or more problems than it solves. Others are born with a naturally-beautiful face or body, which is also completely an illusion, a façade. "Beauty *is* only skin deep," it fades with time — for some of us, a very little time — and, beauty, by itself will never actually solve any of life's problems. You will never realize the true fulfillment life has to offer while focused on one SPESIFC or any of the illusions of "conventional wisdom".

You must face your fears, make the uncomfortable decisions, get off the beaten track, do hard things, and find your own unique path. You must overcome criticism and trials, which will enable you to be true to your higher self and follow the light within (just beware of the emotional illusions within). You have to drop the façade, forgo guilty pleasures, discover and focus on your heart's desire, plumb the depths of your intuition and inspiration, don't let anyone yank your chain and — for heaven's sake — try to avoid tired, worn out clichés like these!

This is the only possibility for consistent miracles in your life. Anything else can only bring you mediocrity at best. As Theodore Roosevelt so eloquently stated:

> Far better it is to dare mighty things and win glorious triumphs, even though checked by failure, than to take rank with those poor souls who neither enjoy much nor suffer much but who live in that gray twilight that knows neither victory nor defeat.

Finding the Path

You have decided to seek the best direction for your life. Your first, obvious, and very legitimate question follows, "But, how do I find my destiny?"

As noted in Part 1, grace is that hand-up that enables us to accomplish worthy goals and objectives that are bigger than ourselves. "Grace" is defined, among other things, as "a manifestation of favor, especially by a superior." Generally, most of us think in terms of the "grace of God" meaning divine intervention on our behalf. Certainly, there's a lot of that in the world (and there should be much more), but grace can also be given by humans — mentors, friends, strangers, etc. — sometimes openly and publicly, sometimes silently and anonymously.

As Bryan Adams (*et al*) wrote, "Search your heart, search your soul, when you find me there, you'll search no more." Finding a soulmate may be as rare as thunderstorms in the Sahara, but some people are sure. By this, I mean that some feel like they don't choose their path in life, they feel the path chooses them. Many artists feel impelled to write, compose, paint, sculpt, or whatever. Others simply fall in love with an idea — science or theology or diesel mechanics or farming — and never want anything else. These are, of course, still choices but, if God sent you to Earth for a purpose, would He provide you help in discovering that purpose or would He just let you to wander in the dark and leave finding your destiny by luck?

As much as it is convenient for most people to believe, there's no such thing as *luck*. Earl Nightingale said "Luck is when preparedness meets opportunity." And Denis Waitley calls it an acronym for "**L**aboring **U**nder **C**orrect **K**nowledge." It may be a fictitious movie, but the principle is real when Obi-Wan Kenobi mentored young Luke Skywalker. Luke was able to "take your first steps into a larger world." Luke knew nothing of the universe outside his uncle's farm on Tatooine. He'd *heard* of the Rebellion, but he *knew* nothing, as later experiences made clear. Only when Kenobi showed him a new way did his universe begin to expand.

Obviously, you can only choose among options if you see them. That is a prime reason to associate with the best mentors you can find. Their lives can show you options that no one else's can, because no one else has been where they are. It is virtually impossible for you to discover all the short-cut on your own, especially without all the time to "reinvent the wheel," as Luke found with Obi-Wan and Han Solo. With your mentors' guidance, you can make wiser, more productive decisions which create much bigger rewards.

Equally obvious, I hope, is the potential for error. Learning to discern which impressions or persons to follow and which to avoid is one of the great challenges of mortal life. Fortunately, there are only two results your decisions can bring, those that make you a better person/increase your potential and those that make you a worse person/deteriorate your potential. I said there were spiritual realms of light and spiritual realms of darkness. However you wish to view or define them, there is good and evil in the world; understanding and recognizing the differences, and where spiritual influences originate, will make your life a whole lot easier.

By the way, along your pathway to perfection, you may have more than one view of your "destiny". Early childhood dreams can be born of inexperience or incomplete information. Have you ever had a dream that felt so real that you thought, at least while you were in it, that it was real? On the other hand, it has been shown, (also by my own experience) that some of those childhood dreams are guidance to your best destiny and will prepare you to better recognize them when the opportunities present themselves. Some of us spend great resources creating a destiny — reading everything we can, talking to mentors, working, getting a college degree — only to discover, after a very few years of work, that it was an illusion, that this path simply wasn't the right one. It may be among your greatest acts of courage to say, "I was wrong, I need to change my path," and, then, to make the sacrifices necessary to discern your true destiny and remodel your life into one that fits that destiny. Or in my brother's case to simply find that the path you have been on will continue to bring you value through your life, but ultimately was for the purpose of guiding you to the point where you could discover that best destiny beyond.

Following the (sometimes bumpy) Path

There are roads available to each of us that lead to poor, mediocre, extraordinary and miraculous results. The lower roads are often the most temporarily enticing to our selfishness, self-gratification, dishonesty and the like. They can be what you were born into and just naturally feel comfortable with. The higher roads you were destined for but in the short-term view seem harder. The lower one's are typically the easiest, at least in the moment, while following the higher roads require deliberate, educated risks and the courage to get onto that horse and ride.

I have definitely discovered that there are carpenters and there are people who work as carpenters on their way to somewhere else. There are coal miners and people who work in the coal mine on their way to somewhere else. There are even doctors and lawyers who are headed somewhere else, whether they know it or not. That probably describes all of us, at one time or another.

There are also folks who are, literally, on their way to somewhere else; who understand there is a higher road but they are where they are for a reason. They may take a job to gain experience or while they obtain education they need for their next step forward. They may be surprised by a layoff or company closing — and find they have to get by while they revise their short-term plan to reach their long-term goal. Setbacks happen, delays happen, almost nothing happens immediately. Being in a poor or mediocre situation isn't a negative if you learn from the event and create circumstances that get you closer to fulfilling your passion.

If this is your status of the moment, remember a few things: You are accountable and responsible, so put your mind and skills to active and productive use. Your future will still be made up of what you are creating now. So jump into any problem and create a solution. If you don't think there is an immediate problem, you need to look deeper and further. You'll find solutions to problems are easier before they cause you pain than after. Be thinking and making the most of things for yourself and your company as far in advance as possible. Whether you are the owner or the janitor, as long as you are there, you owe that company your best effort. They (the other stakeholders in that company) deserve a worker that's an asset to the company. This attitude has many benefits: If or when layoffs are required, your job is more secure. You'll learn more and earn more if you give it your best. You'll earn greater grace by being diligent in every endeavor. You'll enjoy your job more and build relationships with others that may bring you great benefits down the road.

The opposite is equally true. If you're working a job that isn't your passion and you don't put any passion into it — if you just settle for doing enough to keep your job — you are the biggest liability that company has. If you don't quit in frustration, the company will, sooner or later, figure out a way to get rid of you.

When (not if) you find yourself on what looks like a detour of your destiny road, keep in mind that you are, still, on a path to your perfection as long as you are consistently following your Next Best Guess. You may only be able to create small, short-term miracles, but who said that was a bad idea?

You simply have to work through these detours, learn what you can, and remember, your present circumstances could simply be the universe (and, by that, I mean God) testing your persistence or teaching you something you will need so you are ready when the time comes. Remember what Calvin Coolidge said:

> "Nothing in this world can take the place of persistence. Talent will not; nothing is more common than unsuccessful people with talent. Genius will not; unrewarded genius is almost a proverb. Education will not; the world is full of educated derelicts. Persistence and determination alone are omnipotent. The slogan 'press on' has solved and always will solve the problems of the human race."

The Path of Magnificent Obsession

Have you ever shared your dreams, ideas, or plans with anyone who responded with something like, "I wouldn't get to excited about that if I were you," or "Come on, be realistic," or "We just don't want to see you be disappointed or get hurt," or even, "go ahead a live while you're young, life will soon teach you how to be realistic," or "Don't get your hopes up over that"?

As another of my role models and one of the best motivational speakers I've ever heard, Mark Gorman so aptly put it, "You better get your hopes up!"

Don't you love it when someone makes what they believe is a derogatory remark to you like; "You are obsessed with that" or "can you believe that fanatic?" Nothing great was accomplished without someone having an obsession about it! (Of course, there are dangerous obsessions, we can decay from interest to obsession to addiction, but that is another book.)

Clara Shih, founder and CEO of Hearsay Social, declared, "As entrepreneurs, we must constantly dream and have the conviction and obsession to transform our dreams into reality — to create a future that never existed before." French painter Eugene Delacroix had a complementary view, "What moves those of genius, what inspires their work is not new ideas, but their obsession with the idea that what has already been said is still not enough." This one idea has given me more drive to share my message than any other. If you ever intend to accomplish anything miraculous — Earth-shaking, world-changing, future-summoning — you'd better be obsessed with it or you will never overcome all the obstacles that will arise before you accomplish it. The magnificent obsession concept is the mother of all amazing achievement.

The Loyal Opposition

How do you respond when others tell you to abandon your magnificent obsession?

Remember that, mostly, they oppose you out of honest concern, they don't want to see you get hurt or be disappointed. Such are the people who settled for mediocre results. It's a sure bet that they haven't created many miraculous results themselves — they may never have created any — they just do not understand. Most of them don't think you can, because they don't think they could. They've bought into the "conventional wisdom" that miracles belong to the few or to mythology. A few, the truly selfish, don't want you to achieve miracles because they didn't and their ego is stroked by trying to bring you down to their level. These people you must proactively avoid — if you expect any sort of success.

Many have succeeded in something or another while remaining ignorant of principles, so, they cannot advise or teach you properly. They've lucked out with good guesses but, unless they get a handle on principles, their success will be temporary. Inform those who are negative that if one can do it, so can another and that the greatest risk in life is letting fear hold you back from taking the risks that will set you free. If their opposition continues, change associations — fast!

Those who have done it or, at least, who are working to do it themselves, will understand the process and encourage you and assist you to find and follow the right formula so that you can do it also. They know you can, because they know anyone can.

Family can be our staunchest supporters or most degrading detractors.

To all those who "love you" but do not understand, just know that they do not understand. You can simply tell them "Thank you so much for your concern. I appreciate it and that means a lot to me," and never talk to them about it again — until you win, unless their attitude changes. Whether they act out of fear and speculation or from their own failures is irrelevant. Just because some fail and have negative experiences doesn't mean a thing is impossible, it just means what they tried didn't work and they never continued to The Next Best Guess and, so, never discovered what does work.

Of course, you rightly may not want to cut family members off completely, except in extreme situations but you have to limit your associations with anyone who tries to drag you down. Be nice, be encouraging, help them to understand — if they are willing to learn — but, be clear that you are pursuing a course and you're not going to change, so they can accept that or not. If not, you can "agree to disagree" and focus your relationship on things that bring you together but, if they persist in degrading you, you'll have to cut them off. If they choose the lesser path, tell them you love and support them and you'll be happy to welcome back into your life when they make the choice to be reasonable, courteous adults.

And if, by chance, you get a little discouraged (and I know you will), stop, take a deep breath, pop that old John Parr CD into the player, and create a little "St. Elmo's Fire":

> Growin' up, you don't see the writing on the wall,
> Passin' by, movin' straight ahead, you knew it all.
> But maybe sometime if you feel the pain,
> You'll find you're all alone, everything has changed.
>
> Play the game, you know you can't quit until it's won,
> Soldier on, only you can do what must be done.
> You know in some way you're a lot like me,
> You're just a prisoner and you're tryin' to break free.
>
> I can see the new horizon underneath the blazin' sky,
> I'll be where the eagle's flying higher and higher.
> Gonna' be your man in motion, all I need is a pair of wheels,
> Take me where my future's lyin', St. Elmo's fire...
>
> I can climb the highest mountain, cross the wildest sea,
> I can feel St. Elmo's fire burnin' in me, burnin' in me!

Conclusion

Growing up in our family required learning to ride a horse, and learning to ride well happened pretty young. My dad wouldn't let us ride with a saddle until we learned to ride bareback first. Once you master bare back riding, the saddle was a cinch (pun intended). In the process though, I guarantee you will fall off and probably even get hurt but there is no better teacher on Earth than the pain that comes with bumps and bruises, even a broken bone or ten, to force you to sit up and take note and make needed changes. In the long run, your value is amplified tremendously.

I taught all three of my sons to drive a stick shift before driving an automatic. If you are willing to do the hardest work first, then whatever comes next is always easier.

There is no greater teacher than mistakes and accidents to discover principles. It is only by doing things successfully that we understand the process and in the process of learning we have to rely on our next best guess. This process of learning is tried and true throughout history.

One of the biggest mistakes you can make as a parent is to be over protective. I am often amused and sometimes frustrated with all the new policies, rules and even new laws they make to try to keep people safe. From OSHA in the construction field and work places to schools to businesses, to so many special interest groups. It has become absurd.

Our public school system has let us down. I am so heart-sick at how parents in America have let our school system degrade our education system in to a never-ending cycle of rote memorization and test regurgitation. Reading from books and listening to lectures was never education. They were and still are useful tools, but they are not an effective, stand-alone program. The whole Prussian model is debilitating to our children, our young adults, our parents and our communities. What we in America call education has almost entirely departed from the actual definition and goal of that word.

Finding and fulfilling your destiny is something that you must choose to do and then must stay committed to achieving, no matter what. You have to intentionally move it from your "wants" list to your "needs" list. It is necessary in order to realize the life you are divinely destined to have. The fact is that everyone is born into circumstances that make this a challenge. But the challenge is key to discovering and attaining the wisdom to put it together and keep it evolving. Otherwise, like Tom Hanks character in *Extremely Loud and Incredibly Close*, "if it were easy, it wouldn't be worth finding."

Summary

Every person is born into a unique set of spiritual, physical, emotional, social, intellectual, and financial circumstances — our birth SPESIFCs. From these, we gain our initial worldview, our childhood perspective. There are those who would have us believe that this early programming is permanent. While our childhood certainly forms the foundation of our character and plays a part in our entire lives, we are not slaves to our birth SPESIFC. We can alter our initial programming, replace it entirely with new SPESIFCs so powerful that the original programming can be completely overridden. The script of our lives is not unchangeably written. Each of us has a "destiny", meaning a "best case scenario". There are things you are uniquely suited to do; a contribution you can make that is superior to anyone else. If you want your ultimate life, then discovering and achieving this personal destiny must be your prime directive.

No matter what you call it — calling, mission, destiny, karma, purpose, responsibility, inspiration — you have an obligation (to yourself and to the world) to follow it. Your unique individual experience has prepared you for what the universe is calling you to do — the miracles only you can create to bless the world. You might, initially, think this is impossible because you were not born into ideal circumstances. Well, who was blessed with ideal circumstances?

Everyone was. If it wasn't so, God must instantly cease to be God. He sent you to Earth with a purpose (which you volunteered for!) and the challenges of your life were designed to prepare you to complete that purpose. They give you strength, flexibility and integrity. It has nothing to do with *what you go through* — the events of your life — it has everything to do with *what you take away from* and create from what you go through — the circumstances of your life. We all experience tough times but those who perceive the tough times as learning opportunities also see themselves enhanced and tempered by those times. Most people call those "bad" experiences but how in the world can they be bad when they are the very things that cause us to grow faster and stronger and, if we let them, more perfect?

Finding that path may not be easy. By grace — of God, of mentors, of many others — you can be guided to your first, best destiny. There are positive and negative spiritual influences, the darkness will try to lead you astray, but your heart and spirit and conscience already knows the truth and they will, if you learn to really listen, keep you on the path you need to follow and bring you back when you stray. You will get sidetracked, we take a few detours but these, too, can be learning experiences.

There will even be people who, because of their illusions or selfishness, try to pull you away from or down from the mission you aspire to complete. They will tell you to be realistic or they'll try to soften the blow of (what they perceive to be your inevitable) failure. They may even claim to try and dissuade you from your fanaticism out of love. These are the people who settled for mediocre results; they've bought into the "conventional wisdom" that miracles belong to the few or to mythology. If you have found your destiny, there will be a fire within you that others cannot quench — unless you help hold the hose. Let your magnificent obsession burn within you like St. Elmo's Fire and create a future that never was possible before.

Chapter 13
The Fire Principle

This thirteenth secret, ancient principle will allow you to harness the two most powerful forces on earth. These forces must be deliberately controlled in order to achieve your biggest goals or they will by default, control you and a little or a lot at time, strip you of honor and dignity and trample you-even to death.

Fear — the Fire on the Mind

You've all heard stories about "the little grandma" who picked up a 1,500-pound car to save her grandchild or the caveman who killed a saber-tooth tiger with his bare hands when his family was threatened. We all know the motivation and power in these kinds of stories is fear, which floods our system with impressive amounts of adrenalin. Fear can enable the smallest person to do the largest feats. While this type of miracle event is rare, on a much larger scale, fear stops hundreds of millions of people, every day from doing things that would set them free and enable them to create productive miracles.

A few years ago (in my previous life as a general contractor/cabinet maker), I received a phone call from a potential client. He wanted me to do a remodel project on his home, part of which was to tear out a closet between his living room and dining room and replace it with a beautiful, built-in entertainment center on the living room side and a built in china hutch of the dining room side. Upon inspection, I discovered that one of the walls he wanted removed was a "bearing wall". It was holding up the ceiling and roof so, if we just removed this wall, part of the ceiling and roof above would collapse. The day we started the job, I took my helper and explained the scope of the project. I needed him to work by himself for a few days so I could do some final trim work on another project we were just finishing a few miles away. I explained how to build temporary supports on both sides of the bearing wall and how to install temporary braces in the attic from the roof to the temporary supports below. He could then remove the existing braces, build a new header in the attic across the space where the wall would be removed, install some permanent braces from roof to the new header, and hang the ceiling joists from the new header. He could then remove the wall below and preserve the structural integrity of the house. I gave him all the details he need; in my mind it would be a "piece of cake" project.

I also explained that this work had to be finished as quickly as possible so we would be out of the way of the electricians and keep the project on schedule. This guy had proved to be trustworthy and competent in the past, so I had every confidence I could leave him alone with the task.

The next morning, I stopped in to see how things were progressing and found he had done several other less important things but hadn't started the header project.

A little frustrated, I reminded him about our time commitment and told him this header had to be built and installed today. He apologized and agreed to get it done and I left once more to work on our other project.

The following morning, I returned only to discover again that the header project was still not started. Now I am a fairly patient guy, but this made me a little angry. I had promised the other client that I would finish their project that day.

However, if this header was not installed, the electricians would have to cancel — and who knows how long it would take them to get back. They had their own schedule to keep and I wasn't about to be responsible for their inconvenience or any added expense to myself or my client for any delays, which would've also thrown off the whole project schedule. So I made a hard phone call and apologized to the other client explaining that I had an emergency and would not be able to finish today but should be back tomorrow.

I walked out to my truck, strapped on my tool belt, put up the temporary supports, climbed into the attic, installed the temporary braces, pulled out the original braces supporting the roof, built the header, fastened it in place, attached the ceiling joists on both sides, put in some new braces from the roof to the new header and left in a huff without saying a word to my helper.

All the while, he was scurrying around, looking nervous, working on some other less important projects and never made eye contact with me the entire day. I decided to let it go until I had wrangled in my anger.

A few days later we, were working in the cabinet shop, cutting out the entertainment center and hutch. After a few minutes of trivial conversation during lunch, he turned to me a little uneasy and asked, "Eldon, how do you know how to do so many things?" His comment, completely out of context to our conversation, took me by surprise. I looked at him, puzzled and asked, "What are you talking about"?

"Well, most of our jobs are either doing what other contractors can't or fixing what they've messed up and, regardless of the challenges that arise, you always know exactly what to do — like the other day when you built that header in the attic. How do you know how to do all that"?

It took my mind a few moments to wrap around what he was really asking. I had pretty much forgotten about that little hiccup. As my mind raced, all of sudden an uncontrollable grin broke across my face, I realized that he hadn't done what I had asked because he had never done anything like that before. It seemed overwhelming and he was afraid of it. In fact, he was more afraid of the risk to start that project than he was afraid of the risk of getting fired. In addition, he was afraid to tell me that he was afraid to attempt the project alone. He was trying to stay busy with other things, desperately hoping I would finish my project soon enough to help him with this one. I just looked at him, nodding and trying unsuccessfully to stop smiling for a few more moments. Finally, I collected my composure and replied.

"The interesting thing about the remodel business is that you rarely do the exact same thing twice. Lots of projects end up including things that I didn't see coming in the beginning. Lots of times I end up doing things I haven't done before. Sometimes I don't know exactly how I'm going to finish a project. Furthermore, I really don't care anymore, I just know I will — one step at a time.

I've discovered, over time, that it's easier and far quicker for me to just get started and figure it out as I go, rather than try to plan everything out beforehand. I, obviously, understand in general what has to done when I start but there's really no problem or surprise that I can't figure out. Sometimes I call in a specialist if it takes special equipment or skills but that's just part of building. However, even If I've never faced a particular problem before, and don't exactly know what I will run into, I know that if I just go as far as I can see, by the time I get there, I will be able to see further. You just develop a 'whatever it takes to make sure it's done right' mentality and never give yourself the option to cut corners or quit till it's finished."

He nodded as though he understood but was still looking at me with those wondering eyes.

It reminded me that many people in the world today often feel exactly like he did, they are afraid to begin. They've never "been there before" and can't seem to muster the courage to take that leap of faith — in themselves and their ability — to just get started.

Unfortunately, as a result, most people rarely experience this magic of self-discovery. On one hand, it is critical to design out your life, the further into the future the better, even though your plans are always evolving. On the other hand, there will always be surprises, impossible to predict but you just develop that 'whatever it takes to make sure things are done right' mentality and never give yourself the option to cut corners or quit until you win.

There is also a balance to discover about what you should have someone else do and what you should intentionally put yourself to the task of discovering by way of mentors yourself. Developing that balance is a critical skill, you should never be ashamed or embarrassed to ask questions but, at the same time, to conquer and control your ego, develop the right skills, self-respect and self-esteem to push yourself to task your creative mind to the process of self-discovery.

No one ever became wise without mustering the courage from depths they never knew they had, to face their fears head-on with an uncompromising commitment to solve them. That practical application is the only way to self-discovery and it always takes facing your fears and acting positively in spite of them. That process will also instill the right character and teach you invaluable lessons that will bless your life in countless ways in the future. It only took two words to paint that picture in my mind when I was young, "Cowboy up!"

There is good news in all this. The world is designed so that if you miss an important lesson, it will come back around and around and around and around and continue to get worse until you either learn how to solve it or you keep giving in to your fear long enough so that it helps to kill you. The more you run away from these lessons, the more it is impossible to calculate the expense to you in terms of stress and time and energy and frustration and failure in your life.

It was dusk, on an otherwise ordinary day, as I squeezed through the rails of the corral fence. I was on a half-trot, taking a shortcut to help one of my brothers with some chores. Suddenly I heard that all-too-familiar snort and stomping. This corral was usually empty. I stopped dead in my tracks before spinning on my heels to find myself face-to-face with a very cantankerous bull. I was close enough to feel the warm, moist steam from his nostrils.

I was a super-scrawny kid, always the smallest in school classes and often mistaken for being younger than I was. At this point I was in the sixth grade. Here in the corral with an angry bull, my mind raced, and my body was frozen with fear.

That proved to be a good thing. If I had tried to run, that bull would have caught me and pummeled me into the ground before I could have jumped back through the fence. As he snorted, he threw his big head up and down. I remember thinking, "Wow, his is head is as big as me!"

I had heard all the scary stories and had strict instructions to avoid those bulls when not in company with someone older. Luckily, I had also heard about the best ways to deal with them — that I could never give them the slightest indication that I might be afraid. If he charged, I'd better run but, if not, I better stand my ground. Otherwise, I would end up hurt or maybe even dead. Not only that, but running would make the bull even more aggressive the next time someone else had to deal with him.

Even though I was shaking in my boots (literally), my bluff was good enough as I stared him straight in the eyes, leaned a little towards him, and with as authoritative a tone as my pre-pubescent voice could muster, started to shout, "Back off, you big bully, back off!". At the same time, I slowly inched my way to the fence and climbed back through the rails. The moment I realized I was safe on the other side, my entire body began to shake violently and I sat down in the dirt without energy or stability to stand for a few minutes.

Like me, you have probably heard from experts that we are only born with two fears, the fear of loud noises and the fear of falling. I suspect that is true, which also means that every other fear you have was learned from personal experience. Ironically, you learned them all in stages of your life when you were very uneducated about the circumstances that caused the fear.

There are plenty of other people who do not fear the same things. At least some of those people are not afraid because they have discovered the principles that control those situations through practical application. They have proven to themselves that they are competent enough to accurately predict positive instead of negative outcomes. Everything you learned in a disempowering way, you can relearn in empowering ways. Such is the way of the mentor.

Fear affects us in so many ways it is impossible to list them all. There are, however, pros and cons to the "fear factor" — both can either save you or destroy you, depending on how you react.

Debilitating Fear

I've heard that a cat who has jumped on to a hot stove once will never jump on a hot stove again. Nor will that cat ever jump on a cold stove.

I also recall a story about a young man whose father could never get him on a horse. He grew up in a family of horse riders and it was a proud tradition in the family. When the young man was a little boy, he had been nipped by a pony and developed a deep-seated fear of horses. After many tries, the father finally got him to give it another try. Reluctantly the young man climbed back onto the horse and, in a short time, beat his own fear. That young man was Marion Michael Morris, who grew up to become the iconic movie "cowboy" — John Wayne. Imagine what his life would've been had he never gotten back on that horse.

Fear clouds judgement; it can keep you from starting something important. This will keep you from discovering truths that would benefit your life. Living with this fear keeps you from discovering truth and enslaves you. If you don't begin, you will never know where life would have taken you.

Shortly after I graduated high school, several of my friends and I got together to go pay our entry fees for the local up-coming rodeo. When I handed the lady my cash, she asked with a questioning look, "Is this for your bareback or bull entry?"

I looked back in surprise, "What? I didn't sign up for bulls!" At that point, a couple of my friends shifted uncomfortably beside me. Processing for a couple of seconds, I turned and said "You guys signed me up for this. You bone heads, I'm not riding no stupid bull!" These friends had been trying to talk me into riding bulls for the months, trying to convince me that I'd be good at it.

"Come on" they pleaded, "at least try it once."

I repeated my usual response, "Riding bulls is stupid. There's no rhyme or reason to it. At least riding horses has a purpose, horses are meant to be ridden. But bulls — that's just brain dead! That's not a sport for cowboys to see how many bulls they can ride but a sport for bulls to see how many cowboys they can trounce."

The lady taking our entry fees was a friend of my parents and chimed in, "You know Eldon, if you wanted to give it a try, you drew-out for a really good bull. He's not mean and he scores high. He's a good bull for anyone to ride and a great one to start on."

I was 18 years old and had a reputation to uphold of not being afraid of anyone or anything. At that point, I had no choice, right? Wrong! Of course, I had a choice — I could face the bull or face risking my friends thinking I was afraid. At that moment, that choice felt like jumping from an airplane at 12,000 and wondering, "should I wear the parachute or jump without it?" Since they had taken away all my "logical" excuses, I paid another entry fee. To my surprise, I enjoyed the ride and that ride completely changed my thinking about that event.

Only when you learn to face your debilitating fears can you discover the right formulae to free yourself from those self-imposed hobbles. Fear of looking foolish keeps you from asking questions that would provide solutions you need to develop skills and create circumstances you want. You've all seen those students in class, the ones afraid to raise their hands (that was me). It's a symptom of an out-of-control ego. Ego exists to protect us from many things but, inevitably, unless we take control of it, ego will be over-protective and control us by preventing small pains that could have been valuable growing pains.

Protecting Fear

This is our God-given "fight or flight" response, designed to remove threats from us or remove us from threats. It enables us to act quickly, like "the little grandma", to protect ourselves and those we care about.

Did you hear the one about the driver who was pulled over by the highway patrolman? As the officer approached the window, the driver rolled it down and said, "Just so you know, officer, I have a concealed carry permit in my back pocket, a .380 holstered under my left arm, a .45 in the glove box and a 30-06 rifle in that case on the back seat."

The patrolman was taken aback. "What are you afraid of?" he asked.

"Not one thing," the driver replied, smiling.

On a different note, perhaps you're aware of counsel that leaders of The Church of Jesus Christ of Latter-day Saints (the Mormons) have been giving their members for six or seven decades: Have a one-year supply of food, clothing, fuel and other necessities in your home for emergencies. This advice is an impractical goal for many, and the church leaders have been clear that, if a full year's supply isn't possible, then keep six months or one month or two weeks or whatever the family circumstances allow. Not to be so obvious as to be insulting, the point isn't perfection — that full year's supply — the point is doing your best to reach perfection — doing as much as you can do to protect yourself.

Protective fear causes us to be aware of potential threats and prepared to act responsibly in softening those potential threats. It's the same emotion that causes a responsible teen to call home and say, "Some of the kids at this party have started drinking, please come and get me." Fear can sometimes be the secret to survival and achievement.

Up until my mid-30s, I was so afraid of failure and rejection that, if I was driving at dusk, I wouldn't even turn my lights on if there were other cars coming toward me with their lights already on. That would have meant (to me) that I would be admitting that they must be smarter than me because they thought about it before me. So I'd wait till I thought no one else could see me before I turned mine on. Now, seriously, did any of those other drivers care? Did any of them look at my car (they couldn't actually see it was me, you know) and say, "What a bonehead, he's so dumb he couldn't remember to turn his lights on at dusk"? Looking back, that seems so foolish. I'm sure they never gave me two seconds' thought. That's why we call them "irrational fears"!

A tremendous step forward occurred for me when I was attending a seminar by Donald S. Wolfe (another role model). He was taking us through some "breaking through fears" exercises. At one point, he gave us an assignment to face and break through a significant fear during our dinner break. I kept thinking, I'm really not afraid of much but all of a sudden a rush of feeling flooded over me and I recognized for the first time how totally afraid I was of not measuring up to others, which is fear of rejection.

It was so significant that I didn't wait for dinner, I took the course manual up to the front and explained to Don the insight I'd just experienced and asked him for his autograph. I told him that I had never asked anyone for an autograph in my life before that day. I explained how I had told myself that autographs were stupid and I never wanted one. As I sat listening to him, I realized that I called them stupid because I felt that, if I ever asked anyone for an autograph, it meant I thought they were better than me.

I remember his words, "Wow, that's a big one." He was happy to autograph my book. What he didn't know, however, was that I skipped the dinner break. I just went to my hotel room, overwhelmed, even shed a few tears, coming to terms with many of my own suppressed feelings of inadequacy. Throughout my young life, I never felt like I was good enough and desperately hoped no one else ever found out who I really was for fear they wouldn't like me anymore.

I flunked junior high and barely graduated high school simply because I would never ask questions for fear others would think I was stupid. Today however, asking questions of people who know more than me, or may know more than me, is one of my very favorite activities!

This won't come as any surprise because you've heard it lots of times, directly or indirectly since you were old enough to understand, "You have to face your fears!" and do whatever it takes to get yourself to take action in spite of your fear. Like facing the bulls, once you do it the first time, the next times will be easier.

As John Wayne often said, "Courage is being scared to death, but saddling up anyway."

Many times you can overcome your fear by simply realizing that you have out-grown it. Regression therapy is not effective just because you go back in time and re-visit the experience, but rather because you now take back with you greater intelligence and a stronger and more mature character. You don't need that fear for protection anymore and now it is a problem instead of a perceived solution, so you leave it behind forever. You may have even forgotten the actual experience that started the fear and have been simply responding subconsciously on a habit. But now you can handle the situation and don't want or need the fear anymore. The moment your brain really 'gets that,' you have discerned the reality from the illusion and the fears just float away, never to return — at least not enough to keep you from creating different circumstances needed to achieve the better things you want.

Several years ago, I was having a bit of a tense conversation with one of my brothers about fear. He was contending that fear is a good emotion that we need and that it can be very helpful. I agreed, but only to the extent that we are naive about the world. When we get ourselves in trouble, it can help keep us safe but, I added, fear is an emotion that we must control in the beginning and eventually learn to completely live without. Fear is designed to provide short-term security when we find ourselves in trouble and need to fight or flight. Let it linger and it guarantees an early grave — even if you live to be 100 years old. In the long term, fear will always shut you down and rob you of your ability to access your creative power.

Passion — the Fire in the Heart

For almost one year, I deliberately thought about fear and the tremendous boost of potential that adrenaline gives you in times of extreme fear. I thought, "There has to be a positive resource that provides the same super-human strength and heightened senses to allow us to achieve something positive we want and not just to protect us. The universe could not exist without a polar opposite because the entire universe would be thrown out of balance without it."

Then one day, while reading in the New Testament, something struck me. Every time someone came to Jesus for help, he responded with something like "Fear not." In fact, a similar phrase appears over 100 times in the Bible, and many hundreds of times, if you count synonyms like "Peace be unto you". It was always about getting people out of fear and into hope, possibilities, and faith. Instead of worrying about the past and fearing the future, we should learn from the past, project it into the future, focus on opportunities and create miracles. The mindset, the spiritual trajectory, had to change before the physical reality could change to match it.

Jesus gave this counsel to many people, some of whom were in the darkest hours of their lives, yet His response to their pain was a focus on what can be and not their illusions of how things were. Why would He give such advice? We've all been taught to empathize, be understanding, don't try to change other people. Jesus had an entirely different plan. When facing tragedy, He gave a perspective about how to achieve greater things today than yesterday and how to prepare to achieve more tomorrow than today. We've got to focus on where we're going, not where we are or what we're going through. I heard one person say, "don't think about what you're going through but about what you're going to."

So, as all this is rolling around in my mind, the lightning of inspiration flashes. There *is* a positive flip-side to fear that fills us with the same heightened senses, super-human strength and ability to create miracles. *Passion* enables people like you and me to build empires and leave a legacy for our families and loved ones. The key is to make sure you never give passion its own head or it will take you where you don't want to go. But to deliberately train, direct, control, and utilize it to its full potential.

Passion is definitely the most powerful force on earth, much more powerful than fear because fear can only take you backwards but passion can take you anywhere you truly want to be. Beware though, passion is a double-edged sword. Wielding it with wisdom will give you the power to carve your way to miracles. If you wield it with your unbridled ego, it will drag you through obsession to addiction then strip you of everything dear and, finally, it will execute you. With passion, there are only two realities — you control it or it controls you.

Like fear, passion shows two completely different faces and personalities — the deceitful and destructive passion on one hand or the creative and constructive passion on the other. Napoleon Bonaparte wrote that "Great ambition is the passion of a great character. Those endowed with it may perform very good or very bad acts. It all depends on the principles which direct them." M. Scott Peck compared our ego to having several big Clydesdale horses in your backyard. The same example is true with passion. If you allow them to remain wild, "they will knock your house down" but, if you train and control them properly, they will take you places and enable you to do things that would have been impossible otherwise — and I'd add that you will look extremely cool while doing it!

Unbridled Passion

Benjamin Franklin said "a man in passion rides a wild horse." If you fail to master your passions, you really will feel like you're riding a powerful wild stallion and it will take you where it wants to go, completely out of your control. You will definitely experience a thrilling ride. You will believe in the beginning that perhaps you have even "died and gone to heaven". Sooner or later, however, you'll realize that horse ride is dangerous, unstoppable, and bound for disaster. You'll also realize you're tiring but the horse isn't. if you are lucky, perhaps it will run your face into a low hanging tree branch and sweep you off. If not, and you don't get off, at any risk, it will get harder and harder to stay in the saddle and, when you have no more strength to hang on, it will buck you off and trample you under foot without regard.

Unbridled passion is a cancer that cares only for itself and sucks the life out of you. It sustains only its own life at the expense of yours. It does not care about your feelings or values or intentions or wellbeing whatsoever. It is completely self-absorbed. It will feed off of you for as long as you give it life.

I will always remember what happened when I started studying personal development. People started treating me differently. The only thing I wanted to study, to do and to talk about was personal development. They started to believe that I had become an eccentric and had "gone off the deep end." They were right! I had discovered the great treasure map of universal and unlimited abundance and the more I designed my future, the brighter and more powerful my reality became. My unbridled passion for the subject unbalanced my life. My leadership of self was lacking. Actor Charlie Sheen may be the poster child for that concept. His idea that "I think my passion is misinterpreted as anger sometimes. And I don't think people are ready for the message that I'm delivering, and delivering with a sense of violent love" borders on delusional. His near-death drug abuse, multiple rehab commitments, failed marriages, and, ultimately, firing from his hit sitcom *Two and a Half Men* are ample evidence that his unbridled passion rules him, to his frequent and repeated ruin.

Canadian businessman and venture capitalist Kevin O'Leary would say that attitudes like Sheen's have sunk many potentially miraculous ideas.

> I have met many entrepreneurs who have the passion and even the work ethic to succeed but who are so obsessed with an idea that they don't see its obvious flaws. Think about that. If you can't even acknowledge your failures, how can you cut the rope and move on?

Think about that. Each of us wants to believe he or she is brilliant — that's the ego talking — but practicality is an absolute necessity in any venture. Can you examine your product or project — and yourself — so you can see your own mistakes and correct them or does your unbridled passion overrule your measurement principle?

With the help of wise mentors, I learned more and more control over passion instead of allowing it to control me. I am still learning to effectively harness its power, so that we become one. Together, we are building an empire that will expand for generations to come. It has propelled me into a state and life that I could never have imagined before. The more I discover, the more I harness my passion into a directed discovery, and as you do the same, the more your passion will become your path of magnificent obsession.

Bridled Passion

I have asked many audiences, what it means to "bridle your passions?" Most of the time I hear something like, "It means to not act on them" "to bury them" or that passions are bad because they are based in unrealistic emotions, mostly associated with unhealthy sexuality. I then ask, "So, what is a bridle?" Following a short conversation, most of them get the picture; to control and direct it to a positive outcome.

A few years later, I was introduced to and began studying Steven K. Scott's program entitled *Master Strategies of Super Achievers*. As I mentioned earlier, in its own way, it is one of the finest program I have ever studied and I highly recommend it to you. Through it, Steven helped me understand more clearly the power of passion.

I love what Einstein said, "...a student of science and life must first learn how not to define any process or potential until it defines its self and then to know when that self-definition has occurred." Many potentially-great mentors speak about bridled passion in a variety of terms, all of which are compatible with the principles I have outlined.

Indian composer, singer, musician, and philanthropist Allah-Rakha Rahman believes that bridled passion is synonymous with your first, best destiny, "Success comes to those who dedicate everything to their passion in life. To be successful, it is also very important to be humble and never let fame or money travel to your head."

Cellist Yo-Yo Ma is a devotee of taking you next best guess, "Passion," he said, "is one great force that unleashes creativity, because if you're passionate about something, then you're more willing to take risks."

I mentioned the fear that debilitated my helper on that home remodel and how I typically make it up as I go along. I reminded you that what you want also wants you just as badly. I highlighted my brother's career change and how challenging, but rewarding, he found that move. J. Michael Straczynski, creator of the television series *Babylon 5* and screenwriter for *Thor*, summed up these ideas beautifully, "Follow your passion. The rest will attend to itself. If I can do it, anybody can do it. It's possible. And it's your turn. So go for it. It's never too late to become what you always wanted to be in the first place."

I would add a word of wisdom. Don't just run out and quit your job and put yourself and your family's welfare at major risk. Start by finding a mentor (or two or five) who is the best you can find and has achieved the kind of results you want. Then do exactly what they tell you. If that is starting your own business, remember that far more than 50 percent of businesses fail within two years and many more within the first five. Of those that survive, only a very small number ever make it to support their owners with the kind of business that is really fulfilling for them. Make sure you have a workable plan for at least three years — much longer is even better.

Blue-collar guru Mike Rowe adds some practical advice to the dream team:

> Like all bad advice, "Follow Your Passion" is routinely dispensed as though it's wisdom were both incontrovertible and equally applicable to all. It's not. Just because you're passionate about something doesn't mean you won't suck at it. … When it comes to earning a living and being a productive member of society — I don't think people should limit their options to those vocations they feel passionate towards, at least at first. I met a lot of people on *Dirty Jobs* who really enjoyed their work. But very few of them dreamed of having the career they ultimately chose. I remember a very successful septic tank cleaner who told me his secret of success: "I looked around to see where everyone else was headed, and then I went the opposite way," he said. "Then I got good at my work. Then, I found a way to love it. Then, I got rich."

There's a constant debate in engineering — form follows function versus function follows form. In other words, do you build what works then create a casing around it or do you determine what space you have to work in then build what will fit in the space? The answer is (or should be) obvious, "It depends." So it is with passion. Some of us will figure out our first, best destiny then build our lives around that destiny. Others will build our lives and find, within those lives, something that moves us more than anything else. Both ways work.

Sadly, for many years, the statistics have shown that around 80 percent of people hate their jobs. That is a clue about how most are trained to choose careers today and the practical preparation for them. Also a clue that we haven't developed the character or sense of personal accountability and responsibility — that nothing is ever all "fun and games." Every vocation has times of starting at the bottom, difficult learning curves, the mundane, etc., and we have to work through those things in order to become leaders and do the "fun" things.

Conclusion

Your humanity naturally includes *fears* and *passions* — they are a part of your soul. A huge part of the purpose for this university of life is to overcome your fears and bridle your passions. Harnessing these attributes, becoming the compete master of them, allows you access to the magnitude of your potential. Fear, though valuable, can only take you backwards to the past, to a safe place; passion, though dangerous, is the jet fuel of the soul, if used wisely, it will be a source of perpetual, even compounding energy and brilliance that will take you anywhere you want to go with lightning speed.

Remember also what James Allen said "…so be not impatient in delay, but wait as one who understands, when spirit rises and commands, the Gods are ready to obey."

Summary

Debilitating fear is the cat who has jumped on to a hot stove and will never again jump on any stove, hot or cold again. Such fear clouds judgement; it can keep you from starting something important. This will keep you from discovering truths that would benefit your life. Living with this fear keeps you from discovering truth and enslaves you. If you don't begin, you will never know where life would have taken you.

Only when you learn to face your debilitating fears can you discover the right formulae to free yourself from those self-imposed hobbles. Fear of looking foolish keeps you from asking questions that would provide solutions you need to develop skills and create circumstances you want. Often fear is a symptom of an out-of-control ego. Ego exists to protect us from many things but, if you don't control it, it will control you like an overprotective parent and prevent any small pains that could have been valuable growing pains.

Protecting fear is our God-given "fight or flight" response, designed to remove threats from us or remove us from threats. Fear can sometimes be the secret to survival and achievement. It enables us to act quickly, and, sometimes, in miraculous ways, to protect ourselves and those we care about. Never can we be perfectly safe, nor can we create a completely safe environment for our families. We can however do what we can with what we have, and use what we have to create ever improving circumstances.

As you've heard many times, "You have to face your fears!" You have to proactively reprogram your childhood paradigms, take action in spite of your fear, and realize that every time you do, the next time will be easier. Eventually, you will find the irrational basis of your fears and they will cease to be fearsome.

The Two Most Powerful Forces on Earth

Fear

Quickens reflexes

Sharpens our 6 senses

Super-human strength

Always backwards to a safe place

Tears down/is hard on our body

Negative emotions

Survive

Passion (Bridled)

Quickens reflexes

Sharpens our 6 senses

Super-human strength

Always forward to places we've never been

Builds up/is healing to our body

Positive emotions

Thrive

Chapter 14
The Real-Economics Principle

This fourteenth secret, ancient principle has always been, and always will be, the most sought-after among the great hidden wisdoms of the world. Literally tens of thousands of people advertise that they can teach you this principle. Ironically, few of them have it themselves — just check their bank balances — and even if that looks good, check their character. You will find only a small handful who made it because they truly understood the principles of economics. Many got rich by convincing you that they could make you rich, with no refunds if you don't. But then being rich and becoming truly wealthy is a very different matter. We see hoards, every day, flocking down dead-end roads while the only way to become truly wealthy is down "the road less traveled" and not nearly so readily advertised or available because it is a "hard-sell" (that is that it isn't promised to you on a "silver platter"). That means the chances of finding it is rare because:

1. There is so much false information out there.
2. *All* true success comes from "unconventional wisdom".
3. Very few people actually have the truth.

True economics extends far beyond money, however, learning to deal properly with money can teach us to understand true economic principles, so money will be our teaching tool.

Like all "conventional wisdom", the economics you studied in high school or college is founded on a completely false idea. You may be of the opinion that economics is based entirely in mathematics and mathematics can't lie. Since I am neither an economist nor a mathematician, how could I have the audacity to make a statement that sounds so obviously absurd?

My conclusions are based on years of intimate involvement with businesses — some that struggled and failed and others that prospered and succeeded. Also from many business coaches and mentors over the years, I saw clearly that academia's "Ivory Tower" attitudes are not how successful business owners and leaders build their businesses, but far beyond my experience is the best advice and experience of the most brilliant business and economic thinkers through history.

All money — that is, prosperity — comes from commerce. In fact, every bit of money (wealth, value) that exists on Earth today was created by entrepreneurs. It was *not* created by economists and *not* by governments or government officials — even though they do their best to convince you otherwise. Ever since I began to understand this, it has been extremely interesting and irritating that most government officials or economists don't see eye to eye with business people and yet it is the business people who create and run our prosperity and created our economy. Go figure.

With that background, the question arises: How can I create life-long security for myself and my family, especially in today's economic chaos? (According to Rogers and Hammerstein) — "Let's start at the very beginning, a very good place to start, when you sing you begin with Do, Re, Mi" and reading begins with "A, B, C"; but, if you want learn about money, you must study "His, To, Ry" (history).

The Law of the Harvest

Among Paul's writings, he gave this warning to the Galatians (6:7,9, KJV), "Be not deceived; God is not mocked: for whatsoever a man soweth, that shall he also reap. ... And let us not be weary in well doing: for in due season we shall reap, if we faint not." Some people have referred to this as the classic statement of "The Law of the Harvest". Paul is definitely explaining that this is a universal law — you get out of life what you put in. But this "Law of the Harvest" has always been and will always be the essence of reality (that is the forever unchangeable truth of the universe). It is what the universe and everything in it is and how and why it all works, seen or unseen, understood or not yet fathomed.

Everything in this book is directly pertaining to this "Law of the Harvest" and how you can make the most of it. For example, if you are honest, you will have a free conscience. If you are charitable, others will speak your name with reverence and gratitude, etc. For this conversation, we are talking about the economics part. Thus, if you work on your business, honestly, in yours and others best interest, diligently and intelligently, you will earn respect and loyal customers. If you learn and live by principles that harmonize with the great universal laws to your best ability, you will become wise.

If you study and learn principles of money, you will have money. If you use money for good, it will return to you in multiples. Money used to bless your life and the lives of those you love is a worthy goal and obtainable to the masses, not just the few. Nothing in this book can prevent or solve your life's problems. You must take it from this book and cultivate it into your life and when you do, your problems will begin to diminish. The more you discover and practice these principles, the quicker you will solve your own problems and the easier your life will become. Economic success is as simple as baking a cake. If you learn and follow the recipes, you will have as much money as you are willing to have. I have talked to many, many people who have said things to the effect that "there are no guarantees in life." That very comment, however, defies logic and common sense — as I would hope you understand by now. That is the great "conventional wisdom" misunderstanding and lie.

That is as naive as if to say there is no guarantee that when you wake up in the morning, you may not be able to tie your shoes anymore because the laws and principles of the universe have changed while you were sleeping. Finances follow the exact same laws as every other SPESIFC of life.

At face value, it seems that flood or drought, disease or blizzard, market conditions, or a hundred other things can take you down despite your best efforts. But again, that is the great lie of "conventional wisdom". All the schooling and book learning in the world can never get you past that short-sighted, poverty mentality. Everything in this book is designed to show you how to open your eyes and see through the smoke and mirrors of those illusions into reality and set you free of those self-imposed limitations.

Your employment is one more subset of your life. A few years ago a psychologist acquaintance of mine asked me if I would give a talk to a group of workers who had been down-sized from the Boeing Corporation. He was hired by the company to help them though this difficult transition and find new jobs/careers. It was evident that he was concerned about those people and stressed about his responsibility.

I asked how much time I could take. He said, "See what you can give them of value in about 15 minutes." With raised eyebrows, I asked, "Are you joking?" He said something like "well you know, the world is changing, people have shorter attention spans today than in the past, and they demand better information and in a shorter period of time."

So I asked. "Are you telling me that these people really expect someone to give them something of intrinsic value in 15 minutes?" He looked at me a little funny and said "Yes, they do." And I immediately responded with something like, "In that case, I can clearly see why Boeing decided to lay them off. They are a liability to the company and not an asset. I would have fired them long before Boeing did." With that kind of mindset, they have only begun to experience the pain and suffering that is on its way into their lives.

I can teach them how to be the kind of employees that their future bosses will fight for and do almost anything to keep so they will never worry about supporting themselves and their families again. But in order to do that, they are going to have to think like they've never thought before, do things they've never done before, develop skills and habits they've never had before and cultivate character traits and paradigms they've never imagined before. There is no such thing as microwave success.

Before they will ever solve their problems, they need to recognize that being laid off has nothing to do with the company or bad luck or anything else they would rather blame it on. It is a problem that they created for themselves. My coming in for such a short time will only waste everyone's time and perpetuate the great lie that got them laid-off to begin with. The same lie that will also get them fired from all their next jobs until life beats them up enough to make them cry "Uncle!" and realize that if they want their lives to change for the better, they will have to change their lives for the better. Fifteen minutes might suffice for a mediocre advertisement at best. But even a reasonable infomercial takes longer than that.

Even though other people create a lot of events in your life, you are far more in control of those events than you can realize. Other people will always treat you just like you train them to. Plus, the circumstances you create in response to events will determine your success in every SPESIFC of life — and that includes financials every bit as much as any other area. (Yes, I say that a lot. It's *that* important!). Having money is as simple as tying your shoes. If you understand the laws and apply the principles that put you in control of your results, you will have it. If you don't, you won't have it. It is that simple.

I have also heard more times than I can count that "Life success isn't all about money" and "Money can't buy happiness." So I will take those one at a time.

I don't know who came up with this first, but I have heard numerous amazing, good hearted and miraculously successful people say in some form or fashion, "It's true that money isn't everything but I rank it right up there with oxygen."

About three years ago I was attending a very enlightening and powerful conference by James Malinchak, another of my mentors (if you want to be a speaker, he's the guy to study). During that conference, He introduced us to a friend of his who years earlier had built a multi-million-dollar business. When Hurricane Katrina devastated New Orleans in 2005, Scott was overcome with compassion, opened his own personal checkbook and wrote a check for $500,000 to start his own charity relief program. He personally took time off work, went to New Orleans, and helped feed, clothe and relocate about 25,000 people.

Now let me tell you, if money wasn't important to him, many of those people wouldn't have been helped. If you squabble that money isn't as important as other things, it's clear you will never have enough to really do as much as you would like to do. As the great Earl Nightingale said, "In the area in which money works, nothing will take the place of money." So *stop* sabotaging your own financial success. If you would like more, figure out which parts of the formulae you do not understand, adopt them into your life and character and the laws of grace will help you after you have done all you can and are still willing to take that leap of faith.

Again God said, "Seek ye first the kingdom of god, and his righteousness, and all else shall be added unto you." Remember the laws of grace. When He said "all things" He meant "all things". He didn't make a mistake and forget to say "except money." I will discuss Exponential Returns in the next chapter, which is also part of the laws of the harvest, as is His promise of a blessing so great "that there shall not be room enough to receive it (Malachi 3:10, KJV). That includes money and increase of all kinds. So, when you get there, read very carefully.

Next, "Life success isn't all about money." Of course not. Money is only one of the seven core areas in your life — the SPESIFCs. That's like saying "Life success isn't all about time management, or about relationships or any other one thing for that matter." Finances are every bit as important as any of the other six however. Just try to pay your bills or fill your gas tank with kindness. It doesn't work. A lack of money will bring you unnecessary pain and suffering. If you have a gift to create money, you better magnify your gift. If you don't, you can develop it and it will afford you freedoms and opportunities to increase the good that you do in ways impossible to calculate.

Valuta

What is *money*?

Money is a form of *valuta*, something of worth used as an exchange. Historically, gold is *the* valuta — the most enduring and universal standard of wealth and medium of exchange. Another example is salt. Prized for its intrinsic value — it's a preservative, a seasoning, a necessity for good health — for thousands of years, salt was a currency. In fact, Roman legionnaires were sometimes paid in salt, giving us the modern expression "worth his salt" and the word "salary".

In addition to valuta, we have *fiat currency* — paper money, data bits, stocks, bonds, bitcoins, and other forms of payment traded all over the world. These are worth nothing by themselves, they function as currency only because we accept them as representing value.

Where did it come from, what function does it perform?

To make a long, complex story short and basic, money is a convenience. It arose from the inconvenience of barter. Anciently, if I was a herdsman and you were a blacksmith and I needed less than a whole cow worth of iron work done, I had a problem because cows don't really subdivide conveniently in societies that lack refrigerators. As people formed larger and larger groups which developed into cities and societies, barter became less workable because more people became involved in each exchange but each exchange had to be based on the largest single valuta in the transaction.

Money relieved this problem because it had its own value and the value of everything else could be related to money's value. If I received one cow worth of silver, for example, I could spend part of that silver on iron works and another part on vegetables or wine. The concept of an independent monetary system created the flexibility producers and consumers needed to create a vibrant economy.

Is money good or bad?

It is neither, it is simply a system to facilitate exchanges of value. You have probably heard the "conventional wisdom" proverb, "Money is the root of all evil" — *that is a bold-faced lie!* (Hey, it's "conventional wisdom", what else did you expect?) The phrase comes from one of Paul's epistle, "For the love of money is the root of all evil: which while some coveted after, they have erred from the faith, and pierced themselves through with many sorrows" (Timothy 6:10, KJV). This simple phrase goes beyond the common misquotation — the problems are coveting money (selfishness and an out of control ego), lack of faith in the law of the harvest, and the unhappiness that ultimately follows bad behavior.

The fact is that many of the most kindhearted, philanthropic, generous, and charitable people actually love money. That is to say, they love the education and shelter and food and convenience it provides as well as the poverty, and illness and pain that it cures. Also, contrary to public opinion, most people who are guilty of "the love of money" are people who have very little or, at least, not as much as they want and, so, that love of money rules them instead of them ruling it.

Here is a side note: Some people's love of television or love of food or being lazy or any number of other things is "their" root of all evil. Whatever you love that takes you out of balance and distracts your focus from truly important things is the key. Again, it is your attitude that stems from your paradigm and character toward some object and not the object itself that is important.

Capitalism

Capitalism is one of many economic systems. *Capitalism.org*'s website offers a concise definition:

> Capitalism is a social system based on the principle of individual rights. Politically, it is the system of *laissez-faire* (freedom). Legally, it is a system of objective laws (rule of law as opposed to rule of man). Economically, when such freedom is applied to the sphere of production its result is the free-market. Capitalism is moral and practical as it leaves the individual free to think rationally and act productively to sustain one's life and experience happiness on Earth.

American economist Walter Williams adds a historical perspective, "Prior to capitalism, the way people amassed great wealth was by looting, plundering and enslaving their fellow man. Capitalism made it possible to become wealthy by serving your fellow man."

History teaches us clearly that capitalism, even the increasingly regulated and ever-more imperfect version currently practiced in the United States has produced more wealth for more people than any other society in recorded history. Every person on the *Forbes'* 400 list is worth at least $1.5 billion. The magazine also notes, "It takes money to make money, but nearly two-thirds of the 1810 entrants on *Forbes'* 2016 World's Billionaires list are self-made entrepreneurs who started with little more than a vision. Some had money, others had none to speak of. Today their empires range from fashion and entertainment to real estate and telecom."

One of the biggest problems with entrepreneurs is that most become self-employed because they get good at their craft (or production). Rarely do they understand that there are 3 crucial parts of business.

1. Production
2. Back-end business practices (and culture)
3. Marketing

If any one of these 3 parts go un-nurtured, you are left with a crippled business that will work you instead of you working it and will only return a fraction of what it could to you. Are you over-worked, under-paid, not getting all you would like from your business or your life, or even from the business you help to run or that you work in? Give us a call, we can help you change that.

When I started my first business, I was a great carpenter/cabinet maker. It took a few years however before I realized that I had only created myself a very labor-intense job instead of a lifestyle and it almost cost me everything of significant value to my life. Thanks to my mentors, I was able to turn that all around.

While getting your picture to replace the little guy with the moustache on *Monopoly* boards is a dream many have but few achieve, it has nothing to do with the industry you are in or limited human potential, but with what an individual is willing to accept as their *education*. Financial security and independence is always possible, if one uses correct principles to harness the universal laws and use them correctly to his or her advantage. The concepts of this principle can be grouped into two basic categories.

Liberty

Many people (conservatives and liberals alike) are finally coming around to recognize that US businesses are over-regulated (it's about time!). Estimates on how much companies spend to comply with federal rules range as high as $1.7 trillion dollars every year. That's money business owners can't spend on wages, advertising, product development, and other profit-enhancing ideas. It's like a college student who is required to spend hours every day in meaningless tasks that not only take away from studying but which have zero intrinsic value to their future. He or she can still succeed, but why make it harder than it needs to be? Like Ronald Reagan used to say, "The most terrifying words in the English language are: I'm from the government and I'm here to help." And also that, "Government is not the solution to our problems, government is the problem."

Regulations also demonstrate a one-size-fits-all attitude that has never posted a positive effect on any venture. To be blunt, the phrase "one size fits all" is just flat out stupid. "One size fits all" clothes fit really big people; the rest of us can wear them but they don't fit and, if you really care about how you look, they don't make you happy. Any farmer will tell you to plant what grows well in the ground you have — wheat or corn die in places where rice thrives, and vice versa. A rancher will tell you to choose the breed that fits your target market — Holsteins for milk versus Angus for beef or Quarter Horses for working cattle and Clydesdales for pulling beer wagons. It is up to you to discover which rules will return the most appropriate rewards for your business and your life. That is also where a wise mentor will pay you exponential returns.

Economist Murray Rothbard, one of the grand masters of capitalism, wrote, "Freedom can run a monetary system as superbly as it runs the rest of the economy. Contrary to many writers, there is nothing special about money that requires extensive governmental dictation." Percy L. Greaves, Jr., a historian as well as an economist, added, "The free market is in accordance with the Golden Rule: We advance ourselves as we help others. The more we help others, the more we receive in return."

I should point out a common joke that no one should be laughing at, "The New Golden Rule: He who has the gold makes the rules." That's anarchy, not liberty. As writer Phoenix Roberts points out, "Law without agency is slavery; agency without law is anarchy."

Too many people, including both the Bernie Madoffs and his victims, cut corners for two reasons: First, because they think they will win big. Second, because they think they will get away with it. In the short term, both are true; crime does pay and, sometimes, it pays big, for as long as you get away with it. In the long term — especially in the eternal scheme of things — neither is true, "For what shall it profit a man, if he shall gain the whole world, and lose his own soul?" (Mark 8:36, KJV) and, likewise, "For nothing is secret, that shall not be made manifest; neither any thing hid, that shall not be known and come abroad" (Luke 8:17, KJV). Oh, and, by the way, the victims lost billions of dollars and Bernie's doing hard time at Club Fed, that's called lose-lose.

Responsibility

Ron Chernow, in his biography *Alexander Hamilton*, notes that, as the first Secretary of the Treasury:

> He did not create America's market economy so much as foster the cultural and legal setting in which it flourished. A capitalist society requires certain preconditions. Among other things, it must establish a rule of law through enforceable contracts; respect private property; create a trustworthy bureaucracy to arbitrate contracts; and offer patents and other protections to promote invention. The abysmal failure of the Articles of Confederation to provide such an atmosphere was one of Hamilton's principal motives for promoting the Constitution.

In Chapter 6, I stressed the need to find shortcuts to save time, effort, money and other resources. This is crucial for any businesses hoping to maximize profits. The danger comes when short-cutting turn into cutting corners because those corners often end up involving felonies and the legal community tends to have a zero-tolerance (and no sense of humor) about that sort of thing. It always *looks* harder and less profitable to play by the rules. It always *ends up* easier and more profitable to play by the rules. One of the reasons I loved Jon Huntsman's book "Winners Never Cheat."

There is a fast sweeping distain for our capitalistic, free market system, even among Americans, but the problem is not with the system, it is with our general population that is more and more ignorant about the system and their personal responsibility to understand and hold themselves accountable. As John F Kennedy said, "Think not what your country can do for you but what you can do for your country." It is true that "freedom isn't free." Liberty is a pearl of the greatest price but one that can only be purchased with the currency of responsibility.

Hand-outs vs. Hand-ups

I covered this concept in Chapter 6 but it bears repeating, briefly, because of its importance to our economic reality.

Everybody needs help at times. Sometimes, this help is to provide basic necessities due to unforeseen or emergency events. A friend once told me of his father, an audio engineer who did extraordinary to miraculous work for many major companies. One day, he visited a client to deliver the final pieces of a $100,000 project and was told there would be no payment — the client company was filing bankruptcy. No warning, no real apology, little more than a quick statement of the facts and the door. As a small consulting firm, the engineer could not absorb a $100,000 loss, so his company also went under. The engineer was talented and experienced and he found work in a fairly short time. During that interval of unemployment, however, he needed help and gratefully accepted it.

I never heard the end of the story but hopefully this engineer chose not to be a victim and blame anything but himself for the problems he created but rather recognized his own responsibility of putting his business and family at such unnecessary risk. Stories like this are all too familiar and created from lack of understanding sound business principles. Never the less, we all make mistakes and when we do, hand-ups are so appreciated.

Hand-ups provide temporary assistance that gets people through hard times. A hand-up enables and encourages people to discover what created their problems and how to evolve beyond them. In other words, hand-ups are shortcuts. They are part of the principle of giving and receiving grace that every human being must participate in, to grow and evolve.

Maybe you read about the couple in the state of Washington where I live who received over $100,000 in welfare payments while living in a $1.2 million home. Federal prosecutors allege they lied about their residences, marital status, income and just about everything else. If convicted, they will spend a long time in jail.

Hand-outs are freebies, given and received with little or no accountability in either directions. The recipients are supposed to be accountable but billions of dollars have been wasted on people who got undeserved help. Many recipients grow dependent and that dependence lasts for generations. In fact, many of them fight to keep their "benefits" (hand-outs) with a zeal that would have made them very successful in any industry — if they simply applied that creativity and energy to a useful endeavor. Hand-outs also hurt the giver. Most hand-outs are government welfare and, when the people place their trust in the government, there's little public oversight, outside of elections, where most incumbents' sail back into office because few people do the due diligence to see if these "public servants" are actually serving the interests of the public. Private charities often, but not always, receive the same low level of scrutiny. When people give money through public or private charity they rob themselves of the opportunity to grow through direct involvement in helping someone else succeed.

Wealth and the Wealthy

It is an absolutely, unquestionable, fact of history that the rich get richer and the poor get poorer. It always has been that way and it will always be that way. There is no other way it can be. Why? Because only a few people really understand the principles of true wealth. That means that real, worthy mentors are few and far between. Coupled with the fact that our society and "formal education" system is filled with people who have never been taught those principles themselves and thus cannot help their students discover them.

Add that to what I described earlier about how our egos are determined to make us believe that we know more than we really do and it sheds significant light on why, "it is easier to fool people that to convince them that they have been fooled." As Mark Twain warned. "Thus we fall into a false sense of security and before we know it, we are settling for a life far below our potential, opportunities and privileges." Very few people will push themselves to discover things that they have been taught does not exist, or have been taught, out of others sense of self-preservation is bad.

Now, so that I *cannot* be misunderstood: This is the biggest lie of "conventional wisdom" economics — one being shoved down humanity's collective throat with Earth-shattering muscle. This concept *does not mean* that the poor get poorer *because* the rich get richer. These two facts are entirely unconnected despite the immense resources some are expending to convince you it is true.

In fact, when the rich get richer, the poor and middle class also benefit. The enemies of truth would have you believe that, when "the rich" get money, they hoard it in vaults and treasure rooms like Smaug the dragon. They sit there, letting the coins and jewels slide through their fingers while they laugh at the little people who don't have enough to eat. That metaphor does sound ridiculous, doesn't it? It does, and those who want you to believe it use media-friendly language, but what I describe here is exactly the lie they want you to believe.

That also does not mean that when the rich make more money, it takes money away from the poor and middle class. Every dollar in a (well-run) society was created by an entrepreneur who came up with an idea to solve other people's problems and the more the business grows, the more money the Federal Reserve prints to keep up with the growing economy. (at least that's how it works efficiently — until completely irrational government officials, who have never built serious businesses and do not understand business principles start printing more money that the economy demands, dilutes the value of the currency and severely damages the system). Just listen carefully and objectively to what they say; you'll catch on.

So, what do rich people do with wealth? They buy big houses, fancy cars, stocks and bonds, and a whole lot of other stuff. Now, think about this very carefully. Who builds the houses, cleans the houses, maintains the houses? Mostly the middle class. Who builds cars, sells cars, and maintains cars? Mostly the middle class. Who goes to work for the companies that investor's fund? Mostly the middle class. Who goes to the theater, the opera, the symphony, parks, zoos, museums and other places funded by the donations and taxes of rich? The rich, the poor, the middle class and their families.

Here's another point you shouldn't miss: If they (the poor and middle class) were rich, they (the poor and middle class) would be doing exactly the same thing that currently rich people are doing. Just ask them, "What would you do if you were rich?" By the way, what would you do, if you were rich?

"Conventional wisdom" has so commercialized our society by urging instant gratification of unbridled passions, society is quickly corrupting our population. Those producing poor to mediocre results are quick to point fingers at those who produce extraordinary and miraculous results as the source of their problems. Unfortunately, they are entirely oblivious to the fact that they have created their own reality. Even those who produce extraordinary and miraculous results are not immune to this addiction of self-indulgence. The stories of those who "fall from grace" are too numerous to ignore. If you truly want to create miraculous circumstances, you have to remember that you are always in advance or decay, you never stand still.

Wealth and Politics

Again, Mark Twain was right when he so brilliantly observed that "It is easier to fool people than to convince them that they have been fooled." Adolf Hitler, for example, understood that fact as few men ever did and took advantage of it as few men ever did. As I talked about in Part 1 Chapter 1, we can be so blinded and confined by our unchecked egos that we will allow ourselves to be led into insane acts rather than admit that we've "had the wool pulled over our eyes" by some unscrupulous person or group. In Hitler's case, despite the fact that he had no morale foundation or positive character he convinced tens of millions of people to follow and support him in one of the most devastating and despicable catastrophes in history.

In modern politics, in the Unites States and every other country, citizens must awake and grasp a few of these great hidden wisdoms. If they combine common sense with intelligent observation, they will quickly see through the propaganda and realize that they've been fooled. It will become so blatantly obvious that our current leaders (who are not really leaders by definition) are leading us down that proverbial "primrose path". It's the same path that Adolf Hitler, Joseph Stalin, Ho Chi Minh and so many others have led their people down. The citizens of those countries were every bit as smart as our citizens are today. But because they were blinded by clever lies and evil propaganda, they did the exact same things that our citizens are doing today. Don't wait too long to recognize what is inevitably at the end of the road they are leading you down.

Understand, I am **not** saying that every modern political leader is as evil and ill-intentioned as those past tyrants. I am saying that most are trying to take us in exactly the same direction — more power for them, less freedom for us. I also remind you that the more government has control over aspects of our private and business lives, the more the government attracts people who will deliberately misuse and abuse that power and the more difficult it becomes to take back that control for ourselves.

This leaves us with a question: Are our leaders doing this because they are naive or because they have the same deceitful agenda? In the final analysis, it doesn't matter because, sooner or later, the results will be essentially the same — unless you and I change it. So we must act while we still have a voice, to elect people who pledge to repeal these unconstitutional laws and then hold them accountable to that pledge. At the same time, resolve to discover how you can keep power over yourself and build a legacy for yourself and your loved ones. This book will help you in that journey and I look forward to personally meeting you and showing you exactly how to take whatever you want to the next level. Keep in mind, in our society, those who have the gold, make the rules. So get the education you lack and go out and get some of that gold for yourself and help to bring back the rules that made our country a world power. In the process, do everything you can to help everyone you know understand the truth.

Wealth and the Camel

Jesus said, "It is easier for a camel to go through the eye of a needle, than for a rich man to enter into the kingdom of God" (Mark 10:25, KJV). We are seeing proof of this statement every day, as we see the truth of "the love of money" (that is, selfishness) is behind evil. Do you remember the media uproar over Daraprim? That's an aids drug manufactured by Turing Pharmaceuticals. When Martin Shkreli took over the company in August 2015, he jacked the drug's price from $13.50 per tablet to $750, a 5,000-percent increase. Shkreli was arrested that December on charges of securities fraud — he'd been (allegedly) cutting corners, with other people's money! There were a lot of people who were very surprised at this news and, based on his past actions, a few who were not. Greed, selfishness and dishonesty know no boundary's from one area of life to another.

Let's again be very clear however that "riches" will not keep you out of heaven. If fact, in many cases, a lack of it could keep you out if you fall into the trap of blaming others for your struggles and/or bury your own talents and don't create enough of your own.

1+1=2 Only If You Want A *Settle-For* Life.

Many people (including lots of economists) have a hard time understanding this principle, because their foundation is built on this erroneous idea that 1+1=2. Why do I say that? One of the "jobs" of an economist is to count our known reserves of "scarce resources" and then try to allocate those resources most effectively. Parents, teachers, and so-called leaders of all kinds fall into the same trap. Truly wise people, on the other, hand have never believed that because they know, as Paul Zane Pilzer so brilliantly and unquestioningly illustrates in his book *Unlimited Wealth*, there is always an endless supply of resources. All resources were invented in the human mind as well as the technology we can improve to use them more effectively.

I remember vividly as a youth, I must have been in the fourth or fifth grade. I was in the barnyard looking out at the cows in one of our pastures. I started thinking to myself, "One plus one does not equal two. What a dumb idea. If that were the case, our farm wouldn't work." If you put the right cow and the right bull together, that equals three (maybe four), not two. Then, if you add another cow and another bull and manage them properly (with correct principles), in a few years that will equal a nice small heard. As the years went by, that memory returned many times as I recognized that same principle everywhere I looked. Take two kernels of corn, plant them and take care of them and that can equal several hundred kernels

(I got in trouble trying to explain that to a couple of my school teachers and learned, first, not to share my ideas and, second, that teachers aren't as smart as they want us to think they are, but it never changed reality. Unfortunately, it took me a long time to out-grow that resentment and also to grow out of holding my tongue).

One of our jobs when we were young was picking up rocks and removing them from the fields because they interfered with watering and were very bad for the machinery. Sometimes, my siblings and I would have races to see who could find and throw 50 or 100 rocks out of the field first.

One day I looked at one of the piles of rocks we'd created on the other side of a fence. It struck me, "Wow, that is not just a pile of rocks." Instead of being a problem, we used them for good, to regulate the water for irrigating. Some people use those rocks to build fences which keeps their livestock safe and secure. In olden days, even today, people used them in all kinds of ways, for hunting to keep their families fed, to protect themselves from dangerous animals or bullies, prepare meals and for all kinds of tools. What is the result of any of that? Those are exponential results, nothing to do with "1+1=2". I remember visiting my grandmother whose home was built of cobble stones, just like many of those stones we removed from the fields. Take a truck load of these stones and build a home. All of a sudden, you can provide shelter and convenience for your family and even for generations to come — a place to protect you with warmth in the winter and shade in the summer, a place to prepare meals, provide comfort, security, learning, nurturing and all those things. The returns and rewards from these stones, when we use them wisely, are impossible to calculate. For many, they have meant the difference between life and death. How do you measure that in "1+1=2"?

Scarce Resources

I was going to go into a little more detail about this, but decided to just give you a brief explanation and refer you to Paul Zane Pilzer's book, *Unlimited Wealth* (the most powerful thing I have ever read/studied on the subject). Professor Pilzer is infinitely more qualified than I am on this subject; he's a world-class economist and a front-runner for some of the most dramatically, mind-shifting discoveries about Real Economics.

The German philosopher, Arthur Schopenhauer, observed that "All truth passes through three stages. First, it is ridiculed. Second, it is violently opposed. Third it is accepted as being self-evident." Professor Pilzer's *Unlimited Wealth* went through that process, flying in the face of the "conventional wisdom" of mainstream economics, until Sam Walton, then the richest man in the world, read it, praised it and helped promote it. Today, years after its publication, many economists still have a hard time with the principles spelled out in *Unlimited Wealth* but, among business people it is "self-evident."

Most economics books put forward the idea that resources are scarce and society is responsible to allocate those resources. Dr. Pilzer demonstrates through dozens of irrefutable historical examples that there are no scarce resources because all resources are an invention of the human mind and increasing technology enables us to utilize those resources more wisely. If a particular resource gets dangerously low, that emergency muscle called human creativity and ingenuity simply finds another, typically even better resource. I highly recommend all of Dr. Pilzer's books and trainings.

On a personal level, *Unlimited Wealth* was the finest education I ever received about economics and enabled me to evolve my understanding and results of economics in miraculous ways. His personal story is also one of brilliance and miracles. His books *God Wants You to be Rich* and *The Wellness Revolution* have also had huge impacts on my understanding of principles. If you study them, you will be glad you did. After extensive study, I also recommend Robert G. Allen, Robert Kiyosaki, Dave Ramsey, Loral Langemeier, Steven L. Down and Brian Tracy. If you want financial independence or even financial freedom, you can have it as long as you study the right people and apply the right principles.

One More Quick Note

From the day I was married, I completely turned responsibility to keep track of my finances over to my wife. I hardly ever payed attention to them. When I started my first business, I continued to let her take care of all the finances and she did a good job of keeping track of them. A problem developed: Not only did I not understand the finances but I never knew exactly where I was financially. Several years later, I found myself in so much trouble in every area of my life. One of my first mentors told me very emphatically that I am responsible for the finances and I need to know, at any given moment, exactly where I am financially.

It was okay to delegate but it was also 100-percent my personal responsibility to understand exactly where we are and how things are going. It was amazing to me within only a few months at how things started turning around. It was nothing to do with my wife, it was all about how I looked at everything else in the business, based on a much clearer perspective of what were intelligent versus foolish decisions on my part.

From that experience, it began to dawn on me that if I didn't understand something that effected the results in my life, business, etc. I obviously couldn't make sure it functioned well. I started learning as much as I could about everything that had bearing on my business, my family, my health, relationships, etc. The more I discovered, the more I realized that everything really does affect everything else and that even beginning to understand one principle, increases the success of everything else.

Along those same lines, especially since studying Paul Pilzer's and other brilliant mentor's advice, is our society's idea of retirement. By in large our whole "conventional" system of retirement, is based on someone else being in charge of your retirement portfolio. I'll repeat, if you don't understand it in clear detail, and take personal accountability for it, don't feel cheated or taken advantage of or like a victim if you lose it. Don't ever let any other person try to convince you should let them take better care of your finances. If you do not completely understand and at least have a very significant hand in controlling it, just know that you are not in control and either get in control or be OK with losing it.

Your own business venture, understood and controlled by you will always give you the best possible advantage for your own security and peace of mind.

Conclusion

The Wealth of Nations, published by Adam Smith in 1776, is considered the first work on modern economics. Smith set down the rules that still govern real economics, including:

> It is not from the benevolence of the butcher, the brewer, or the baker that we expect our dinner, but from their regard to their own self-interest. We address ourselves, not to their humanity but to their self-love, and never talk to them of our own necessities but of their advantages.

Why do people start businesses? First and foremost, it's to make money. You can't accomplish any other goals until you provide for your family the basic needs of food, clothing, and shelter. Their success is integral to your success because you consume what they produce and visa-versa. To do anything else is living on the edge, as Ludwig von Mises wrote:

> A man who chooses between drinking a glass of milk and a glass of … potassium cyanide [solution] does not choose between two beverages; he chooses between life and death. A society that chooses between capitalism and socialism does not choose between two social systems. It chooses between social cooperation and the disintegration of society. Socialism is not an alternative to capitalism; it is an alternative to any system under which men can live as human beings.

Jefferson's Declaration said, "life, liberty and the pursuit of happiness." In the 18th Century, happiness meant property because property meant freedom. It was the ability to provide for and protect one's family. It was social standing and community respect. It was education for the children and security for old age. It was the means to contribute to the community.

In the final analysis, as George F. Will put it, "Capital is mobile: It goes where it is wanted. It stays where it is well-treated." It is a powerful tool in creating circumstances that move one closer to perfection and a measure of how successfully one is observing principles that harness and organize the universal laws to everyone's benefit.

Stay responsible for your financial security and independence. No one cares about it as much as you. It is wise to have the most brilliant mentors available, but you stay responsible and you will do better. It may even save you from losing everything.

Summary

The laws of the harvest are universal. They will never change. You get out of life what you put in. If you are consistently honest, you will be successful at honesty. If you are consistently charitable, you will be successful at charity. If you work diligently and wisely, you will be successful at your work. And like Zig Ziglar so eloquently stated, "You can get anything in life you want, if you just help enough other people get what they want." In a money context, as long as you understand and apply correct principles of money, including honesty and ethics, you will create a foundation and infra-structure within which it is impossible for you not to become wealthy.

Money is a form of *valuta*, something of worth used as an exchange. Precious metals, salt, paper, stocks, bonds, and many other things have been used as currency, even sea shells. Money is a convenience, it makes exchanging goods and services simpler. It is neither good nor bad of itself, but the love of anything to unhealthy degrees, meaning ego and selfishness, is, ultimately, fatal to your progress in life. Also like Zig Ziglar observed, "You can't have too much money, unless the money gets you."

Jesus gave us the key, "Seek ye first the Kingdom of God, and his righteousness, and all else will be added unto you." What does that mean? It means if you understand and apply correct principles, you will naturally and inadvertently create unlimited wealth for yourself in all the SPESIFCs of your life. That is a universal law.

Capitalism is the best of all economic systems because it is based on the laws of the harvest. It respects individual rights and demands individual responsibility. American capitalism has produced more wealth for more people than any other society in recorded history, not only among the rich, but all the people who produce the things that we buy.

Financial success comes from two basic concepts — freedom and responsibility. Freedom is reduced by regulation and other forms of government control. They waste resources that could be used to move a business forward. Regulations also demonstrate a one-size-fits-all attitude that has never posted a positive effect on any venture. Responsibility in financial matters is just like any other aspect of life. Discover well-researched, intelligent shortcuts and you'll increase the return on your investments. Cut corners and you may end up in jail. But more importantly you are guaranteed, sooner or later, to only cut yourself, your unique potential and resources short and wind up lonely, sad, broken and die because you have nothing left to invest for another day.

Two Ways To Approach Life

Consumer Mentality	Investor Mentality
Default	**Deliberate**
Face Value	Core Value

• What - - - - - - - -	• Why
• Doctrine - - - - - - -	• Principles
• Linear - - - - - - - -	• Quantum leaps
• Line upon Line - - - -	• Precept upon precept
• Duplicator - - - - - -	• Creator
• Trading time for dollars -	• Passive/leveraged income
• Information based living -	• Transformational based living
• Instant gratification - - -	• Long range gratification
• Focus on the past - - - -	• Focus on the future
• Tastes good - - - - - -	• Healthy
• Hearing - - - - - - - -	• Listening
• Knowledge - - - - - -	• Wisdom
• History - - - - - - - -	• My Future
• Inflexible - - - - - - -	• Flexible
• Answers - - - - - - -	• Questions
• Right vs. wrong - - - -	• It depends
• Left brain - - - - - - -	• Right brain
• Dying - - - - - - - -	• Living
• Letter of the law - - - -	• Spirit of the law

Chapter 15
The Exponential Returns Principle

At face value, this fifteenth secret ancient principle seems counter-intuitive and so is mostly misunderstood. Most of those who actually practice it, however, have seen miracles as a result. There are a very tiny few with a little deeper perspective and insight who not only practice it but have caught the real vision, live it and consistently receive such rewards that "abundant" scarcely describes it.

For those of us, myself included, who slept through high school math classes, there are three types of progressions.

- **Arithmetic**, meaning things grow by addition: This year I have a return of 4 units, for example; next year, I have a return of 4+4 or 8 and the year after, 4+4+4 or 12.

- Not bad, but suppose our return is **geometric**, meaning growth by multiplication: The first year's return is 4, the second year is 4*4 or 16 and the third is 4*4*4 or 64 — much better than 12!

- But wait, there is still the **exponential** progression, meaning growth by squares, cubes and beyond. The first year is still 4, the second is 4^4 (4*4*4*4 = 256), and the third is 4^4^4 (imaging 4*4 repeated 16 times, or just short of 4.3 billion!) Impossible, you say! No, I reply, just miraculous and that after all, is what is possible here.

Tithes and Offerings

How it Works

"Tything" is an Old English term, from the Scandinavian words for "ten" and "assembly". It meant a group of ten men or ten households, the smallest division in English politics and law. One among the ten was assigned or chosen as the "tithing man", who functioned as a constable. Over time, it grew to mean a tenth of anything and the translators of King James' Bible used it to describe offerings made to prophets or priests in support of God's kingdom on Earth. It's most famous usage is, "Bring ye all the tithes into the storehouse, that there may be meat in mine house, and prove me now herewith, saith the LORD of hosts, if I will not open you the windows of heaven, and pour you out a blessing, that there shall not be room enough to receive it," Malachi 3:10, KJV).

Many people of many faiths practice some form of tithing today, with definitions ranging from a very specific one tenth of one's income to a very general offering of any size. Many of them feel they have experienced miracles from practicing this law. Some report financial miracles like unexpected money arriving in the nick of time to pay their bills or to deal with an emergency. Others simply report a general spiritual awakening, comfort, or strengthening of their faith. Among the stories about people who have diligently participated in tithing and received miraculous help, I've noticed that a huge majority of those people believe that tithing is so simple and basic that it is one of those areas in life that you can live perfectly. Just pay 10 percent of your increase and you're done. What could be simpler?

I started to get to know others who have done things like start major businesses, launch and grow worthy nonprofits, foundations, etc.. They have told me that paying tithing enabled so many miracles that it has made their causes thrive and they made and/or raised millions of dollars — even tens and hundreds of millions. Could the rest of us be missing something? Is tithing part of the cure to what ails many who are failing in their lives to achieve the miracles they could achieve? Perhaps the kind of miracles that are so great that "there shall not be room enough to receive it."?

Those who live this concept expecting a return on their investment are not considering that tithing is primarily a spiritual investment rather than a monetary one. Just as "faith without works is dead" (James 2:17, KJV), so acts of faith without spiritual understanding have significantly reduced results.

In other words, at its very core, tithing is a part of the twin concepts of service and charity. James' comments on faith follow from a larger, greater statement, "Pure religion and undefiled before God and the Father is this, to visit the fatherless and widows in their affliction, and to keep himself unspotted from the world" (James 1:27, KJV).

The purpose of tithes and offerings is, primarily, to take care of Gods' children. In its fullness, tithing is a way for the faithful to remind themselves that they owe everything to God, that sacrifice is necessary to growth and charity is necessary to exponential growth. For those not religiously inclined, it can be an acknowledgement that we do not succeed alone, we are part of a community, and we have community members that need and deserve our help. Once again, we live in a world of hand-outs; we would rather "mask" a symptom for someone rather than teach them to fix their own problems. The modern welfare system is "conventional wisdom" in its perfect idiocy. In the beginning, the welfare system was put into place for women and children who had lost their spouses in war or some other disaster. The system would provide a hand-up — support for the family while the widow learned skills needed to fend for herself and her children.

Over the years, that system decayed into today's void where men and women who can work just sit at home collecting a check and teaching their children to take the easy road, creating generational welfare recipients. What happened to allow this to take place? Simple, the American public elected politicians who figured out that they could give hand-outs in the form of "free" ("other people's") money then threaten the recipients — "If you elect my opponent, your benefits will be cut off" — and almost guarantee their re-election. Just look at the difficulty statesmen face when attempting "welfare reform". It always polls well among those paying for it but not among those receiving it—and not even among those who don't understand the difference between hand-outs and hand-ups.

Today, that same cancer is spreading into the hearts and minds of those who do not understand the intrinsic value of money, business or even personal value and thus feel entitled to more wages than they've earned, demand more respect from others than they have cultivated, desire to win or get something for free or at least for less than its value, and so on.

For many years, people considered tithing a strictly religious concept. They evaluated it based on the good it does for "the church" (whatever church they choose) but it used to go so much further than that. In earlier times, tithing meant giving 10 percent of your earnings *and* 10 percent of your time. It was seen as an investment in your future in heaven, but also as an investment in the earthly community. Today, that 10 percent of your time could mean a huge difference in the future of our society. Part of this tithe of action is ideally sharing your talents and abilities through *mentoring* which brings far deeper understanding of that 10 percent and creates exponential returns.

Imagine that you set a goal to mentor four new employees at your business over the course of five years. Part of the mentoring includes their setting the same goal. Imagine, over the next half decade, that those four each mentor four — plus a new four mentored by you — we now have a second generation of 20 mentored workers. Over the next half decade, these 25 each mentor a new quartet. The group now totals 125. Now, imagine that it wasn't just one person doing the initial mentoring but ten. The numbers get very big, very fast. Big enough to change the world? Why not?

By the way, do you think your mentoring will go unnoticed? Not likely; it will probably mean you get promotions, with increases in pay, perks and other rewards. It could mean significant publicity for your business which would bring new respect, admiration, and a flock of new customers. Remember the butcher and baker from Chapter 14? You aren't doing this solely for other people's benefit.

Almost every super successful business person I have ever studied understands well that when you give, you receive more in return. It is a law of the universe. From Moses, Abraham, King David, King Solomon, Joseph (in Egypt), Buddha, Jesus, Aristotle, America's Founding Fathers, Andrew Carnegie, John D. Rockefeller, Helen Keller, Jay Paul Getty, Ronald Reagan, Sam Walton, Jon Huntsman Sr., Bill Gates, just to name a very tiny few, they all understood that the more you give, the more you receive. It doesn't happen in ways easy to measure, but a study of their lives has proven over and over again that the character based in charity pays dividends. When you give with a good heart (that means giving hand-ups), the universe gives back more, to the point that it is impossible to not reap the rewards.

I add that the bigger your thoughts, goals, expectations and wise actions, the bigger your return on investment.

Why it Works

Remember, also, *spiritual egoism* from Chapter 10, "If you will elevate others, the very work itself will exalt you." This principle has nothing to do with your belief in a return on investment. In fact, if you give with the intent to receive, you're cutting corners. Greedy people can't reap the benefits of these laws. I don't want to sermonize, but there is no better explanation of this than Jesus' parable of the unrighteous almsgiver:

> Take heed that ye do not your alms before men, to be seen of them: otherwise ye have no reward of your Father which is in heaven. Therefore when thou doest thine alms, do not sound a trumpet before thee, as the hypocrites do in the synagogues and in the streets, that they may have glory of men. Verily I say unto you, They have their reward. But when thou doest alms, let not thy left hand know what thy right hand doeth (Matthew 6:1-2, KJV).

Your intent and character in giving, regardless of what or how much you give — money, time, compassion, service — do it with genuine love for others and a legitimate desire to enable others to live better and you will see the magic.

If you don't need miracles to accomplish your goals, you won't get any. If you need only small miracles, you will reap small ones. But if you diligently plan and execute goals and objectives that require massive miracles, as long as your goals and plans are in harmony with universal law and principles and your character is worthy, you will receive massive miracles. Your returns are also relative to the amount of faith which is required for the size and scope of your plans.

Unfortunately, the majority who are giving by nature, never plant and cultivate big enough plans so their returns are only enough to cover their small intents and expectations. It works the same in every SPESIFC areas of your life. Your returns are equal to the quantity and quality of miracles that your goals, plans, strategies, intentions, expectations, character and exercise of faith demand. Part of this higher extension of cause and effect is based on how much of your potential you are activating.

On the other hand, when people give grudgingly, it only depletes their SPESIFC accounts. That is Real Economics as opposed to the illusion of economics taught in most formal education today.

Likewise, take time to help another in their spirituality and yours grows exponentially, get involved to help others with their physical health and yours will increase more. Help others improve their emotional health and yours will be multiplied, it works the same socially and intellectually. Give of your own time, your intelligence, skills, character, insights and help others understand principles of time and events planning and you will become its master. But you must give that help with integrity and dignity and from your heart.

I haven't made a habit in this book of simply sharing many quotes to make a point. In this principle however, it seems appropriate because these words speak loudly and clearly to me about the abundance that can be achieved when putting this principle into play:

> He who possesses virtue in abundance may be compared to an infant (Lao Tzu, legendary founder of Taoism).

> You pray in your distress and in your need; would that you might also pray in the fullness of your joy and in your days of abundance. (Kahlil Gibran, poet)

> Your most precious, valued possessions and your greatest powers are invisible and intangible. No one can take them. You, and you alone, can give them. You will receive abundance for your giving (W. Clement Stone, business executive and philanthropist).

> Abundance is not something we acquire. It is something we tune into (Wayne Dyer, counselor).

> People with a scarcity mentality tend to see everything in terms of win-lose. There is only so much; and if someone else has it, that means there will be less for me. The more principle-centered we become, the more we develop an abundance mentality, the more we are genuinely happy for the successes, well-being, achievements, recognition, and good fortune of other people. We believe their success adds to … rather than detracts from … our lives (Stephen R. Covey, management consultant).

> Life is a field of unlimited possibilities (Deepak Chopra, alternative medicine advocate).

> Abundance doesn't follow giving until giving becomes its own reward (Jan Denise, relationship consultant).

What do all of these quotes have in common? The principle of exponential returns. We have to see our tithing, or giving of ourselves, as an opportunity to provide a hand-up to not only others but also to ourselves. We have to give of ourselves on a universal level so that we are then allowed to also drink from the same well.

Conclusion

This principle is simple: Give of yourself; invest in your future in a very hands-on, human way — it will be returned to you, making you the recipient of miraculous results. The key, however, is to be deliberate in your tithing of money, time and other resources. Every part of life that is not intentionally and deliberately designed to improve will inadvertently decay by default. All default results end up in chaos. We have to tithe by design in order to see results. We have to actively seek out those situations where we can contribute to the hand-up concept. If we don't, there is simply no return on the investment.

One key element in this principle is the expectation of abundance. How many times in our lives have we seen someone give of themselves only to watch them then lowering their expectations for their own lives. While this can easily be misunderstood as humble, it is nothing of the sort but is self-defeating. This principle demands that we tithe while expecting the returns in order to be in tune with our first, best destiny. Too often we live "lives of quiet desperation" (Henry D. Thoreau) doing what we deem is right while not expecting things to go our way. With this principle, we come to understand that we can expect exponential returns but only because that's the way it all works and that's the way it has worked for all of time.

One other thought, if I may: As you have probably often heard, "Go big or go home!" The bigger your thoughts, goals and expectations, the bigger your return on investment. That said, *you* get to determine how "big" is "big" enough for you. I know a lot of people who want to own a small business or run a family farm/ranch or some other modest but perfectly reasonable dream. Not everyone wants to be millionaires or captains of industry. The trick is to follow *your* dreams, make *your* miracles, build *your* paradise, whatever that is for you today. Who knows what you will decide for tomorrow.

Summary

Every effort we make is an investment. Returns on that investment in the world, in life, in business, in relationships, and so on, can be arithmetic (poor), geometric (mediocre to extraordinary), or exponential (miraculous), according to your intentions, goals, plans, character and exercising faith. It is understanding your potential and pushing its limits and following with a passion your best destiny.

The divine law of tithing is the best example of exponential returns on investments. It isn't just a matter of giving money to worthy causes, it is also the giving of yourself to assist your fellow humans in progressing their lives through a hand-up, mentoring, and other ways. This spiritual egoism propels you toward perfection as you assist others to grow in that direction.

Follow *your* dreams, make *your* miracles, build *your* paradise.

Chapter 16
The Temple Principle

Although there is a growing awareness, most people take this sixteenth secret, ancient principle for granted until they develop spiritual, physical or emotional problems. Everyone obviously wants to feel that sense of wellness and many people actually work hard to develop that. But like the preverbal chain, most typically only focus on those links of wellness that are publicized and marketed to us, while most of the other links are neglected. Luckily, as you take a better look at the big picture of optimal wellness, you will begin to discover principles that will naturally become part of how you live and keep you happier and freer.

In Part 1, we talked about the SPESIFC's of life and addressed some very basic ideas about physical health. There are probably more books, articles and programs written and taught on physical health than any other one thing on earth today. Unfortunately, the majority of them are not actually that helpful and many even harmful to your long-term health.

It is easy to see from the outside that many people are unhealthy. Some suggest that as many as two out of three people in the United States are living with health problems at any given moment. Unfortunately, even the majority who look healthy from the outside are not actually as healthy as they appear. Most people today are dehydrated, malnourished, and have cellular decay that just hasn't become physically visible yet. Isn't it interesting that we take so much time and expense to look good on the outside but are willing to significantly cut-corners about staying healthy inside?

Not to mention that there is far more to physical health than meets the eye, like spiritual, emotional, social, intellectual, financial, and chronological heath that all directly affect your physical health.

What is a Temple?

Let's take a small detour: Temples — meaning places set apart for deity — are a near-universal concept. They existed among the Mesopotamians, Egyptians, Greeks, Romans, throughout Asia, Africa, Central and South America, etc. They exist today among the Hindus, Buddhists, Jains, Zoroastrians, Sikhs, and some Christian denominations. Even some non-religious organizations — most famously the Masons — have buildings they call temples.

It is common for people to make significant (even major) sacrifices of time, resources, and money to build, maintain, and participate in these temples. Many times, even after such sacrifices have been made, they have seen their temples desecrated or destroyed by their enemies.

So, here's a question. Was that just poor judgement on the part of their leaders? It can seem so, but only from a naïve perspective. If you look beneath the surface, there is a much deeper question we must address before that one can be answered: Why are temples built? Even if you are currently an active participant in temples, I believe you will be pleasantly surprised at what you discover in this chapter. But that will take some round-about explanation, so stay tuned.

Temples are specifically designed and created, in literal definition, as a "place of worship," specific to a deity or deities. What does "worship" mean? "Honor shown to an object" which has been etymologized as "worthiness or worth-ship" — to give value to something.

Why Are They Built?

Classically, temples exist to pay tribute to, communicate with, obtain guidance and learning from, and to gain favoritism with that deity or deities. The temple worshippers commit themselves to cultivate a higher character, seek inspiration, and discover hidden wisdoms. In short, they act to bring themselves closer to perfection by improving their personal lives and their communities.

How do we do that? Ultimately, regardless of what you call "worth," the value of a temple is the value you add to yourself through a deliberate process of self-evolution. Look back through history and you'll find the entire point of temples is to increase our own value and help others do the same. In fact, if you look at the big picture, that evolution has always been and always will be the fundamental programing of human beings. Unfortunately, the vast majority override that core programming and settle for something less. They *cut corners* instead of finding *shortcuts*; they see the world *at face value* instead of *as it truly is*; they reach for *their* optimum performance (as they define it) instead of *the* optimum performance (meaning the greatness they never recognize within themselves).

In writing this book (and this chapter specifically), I intend to show you, at least, a little more than you have seen before and perhaps provide a track for you to follow to develop more of that programing. I hope to enable you to bring more meaning and purpose and incentive and motivation and results, bringing you the peace of mind and happiness that you have wished for all your life.

So how do we create that kind of worth (or worth-iness)? It can only come to you from yourself. Paradoxically, like we talked about in Chapter 9, everything that will ever come to you in your life is because of other people. The only thing you completely have control over in your life is the people that you choose to associate with. Whether that is in-person or through some kind of media. But only *you* can make something out of yourself — or chose not to by what you learn from them.

If God created the world and sent us here, He obviously knows why and how we can make the most of our earthly experience. Seems as though a temple would be a very good place to discover more about that, don't you think? Especially since they were constructed with that very purpose in mind.

But what about those temples? If they are so important, why have we heard of and seen so many destroyed? There are two sides to that question;

1. As Jim Rohn said, "All good will be attacked." If you don't believe that, just don't tend your garden for a season and see the results of your harvest.
2. Individuals are obviously more important and valuable than the building. So, saving yourself is far more important than saving the building.

I repeat: Consider what these people do in their temples: They seek inspiration; they discover "hidden wisdoms" by participating in sacred rituals; they commit themselves to cultivate a higher character — in short, they act to bring themselves closer to perfection by improving their personal lives and their communities.

Therefore, the answer to the question: Those temples were never built in and of themselves to be special places, the buildings are, simply, a metaphor for you. Everything about *that temple* is only to teach you about *your temple*, the one in which your divine self resides. It isn't about those buildings, or those places. It is all about you. Many of those temples are indeed "holy places" and even "Houses of God." However, none of them, in and of themselves have any intrinsic value. The ideals and values and education you can gain through those temples is worth giving your life for. I don't mean dying for, I mean living for, because of what you can become if you honor what you take from them. Those temples are *all* expendable and replaceable. In fact, they will be replaced, and I don't just mean with a different building.

Are we paying attention to what can be learned in and from temples? Take a look at the results our society is creating today: Are we growing closer together or splitting further apart? Getting wealthier or poorer? Are more or fewer people on welfare? Are they working jobs they love or settling for what they believe they can find, building stronger family relationships or breaking up more often? Increasing or decreasing in physical health? Are teenagers growing up more or less secure in themselves? Are neighbors spending more time on the front porch or in the backyard? Don't fool yourself, the strength and health of a community or a nation is only a reflection of the strength and health of its citizens.

The Dove-tailed Being

Jesus gave us the real key when He said, "Know ye not that ye are the temple of God, and that the Spirit of God dwelleth in you"? If any man defile the temple of God, him shall God destroy; for the temple of God is holy, which temple ye are" (1st Corinthians 3:16-17, KJV).

There are two fundamental parts to this temple of yours, the physical and the spiritual. They are, as we say in carpentry, dovetailed perfectly together. To neglect the health of either is Paul's definition of "defile" because you can't neglect just one, anything you do to your body affects your spirit and vice versa. So that I keep this book shorter than an encyclopedia, I will just touch on some highlights and two personal stories as examples.

Physical Health

In Part One we talked about the seven core areas of physical that if you pay attention to will put you NEAREST to perfection.

1. Nutrition
2. Exercise
3. Activities
4. Rest
5. Environment
6. Solidarity
7. Thinking

There is a lot of talk that some diseases are caused by your genes and DNA, but that is not true. Your natural make up is simply the field on which you have to plant, cultivate, and harvest. What you chose to do on that field is completely up to you and will determine the quality and quantity of harvest you reap, the good and the bad. That's why it is actually as important to see the right kind of doctor when you are in good health as it is when you are in poor health. One who can and will help you measure and quantify your unique make up and then decide how to make the most of it.

N

Nutrition. It is true that "you are what you eat." Your body as you know, is not simply "a body", meaning a single unit. It is, actually, a republic of cells, there are many complicated calculations but arguably about 100 trillion cells in the average human. The only thing your cells have to eat is what you eat, so they can only be as healthy as what you feed them and how well you assure that they have access to what you feed them.

Wendell Berry hit the nail squarely when he explained one of the dire problems with our society, "There is no connection between food and health. People are fed by the food industry which pays no attention to health, and treated by the health industry that pays no attention to food."

Fortunately, there is a fast-growing awareness that we need to eat better and the public is demanding more health-conscious food choices. It's also fortunate that some companies are listening and responding, but there is still a massive pandemic of poor diet, unwillingness to provide or to get the right education. Marketers everywhere are trying to sell you things that are not healthy — mostly by way of very *slick* (dishonest) advertising.

Just be aware that most food companies are not your friend. In fact, many of the foods today have been intentionally modified and specifically created, not to provide you proper nutrition but the extreme opposite, to addict you to them so they create life-time, loyal customers. Others intentionally poison foods with pesticides to kill bugs and weeds but then try to convince us that they are perfectly safe. Also, if the FDA and other government agencies that oversee our agriculture were really trustworthy, we wouldn't have the health problems we have today.

Make sure you become a label reader. Many experts have suggested that, if you can't pronounce it, don't eat it. Eat mostly single ingredient foods, the least amount of prepared and packaged foods as possible. Avoid GMOs (genetically modified organisms) or GE (genetically engineered) foods and eat as much organic as possible, even better, grow your own. Staying hydrated is crucial to long-term health. Avoid fad diets and diet food — if you want to lose weight, make sure you follow a plan that takes account of your holistic health and is something you will enjoy for the rest of your life. Everything that is not reasonably sustainable as a life-style, will disappoint you.

Check out *The Truth About Cancer, A Global Quest* by Ty Bollinger. It is the most extensive researched documentary I have ever studied, not only about cancer but also about how to eat right, live healthy and be at a minimal risk to develop cancer and virtually all other so-called diseases of aging. There are many other amazing people I recommend. Steven K. Scott and his cutting-edge nutritional company Max International, Paul Zane Pilzer's book *The Wellness Revolution*, Dr. Ron Rosedale's *The Rosedale Diet*, to name just a few.

E

Exercise. Find the right program for you, your unique body and your specific (pun intended) needs. Sometimes you need a personal trainer. Again, personal trainers are a dime a dozen but good ones are hard to find so don't settle for just anyone. Make sure what you do is something you love, that will also make it sustainable. Otherwise, like diet, if it is not self-motivating, you will not be able to keep it up long-term and it will do you no good — even waste your time in the short and long-term. A real exercise plan includes strength and endurance training, flexibility training and more — skimping on any area means skimping on the whole plan.

Also keep in mind that for 6000 years fitness companies, exercise machines and work-out routines were not needed when we were farmers, ranchers and hunter/gatherers. Why, because we stayed physically fit from practical and normal activities in our every day lives. Granted most people's life-styles have changed but that doesn't have to keep you from taking the same time you may set aside for exercise to do something productive that serves you in multiple ways.

Plenty of things ought to be done (for yourself and/or service for someone else — like plant a community garden or other a project like the old time barn raising tradition idea) things where you can get together with neighbors and friends to have fun, be productive where you can work up a sweat and keep your heart rate up for a while, keep you limber and serve your whole body, mind and spirit, etc. That way you can serve more than one purpose at a time other than just keeping you fit. Lots of practical activities could give you the practical exercise you need to keep your body and brain in good condition. I know, lots of people will say "that's not practical, but you could make it practical. What is your health and your life worth? Is what you are doing working miracles for you? So change what isn't to what will. Take your next best guess.

A

Activities. Chose extra-curricular activities (hiking, camping, dancing, swimming or a combination, whatever) that fit your personality. Choose what you love to do with family and friends. If you sit at a computer or have any other kind of minimal activity work for example, chose things that get you up and keep you active on a consistent basis. Also, things that are in your passion are the best as long as they are not overly risky. It's immensely helpful to have a friend or two so you can hold each other accountable.

Besides, it will get you out of trivial activities like watching too much television or wasting time on the computer — more physically passive activity that only adds to your already activity lacking life-style. You will be amazed at how much fuller and more exciting your life becomes when you are sharing it, in real-time with others you care about. You will not only be saving and adding more abundance and beauty to your own life, but saving the lives of others that you claim to also love.

R

Rest. See Part 2 Chapter 2: The Omega and Alpha Principle — Recreation.

E

Environment. Remember what Jim Rohn said, "You can move, you're not a tree." Find that ideal place for you and make a heaven out of it. That includes making your environment as clean, non-toxic, and stress-free as possible. Make your home a sanctuary from the busy, noisy, toxic world and as free from fear and stress as possible by choosing a neighborhood filled with honest, good-hearted people.

Technology is advancing faster than understanding. Our world is filling with cell phones, microwave ovens, Wi-Fi nodes, computers and TV screens, and heaven-only-knows what's next. These devices require energy and emit energy and we are a long way from understanding all the long-term effects of the increased energies surging through and around us. Already, studies are pointing to the potential for health problems, including very serious health problems.

Take time away from technology, let yourself de-stress and heal. I know many people will say they don't have enough choices, but that is never true. If you prepare yourself and stay determined, the right place will show up for you at exactly the right time. Remember, contrary to "conventional wisdom," luck is not something outside your control. It is when "preparedness meets opportunity" and opportunity is around us all the time; the trick is recognizing it and being prepared to make the most of it. Also luck is an acronym for Laboring Under Correct Knowledge; don't ever use it, like so many others, as an excuse to stay unhealthy and unhappy.

S

Solidarity. Conversion is a lifelong process. It has often been said that doubt leads to greater faith. That is true as long as you control it for your good instead of letting it control you. Don't worry that you have doubts — explore them, challenge yourself and your belief systems. Keep searching your heart, your mind, and your spirit and you will confirm what you believe as either true or false. That way you will find greater truths, from whatever circumstances in which you find yourself. This search, by the way, cannot be all academic, it also needs to be tangible. Remember "Ask, Seek and Knock."

Again, from Admiral Kirk, "We learn by doing." Do you feel increased balance in your body, mind, and spirit? (If not, either your definition of balance is wrong or your activity choices are wrong — or both. In which case, consult a mentor, however you must. If you cannot contact them in person, go the Internet or sometimes, better the library).

Are you really living and breathing those things which mean most to you? Are you actively involved in critical issues based on your core values and your paradigms? How do you feel after doing things you think are important? Do you want to jump right back in and do more or do you want to get away from it for a while? We don't only acquire new knowledge and skills from what we do, we learn how we feel about things and confirm if they are as import as we thought or not (again however, beware of your own insufficiently educated emotions and false ideas from negative spiritual forces that lead you away from, compared to the positive influences that lead you toward truth and genuine happiness and fulfillment. The more you practice, the better you will get at telling the difference). When you establish solidarity in your paradigms, virtually all your destructive stress begins to evaporate and saves you untold pain and disease, replacing it with genuine peace of mind and enlightenment.

T

Thinking. This is the most crucial of all the seven keys to optimal physical and spiritual health because it dictates, controls, directs all the rest. Your thoughts are the foundation of and drive your actions, which create your circumstances. Schedule into your calendar a consistent, weekly time to study from the best books and the most brilliant minds. Study this book. Listen to our audios, attend our educational programs. Looking back over your past activities, your day, your week, your month, your season, your year and more, you will be amazed at the changes that you make with only a few minutes per week or more if possible. Like my brother, Carter, an amazing teacher said, "Your life will begin to produce sustenance and fragrance that you may have thought not to be in existence or only found in the minds of dreamers."

Medical Care

Diligently seek out and chose your healthcare providers with extreme caution. Find people who specialize in holistic medicine, what we call the "wellness" profession not the "sickness" profession. That means people who accept as their primary function the prevention of illness and disease rather than trying to relieve symptoms after your life has already been disrupted and cost you pieces of your life that you can never get back. Compound the effects of that over the course of several years and the benefits are virtually immeasurable.

Here are three very important questions to ask when interviewing and deciding which doctors to allow to help you.

1) What are the chances that this treatment you recommend will cure my problem?

2) What are the likely complications of this treatment? And

3) What is the known death rate of people using this treatment?

Don't be surprised if some get angry at your questions. That means they don't have reasonable answers for you. Be polite, thank them for their time and then excuse yourself because you are wasting your time and theirs.

I heard a comment from Ty Bollinger (who has invested many years studying the finest medical professionals all over the world) that: "Medicine is not healthcare. Food is healthcare. Medicine is sick-care. It's time we see it for what it is."

Spiritual Health

This I've discussed throughout several previous chapters. To review:

- Be aware that you are already part of something infinitely bigger than just yourself and you have a very specific part to play. I call it your unique calling. But to clarify,

- This calling is something you volunteered to do, it is not an assignment. It is your passion, whether you know it right now or not. It includes things you knew you wanted to learn the most and things you were most qualified and wanted to share.

It really boils back down to the wisdom you most wanted to develop. The high intelligence, the master level skills, superior character and extreme insight into optimal human potential (grace you put yourself in contact with to receive) and what you were passionate to share (grace you wanted most to give).

Hate — too Great a Burden

I'm going to tell you a story that, for a long time, I thought I would have rather keep in the past and never talked about again. It is not something I'm proud of, but it is an experience that taught me one of the most important lessons of my life and radically changed my perspective for the better, forever — and so I am grateful for it.

When I was 19 years old, I was "dragging Main" with a friend one evening, just hanging out, checking out the girls. I don't remember how it began, but several guys in another car began swearing at us and giving us a hard time. I was never one to back down from a confrontation and took this as a personal challenge. The driver was the only one I recognized.

I told my friend to pull over and we'd see what their problem was. They pulled up behind us, and all five guys got out. I met them half way and asked if they were crazy. They weren't, they were just a little drunk and "feeling their oats". It became obvious that the driver wanted to fight me. To this day, I have no idea why but, with a bunch of buddies as backup, he was feeling pretty safe.

Of course, he was. When I started winning a fight, it would turn into five-on-two instead of one-on-one — and my friend was not a fighter by any stretch. So I said to the driver, "I'll give you what you want but, obviously, not here like this. I will to go with you to any place you'd like to go, as long as it's just you and me. We can dance and, as soon as you've had enough, we'll come back."

As you can probably imagine, he refused. So I leaned forward, pointed my finger at him and said, "I'm happy to fight you any time you're really ready to make it fair but I'm not stupid enough to fight all five of you at the same time."

It didn't affect me nearly as much in the moment as it began to days later. To make a long story short, I didn't see that guy again for about five years. During that time, I became angrier and angrier. In fact, I harbored that anger until it turned to a genuine hatred. On several occasions, I told people about it and vowed that I would have my revenge the moment I laid eyes on him again. A lot of things happened in that next five years but that bitterness stayed, and it festered in my soul. Many times, I rehearsed in my mind what I would do if I ever saw him again. Finally, I did.

I found myself back in that town, helping one of my older brother's remodel his home. Since his laundry room was torn out, I went to the laundromat one evening. You guessed it, he walked through the door — looking old, drunk, and miserable. I recognized him immediately but, at the same moment, I saw he was carrying an old, ragged laundry basket full of dirty clothes. His hair was matted and messy. He was unshaven and dirty and looked like he had been sleeping under a bridge somewhere. My heart instantly melted and sank to the bottom of my feet.

My mind raced. I thought, "How could I ever be angry at and hate this person? He looks like life has already beaten any kind of dignity out of him." I just sat and watched him while my clothes finished drying. He looked and acted like a complete wretch. He, apparently, didn't recognize me, if he even saw me. I never once saw him lift his gaze from the floor enough to recognize anyone in the room the entire time I was there.

For the next several days, my soul was absolutely tormented with all the horrible feelings I had felt and the ill words that I had spoken about him for the previous five years! I vowed then and there that I would never hate another person as long as I lived. For half a decade, my hate did nothing, except embitter that part of my own life. When I finally let it go, it was like I had just seen and felt the warmth of the sunshine for the first time in half a decade.

To this day, I've had plenty opportunities to be angry and, on occasion, to hate someone but no chance. That experience had such a strong impression on my heart that I never hated anyone since. I have, on occasion, been falsely accused, threatened, treated unfairly, even robbed. I still stand up for what is honest, fair, right and make sure others are held accountable but I never hold a grudge — for more than a few minutes. I've fired people for stealing from me, gone to see other parents of kids who bullied my kids, even turned a few people into the police. But I decided that I, would never be offended by anyone ever again and, since that day more than 35 years ago, I never have.

Revenge, the circumstance you might create when you hate, is certainly one of the most dangerous crimes you commit against yourself. That's why I chose it as the example concept. If you seek revenge, you have allowed the actions of someone else to dictate not only your actions but the outcomes of your life. There are few things in this world that can do more damage to your spiritual health. You have given up your freedom and enslaved yourself to someone else, totally without justification — just ask the judge you'll end up standing in front of when you get arrested for whatever act of revenge you commit.

As Dr. Martin Luther King, Jr., said, "I have decided to stick with love. Hate is too great a burden to bear."

Forgiveness — too Great an Opportunity

"Every action has an equal and opposite reaction," just might be Isaac Newton's most famous saying. It is a universal law and one that applies to the spiritual realm as much as to the physical. A little over 15 years ago, I was reminded of the fight-that-never-was and learned an additional, fundamental concept from that experience.

My wife and I had started doing some real estate investment. During that time, we met another gentleman was also doing some real estate investment. As we got to know each other, we decided to do a project together. We bought an old home and combined our efforts to rehab it. I really should've taken a much closer look at some of the projects he had done in the past because his idea of fix-up and my idea of fix-up were polar opposites.

As a former high-end finish carpenter and custom cabinet maker, I wanted to really upgrade the place. He wanted to come in and just roll some paint on the walls and call it good. To my way of thinking, it would've been dishonest to leave things that could later become problems for the new owner. I could no more bring myself to do the bare minimums than I could intentionally jump off a cliff.

So, I spent the next three months turning that trashed house into a very nice, beautiful home. Neither he nor his help had the skills to do what I felt needed to be done, so I ended up doing about 95 percent of the work by myself. When it came time to sell it, however, he still wanted 50 percent of the profits. Well, since he had never even offered to help with much, you know what I thought about that. After several heated arguments, and eventual arbitration with an attorney, we finally settled on something that was much more in his favor than he deserved. I agreed, in part, because I had to admit that my failure to clearly communicate my intentions and expectations was my fault. If I had been a "good steward," this arrangement would have never happened. My wife and I chalked it up to experience and walked away.

Even at that, he left extremely bitter and hasn't spoken to me since. For about 30 minutes, I felt deeply offended. Then the thought passed through my mind that I should forgive him. Of course, I began to argue with myself (or was it with some spiritual power trying to teach me not to be an idiot?) to the point that I decided if I forgave him he would get away with it scot free and that would not be fair. After a few minutes of arguing back and forth inside my own mind, the previous experience with this kid who picked a fight flashed through my mind. Immediately, I had an "A-ha!" moment — an epiphany, you might say — "Forgiveness has nothing to do with him; it's all about you!"

Again, my heart convicted, I vowed that I would never take offense to another human being as long as I live.

Some years ago, I read a quote from Brigham Young, a 19th Century religious leader and founder of Utah. Young said, "Any person, who takes offense, when offense is not intended, is a fool. And any person who takes offense, even when offense is intended, is also a fool."

That's a truth that I deeply discovered by sad and personal experience. Taking offense only hurts you, not the other person. Forgiveness on the other hand is the only cure and likewise it only cures you, not the other person. Do you think my hatred affected that would-be Mohamad Ali? Does my former real estate partner's hate affect me? In both cases, the answer is no.

Jesus said, "Judge not, that ye be not judged. For with what judgment ye judge, ye shall be judged: and with what measure ye mete, it shall be measured to you again" (Matthew 7:1-2, KJV). Jesus didn't command us to refuse all judgement; it is your duty to judge. If you don't, you could never know who to do business with; who to hire, promote, or fire; who to marry or who should teach your children or many other important matters. His statement concerned judging wrongfully, harshly, or unjustly — He said you will be judged the way you judge others. In this, as in every other aspect of life, you will reap what you sow.

You are given a span of some years and it is up to you to make the most of those years for you. You can shorten that life physically or waste that life spiritually or you can enhance that life physically and spiritually. Your quality of life is entirely your choice, it is perhaps the most significant circumstance you will create. As you do, consider: What is intrinsically empowering? What nourishes the soul so it evolves as a natural result of your choices?

Conclusion

Singer-songwriter Conor Oberst hit it on the head when he ventured the opinion, "I really believe in the way the energy can consolidate in certain geographical spots. You can find it in a lot of different places, beautiful natural spots, or if you look at Islam or Judaism or Christianity, these ideas of holy places."

Everybody will have different ideas about what is a holy place and how it becomes one. That's not important, because spirituality, your path to God is a unique and personal thing. He has a "plan-of-salvation" for you, personally. Certainly, it has something to do with where you decide to put yourself. There is not a lot of spirituality in strip joints or gang clubhouses or businesses where profit is their only goal. Likewise, it has something to do with who you chose to associate with. People who degrade themselves with drugs, alcohol, pornography, and other such activities deny their divinity and cut themselves off to spiritual power.

In truth, you could say that there is only *one* holy place in which you have the capacity to stand. I talked about what keeping the Sabbath day holy actually means back in Chapter 2. It isn't about the calendar, it is about what you did on preceding days, what you do on that day, and your commitments to the days following — to access the spiritual realms and draw on spiritual power. So, stand anywhere you want — church, temple, synagogue, mosque, under the beauty of open skies looking up at the great cathedral that is God's creation, in your own home, at work, on the freeway stuck in traffic, etc. I have been in a cigarette filled bar when I was in a holy place and I have been in a temple when I was not in a holy place. Not because of the place but because of why I was there and where I was within myself. Even if the whole world acknowledges a site as a holy place, you can never really be there unless you access the holiness within yourself. Likewise if evil surrounds you, you don't have to really be there if you have a holy place within and are there. Imagine sitting in a lecture in German and you don't speak German — you won't get much out of the experience. Open your soul with all your heart, might, mind, and strength to connect:

- To the divinity within you — "Luminous beings are we, not this crude stuff", as Master Yoda said.
- To the miraculous around you — "[T]o the extent that one communicates with Nature, so one ascends to Divinity through Nature", said monk and astronomer Giordano Bruno.

This weak, imperfect mortal frame is the only real home you have. You take it with you everywhere you go. But it isn't all you are. Within that home lives a child of God guiding and hoping you will do what needs to be done in order to be reborn in perfect form. As Michelangelo reportedly said, "I saw the angel in the marble and carved until I set him free." If you are determined and work for it, you (like Michelangelo) can carve out that divine being who's potential is alive within you. One step, one thought, one decision, one insight at a time, you can grow to be your best possible self. Constantly taking *The Road Less Traveled* as M. Scott Peck said (or "The Road Less Traveled" as Robert Frost said) seeking your first, best destiny through circumstances that will bring you as close as humanly possible to perfection.

Summary

Philosophers in all ages have spoken of a divine nature that is part of every individual. We are physical beings and we are spiritual beings.

Learning to develop the best attributes of our divine nature, while conquering the worst aspects of our earthly nature, leads to peace of mind and gives us access to spiritual power that will transform us.

Circumstances, including your location and your companions, will affect your spirituality but nothing will affect it more than your character. Once you transform your own personal temple into the embodiment of what those temples represents, you will never need those temples again because you will have become the ultimate temple. As a result you will have created a perpetual, compounding return on investment (ROI). If you want it, it is yours, just follow the principles and be open to the miracles that will result.

Chapter 17
The Synergism Principle

This seventeenth is the culmination of the secret, ancient principles and how they work together to create miracles. In and of themselves, each can produce extraordinary results; even small miracles. Combine them and they will create a synergy that will surprise and delight you to the core. They can prepare and set you up for consistent grace and miracles, whereby you will Solve Every Problem In Your Life.

Almost everyone you meet can give you an earful of how they understand these principles, yet their personal results tell a much different tale. People who truly understand them are the most successful people on Earth and, without exception, the results of their personal lives prove it.

However, if you want miraculous results, you cannot pick and choose which parts you accept and which to reject. The fact is that the more parts you include, the more compounded your increase becomes.

And so, just as you get so deep in the complexity of things that you think you cannot learn enough and are about to be swallowed in the impossible black hole of infinite information, the moment you are willing to risk it all to understand and take that next leap of faith into the darkness anyway, it all begins to condense back into this one simple formula to consistently produce miracles for the rest of your life. You will then have begun your journey toward enlightenment, begun to discover principles for what they really are and truly begun your journey into wisdom.

Again, at face value, this formula sounds far too simple to produce such phenomenal results. In order to guarantee that this formula works for you, we need to go through each step and specifically define the real core of each of these words. I know they seem like such common words that the formula to perfection couldn't possibly be so simple, but there again lies another great delusion of "conventional wisdom". Of course, perfection includes everything, but then the ability to learn everything is entirely wrapped up in this very simple formula.

This is what the wisest people through the ages have been trying to show us, so beware before you brush it off as being too simple. None of these words mean quite what you think they mean, regardless of whether you believe you understand them or not. The more you learn about them, the more you will realize there is to understand about them.

1. Belief
2. Vision
3. Plan
4. Faith

5. Hope
6. Charity
7. Passion
8. Miracles

Understand these words and this process and you graduate with honors from this university of life to be accepted into your celestial graduate studies with guaranteed compound, perpetual, and eternal increase.

Jesus gave us some of the steps — faith, hope, and charity — in that specific order and yet, virtually everyone talks about them out of order, which puts the wrong interpretation on what they really are.

So let's briefly go through each step. I say briefly because we could write an entire book on each one of these. For now, however, I only need to address them to the point where you begin to see how they all work together in a synergistic and miraculous combination. It's a very simple and basic place to launch and practice accessing the powers of heaven and creating your own miracles. This is only an introduction to the big picture and not even close to the "end-all, be-all" solution. And, it is definitely not a quick fix!

Remember Kwai Chang Caine and Master Po?

"How long will it take me to learn these things?"

"Only a lifetime ... and, perhaps, a little longer."

You have the rest of your life, and then some, to add one step to the other. This is a lifetime study and practice. Don't be discouraged by that, in fact, be encouraged by it because through the seasons of your life, you will discover how to create bigger and better harvests and never-ending rewards — rewards that no one of us have the capacity to dream.

Belief

At the deepest root of all behavior lies an image of yourself. That image encompasses everything you truly believe about yourself, including the worst of the worst and the best of the best.

The very invisible hands that build the fences that shape the limits as well as the extremes of your own potential are the hands of your own self-image. It is not the self-image you try hard to portray to others, but the one you wrestle with deep inside, even subconsciously. Much of which you do your best to hide from others, even from those closest to you, in fact, even from yourself.

This is the inflated and deflated, the substantial and hollow self-image you have of yourself, combined with the image that God has of you and is consistently sending you glimpses, feelings, and ideas about. This combined dichotomy created the parameters that define and confine your current potential.

Mahatma Gandhi said, "Men often become what they believe themselves to be. If I believe I cannot do something, it makes me incapable of doing it. But, if I believe, I can then I acquire the ability to do it even if I didn't have it in the beginning."

The way you deal with every opportunity in your life is entirely due to how you perceive yourself, consciously and subconsciously. Whether you are willing to take a risk or give in to fear. Whether you take a foolish risk or any worthwhile risk, etc.

Vision

In order to understand what vision actually is, let's go over a few common myths about vision and determine what vision is not.

Vision is not simply a figment of your imagination or random pictures in your mind. They are certainly not just hallucinations, dreams or wishful thinking. Not even things you daydream about, wish you had or likely even things that you have decided you want and work toward.

A vision is the literal spiritual creation and a real, tangible and specific time, space and experience in the future. One that is so clearly defined, that you know and immediately recognize it, even at a distance. You know what it feels like, who is there, the weather, the sounds, aroma's, attitudes of the people, and so on.

In the true sense of the word, visions are often how God communicates to his children. For the good of the individual and of a group, God sends visions to the appropriate people so they in turn will counsel, warn and teach us important things that will enable us to discover principles, avoid tragedy and live at higher levels of wisdom/results.

Vision is a holistic picture in your mind that fills your senses. The process of bringing light to the future where there once was darkness. It brings understanding to ignorance and possibility to hopelessness, organization, form, texture, and consistency to that which is unorganized. Visions are the spiritual blue prints and specifications to physical reality.

Solomon said, "Where there is no vision, the people perish" (Proverbs 28:9, KJV). Now, keep in mind he was the wisest and wealthiest man who ever lived on Earth. He understood that it was not just dreaming that was important to human beings but that those dreams become so real, so clearly described and identified in significant detail that the physical reality was not only recognizable from its spiritual blue print, but the actual first "breath of life" into your creations.

Henry David Thoreau was trying to teach us this same principle when he said, "If you have built castles in the air, your work need not be lost, that is where they belong. Now, put foundations under them."

Once you get this vision clearly identified and defined in your mind, you must then transform this spiritual blueprint into a physical blueprint by portraying it on paper as clearly as possible. There was never a serious vision that has been brought into reality without a written copy hung up or at least in a place where it is visible and often reviewed.

All significant visions given to prophets for the betterment of mankind have been, by divine command, written down. Why do you think that is that the case? Because we need that physical reminder and unchangeable, written down clarification so that it can be referred to often and further clarified as we gain greater understanding and bring it to pass.

Plan

I've heard a lot of people talk about strategies to achieve goals but only a few who actually understood exactly how to draft and design them so they work — without exception. This plan consists of the details about how and when and who will be involved with you to clothe your blueprint and spec-book, that is your spiritual creation, with physical reality. People who have a habit of success are people who are willing to do what unsuccessful people are not willing to do. Among those habits of success is making a notebook and pen (or some other way to make a permanent record) your best friend, from the time of conception until this vision becomes reality. As the old saying goes, "The weakest pencil is mightier than the mightiest memory."

"Is it really that important to write things down?" I hear that question so often, it's never surprising anymore and the answer is always the same. It was important enough for the wisest and most successful people in history but, if you think you are so much smarter and better than all of them, give it a try. When you have fallen on your face and dashed your dreams to pieces on the rocks of reality, maybe you'll decide to train your brain to think. Albert Schweitzer, was once asked, "Dr. Schweitzer, what's wrong with men today?" He responded, "Men simply don't think!"

Thinking is *not* about remembering; it is a creative activity of discovering new ways to organize what is unorganized and consistently organizing better that which was previously organized.

First — set the parameters of your journey. "Parameters" are boundaries and they will, in large measure, help you discover the formula that will take you where you want to go because they will remove a whole lot of ideas or processes that won't work. Part of that comes from the wisest mentors you can find who have already accomplished what you want to accomplish. Make sure you know where you are (Point A); decide where you want to go (Point B). Decide what you won't do to reach the goal — there will be a few obvious things on the list ("anything illegal or unethical") and there may be a few not so obvious things ("work on the Sabbath"). These, you could say, are your line of scrimmage, your goal line and your sidelines.

Second — forecast, as best you can, what obstacles may arise. Consult with others who have already been where you want to go or, at least, who are familiar with the best processes of achievement (at least discovered so far). You never need to take their advice, you are welcome to try to re-create the wheel on your own but in the beginning at least, you will only waste a lot of precious time and energy. Even toward the end, their advice may spark great ideas of your own. Don't be too specific, most of the significant roadblocks will be things you didn't include in your next best guess. (If you're jumping into new territory, you should expect new challenges, trials, and problems. And new territory means for you, not necessarily for others.) Being aware of that and being unconditionally committed to overcoming them as soon as they begin to show themselves are your best defenses against being overwhelmed by these new challenges.

Third — set the time. If you want to do something, you need deadlines. "Well," you say, "I have no way to know how long this will take to do." That's why I decided to call it the Next Best *Guess* Principle! It doesn't matter what date you set as your goal — well, it matters a little — it is far more important that you set a time limit and do your best to achieve within that limit.

All of this includes being realistic about where you are in life and that means setting realistic goals. That may sound contradictory to what I just said about vision, but it's a serious consideration. Let's say your professional vision is a university professorship. One of your interim goals will be to earn a master's degree because there are very few colleges or universities that will hire you without one. If you cannot achieve the degree, the professorship is pretty unlikely, so at least your best guess may be to focus on the degree. When you have the degree, you have a whole new situation — a new Point A. Along the way and afterwards, new possibilities will open up and you will create a far better plan to achieve the next step toward your ultimate goal at that new point. Beware however not to fence yourself into the "conventional wisdom."

Notice that I said "very few colleges or universities". There are avenues to professorship that don't include a master's degree. I have been offered opportunities to teach courses or team teach at college and I've never been to college. What type of school you want as your employer will, to a degree (pun intended) determine your path.

Faith

Faith was a difficult thing for me to really grasp over the years. It has always been intriguing because I've heard so often about how it is associated with miracles. Faith is the one principle that seems to always come up when we want to make changes for the better in our lives. As a result, I decided to make a very deliberate and major study of faith. At first, it seemed so esoteric and difficult to really get a handle on it. Eventually, however, I began to see some light. Finally, I decided to write my own definition of faith because all of the other definitions I ever read, never seemed to explain it in a way that I could actually put it into practice. Faith is a verb, not a noun:

- A calculated, deliberate, and unconditional commitment to and process of achieving your clearly-defined vision;

- The process of clothing your spiritual vision(s) in a physical reality that is so much bigger than yourself that it requires divine intervention for fulfillment.

Faith is *not* just a step before knowledge, but the steps before the knowledge of processes. It is *not* about knowing what things are true or false but about understanding that there are good spiritual forces that we put under our control to provide things that we cannot provide for ourselves. Faith is *not* a lack of understanding of doctrine, it is a lack of understanding of principles. Woodrow Wilson said:

- We grow great by dreams and goals. All big successes are big dreamers. They see things in the red fire of a long winters evening and in the midst of a rainy day. Some of us let these great dreams die, while others nourish and protect them, through the bad days, until they bring them to the sunshine and light that always comes to those who sincerely believe that their dreams will come true.

- Also Goethe, "Whatever you can do or dream you can, begin it. Boldness has genius, power and magic in it!"

- And James Allen, "So be not impatient in delay, but wait as one who understands, when spirit rises and commands, the Gods are ready to obey."

Hope

Hope is a very intriguing word. But to really understand what hope is, we need to first understand what hope is not. It was about 15 years ago when it began to dawn on me that, when people used the word hope, it was almost always talked about entirely from a faulty perspective.

I know because, for the first 45 or more years of my life, I used the word like everyone I know uses the word. It was one day in a Sunday school class. We were reading First Corinthians, where Paul talked about faith, hope, and charity. Even though I'd heard and read that scripture many times before, my first thought on that day was, "I wonder why he didn't say 'hope, faith, and charity', because that's really the rightful order of things."

Almost immediately, I started thinking, "Who am I to think that I know more about this subject than Paul?" I was puzzled about that for some time until a couple of years later, when I started to understand that faith really was not what most people thought it was. Only when I began to really understand what faith actually is, did it begin to dawn on me that hope really does come after faith.

I started thinking: How can a person have a genuine hope in something until there has been a reasonable progress toward a desired objective? This was revelatory for me. Over time, one piece here and there, I began to understand that, when most people use the word "hope" they are, in fact, talking about "wishful thinking". Wishful thinking is a distraction, a form of decay. It is thought without discipline. There's nothing profitable in wishful thinking. It accomplishes nothing except to keep us discontented with things that will likely never change.

A few years after this second epiphany, I heard about Steven K. Scott, who has become one of my all-time favorite mentors. He was the first and only person that I've ever heard confirm what I had discovered a few years before and he explained it in such a profound way, using a brilliant, simple example:

He reminds us about that classic experience we've all had of traveling in a vehicle to a distant place when we were children. Remember shortly after you started when you ask your parents, "Are we there yet?"

"No, we have a long way to go."

"Oh, okay." No hope. Three minutes later, "Are we there yet?"

"No, I told you we have a long way to go."

"Oh, brother!" No hope.

Time after time we asked, "Are we there yet?

Always the same answer, "No." Never any hope.

So, we got ourselves distracted, playing games or going to sleep until one time we ask, "Are we there yet?"

"We are close, only about five minutes."

"Oh, yeah!" Now there is real hope because we know we are going to make it. It is only after we have successfully worked through the trial of our faith and been through enough of the process to know for a surety that we will make it because we can see the "light at the end of the tunnel." When we are virtually guaranteed to make it. That is real hope!

Charity

Earlier, we talked about character being the core trait in your entire life to work on because everything you ever will do or become or accomplish in your life is 100 percent dictated by your character.

Just as character is the most important aspect of you to work on, charity is the core and central character trait that defines and brings meaning to all others. It is the standard by which all other character traits can be measured and from which all other positive character traits naturally and effortlessly flow. Charity isn't the sum total of your character. All other traits are appendages to charity. As we intentionally work on developing positive character traits, all eventually lead to the core trait, charity.

I know you've heard about charity but, as with so much of our language today, we have so diluted and twisted the meaning that the general population does not understand what it really means anymore. Happily, everyone understands one part of that charity — caring for those who are poor, sick and otherwise in need of help. If, however, you actually stop and think, is there any such thing as a person who is not in need? Every single person on Earth needs to learn new things and grow in new ways. Virtually all of the resources we need in order to bring our visions into physical reality are controlled by someone else. In fact, no matter who or where you are, essentially everything you want is only available through other people.

You've all heard the cliché, "No one cares how much you know until they know how much you care." It's true, and that is a simple (incomplete but useful) definition of charity. Part of the human condition, as defined by the Author of the human condition, is the need for cooperation. As Benjamin Franklin told the Continental Congress (on July 2, 1776), "Gentlemen, we must all hang together or, assuredly, we will all hang separately." If you can communicate to the right people, your needs in a way that shows them, irresistibly, why they want to have dealings with you then everything is possible.

Why, exactly, do they want to have dealings with you? Because you care about them as much as you care about you. Because their vision is important to you and your vision and you want to help them achieve it. Because they know you are honest and have integrity; that you will only and always deal with them on an absolute win-win basis. That's what people used to be saying when they spoke of a man or woman of character. (Well, that and a few other very nice things.)

Charity is that all-inclusive process of self-evolution toward perfection through the giving and receiving of grace/ hand-ups. On one hand, it is being excited to share what we have and, on the other hand, being grateful for every opportunity to receive from others so that we evolve and have capacity to share more.

Since charity deals with both giving and receiving in a spirit of genuine love, it could not possibly exist within a person without them understanding how crucial it is to be on a continual program of self-improvement. Charity is that great character trait of ultimate leadership. It is a state of being in which selflessness completely replaces selfishness.

Many years ago, I heard a powerful metaphor by Zig Ziglar. He used it in a different context but the metaphor brings out a part of charity that is critical to understand and, so, I will paraphrase:

> Your heart is a most remarkable muscle. Every minute of every hour, every hour of every day and every day of every year for your entire life, your heart continually pumps blood, delivering the crucial, life-giving oxygen and nutrients to every part of your body. It never rests, never sleeps, never takes a break. It is completely and utterly selfless and serves literally every cell of your body, every moment of your life.

> But do you know where the heart pumps blood to first? It will probably surprise you, no, not to the brain, not to any other vital organ but — to itself! Now why would it do that? Because, like you, if you don't have something, you can't give it to anyone else. Also, you can only share with others the amount that you have.

Charity encompasses the entire spectrum of every facet of the purpose of our lives. There are only two perspectives from which all our intentions and behaviors stem — selfishness and selflessness. Selfishness is the opposite of charity and the opposite of love. Selflessness to others and to yourself, to the greatest expanse of its potential is the essence of charity.

Charity is the core character trait that enables this system of Earth life to function properly. It enables us to ultimately, find that perfection they seek. There is only one other possible result — if people do not develop charity, they will by selfishness decay, eventually to complete ruin.

Passion

Passion, as we discussed earlier, is that self-perpetuating fuel that supercharges everything you do. It enables you to go as far and high as you are willing to. Passion is the direct by-product of following this formula for miracles. It is a self-renewing energy that gets you up early and keeps you up late to specifically be involved with your calling and purpose. You might think that kind of activity would tear down your body but it actually heals your body and extends your life and vitality.

The more you believe in yourself, the clearer your vision becomes and the more carefully you plan and design to bring those visions into reality. The more clarity in your plans, the more faith you have to exercise and the more hope is naturally produced in your life. The more hope, the more you see how you can bless other people's lives' and the more others will be motivated to join your cause and charity begins to form. The more you come to love other people and the service you can offer, the more you realize how others can participate with you to bring more blessings to others and the more passion you exude — which in-turn brings you more belief into yourself and that becomes an eternal compounding return on your investment.

Miracles

If you want something that you've never had before, you will have to do things you've never done before, develop skills and habits you've never had before, and become someone you've never been before. But if you are willing, one day you will wake to find that what you wanted is now in your possession but, when you look closely, you'll discover that you actually didn't get it for yourself. Rather, it was a gift and came to you the moment you were prepared to receive it and now it is yours forever for you have become its author.

The Buddha said, "We are shaped by our thoughts; we become what we think. When the mind is pure, joy follows like a shadow that never leaves."

God's commandments are nothing more than opportunities to discover much deeper, broader, more inclusive universal laws and the principles that enable us to harness them for good. It comes back to this basic.

One of my favorite quotes is from William Hutchison "W. H." Murray:

> Until one is committed, there is hesitancy, the chance to draw back, always ineffectiveness. Concerning all acts of initiative (and creation), there is one elementary truth the ignorance of which kills countless ideas and splendid plans: that the moment one definitely commits oneself, then providence moves too. A whole stream of events issues from the decision, raising in one's favor all manner of unforeseen incidents, meetings and material assistance, which no man could have dreamt would have come his way. [Then, quoting Goethe, he finished,] "Whatever you can do or dream you can, begin it. Boldness has genius, power and magic in it!"

Another is from James Allen:

> You will be what you will to be.
> Let failure find its faults content
> in that poor word environment,
> but spirit scorns it and is free.

It masters time, it conquers space,
it cows that boastful trickster chance,
and bids the tyrant circumstance,
uncrown, and take a servant's place.

The human will, that force unseen,
the offspring of a deathless soul,
can hew away to any goal
though walls of granite intervene.

So being not impatient in delay,
but wait as one who understands,
when spirit rises and commands,
the gods are ready to obey.

Conclusion

I once had some conversations with a life-long student of the great Buckminster Fuller.

> This gentleman asked me, "Will humankind survive and thrive on spaceship Earth?" Or, was his real question, will we damage it to a point beyond recovery? I replied:

> "We will not only survive but thrive on Spaceship Earth! For 6,000 years, history has proven that the fundamental programming of the human spirit is nothing short of thriving. Surviving is only another word for mediocrity and decay, but thriving is evolution and though the majority override their destiny to evolve, there will always remain those on earth who are willing to follow their best destiny and evolve, whatever the cost. These will always be our great leaders and they will always have faithful followers.

Human beings do not lack capacity, only incentive. Unfortunately, the masses typically require a catastrophe to muster enough incentive to activate their virtual unlimited creative potential to evolve but, regardless of what triggers it, those creative powers are capable of what is now improbable and even impossible.

However, there is a much deeper question that must be reconciled before this one can be addressed with any significant foundation whatsoever: "Is there a purpose to 'spaceship Earth'?" If there is no purpose and we are only the result of a random "big bang" in space, then it is, ultimately, of no consequence whatsoever whether an individual or our entire species lives or dies.

On the other hand, if there is a purpose, (and there is, whether you believe it or not!) then all the rules change and human potential expands exponentially with access to miracles! And that pertains as much to personally creating the life you dream about as it does to our collective success."

There exists but one ultimate question of life: Will you graduate with honors from this University of Life by accepting your birthright and taking your rightful place as an active participant with those who thrive?

If that is your desire, you have exactly one path to achieve that vision: To proactively and wisely invest your priceless resources — time, energy, and potential — in such a way as to realize an ever-compounding and perpetual return of additional resources. Remember, only results count. Or, by default, will you consume all of those priceless resources and die because you are depleted and broken, with nothing left to consume or invest in order to purchase another tomorrow?

As for me, I guarantee that, especially if you have actually read or listened this far, you have capacity to become a leader of leaders and create miracles. Again, to quote Dave Ramsey, "If you are willing to live like no one else, you will be able to live like no one else." Also one more role model that I have come to greatly admire is Dexter Yager who said "Every person in life will pay one of two prices. Either they will pay the price of discipline or they will pay the price of regret. And if the price of discipline weighs ounces, by comparison, the price of regret weighs tons." Just remember that God said, "Fear not for I am with thee" (Genesis 26:24, KJV) and "According to your faith, be it unto you" (Matthew 9:29, KJV).

I believe in you. I know for a fact that you can do it. Whenever you need an extra

push or pull, you will find me on your shoulder cheering you on. You will hear my voice saying, "Get up! Go on! You can do it! Just one more step…and then one more step. Success is waiting for you."

So fall and the one you want, the one you will become will catch you." I personally look forward to hearing from you about your most significant wishes, dreams and ambitions, those you are willing to turn into reality — the ones you are no longer willing to live without. I look forward to being a guide on your quest to discover more of these secret ancient principles on your incredible journey to find and fulfill your destiny to live a rich and abundant life and accomplish things that are so much bigger than yourself that they require divine intervention for their fulfillment.

So God Bless You, Enjoy and Go Catch Your Dreams!

About the Author:

How did I become "America's Wisdom Mentor and Master Problem Solver"? I certainly never planned on that and, only a few years ago, could not have even imagined such a thing. I am very much in awe and humbled by it. However, by the time you get to the end of this book, you too will begin to recognize how a few secret, ancient principles can put you on track to achieving more than you have ever imagined possible for you. It is my honor to share this journey with you.

I grew up a hard-core Utah cowboy. I learned a lot from my dad and also my older brothers, about the laws of the harvest, about what makes things die and what makes them grow. About how to ride, rope, break horses, work with animals, operate farm equipment and tend crops. I also learned how to love and serve people and developed a deep respect nature and all life within it. Despite all the good example and direction from family I was a bit of a "hard-case."

Our family moved a few times within Utah during my school years: from our Layton/Kaysville dairy farm to another farm in Hoytsville, where I attended 3rd through 5th grade. Finally, we moved to Roosevelt, and a smaller farm, where my dad also opened a small custom cabinet and furniture shop. That remained his vocation from that point on. The shop in Roosevelt is where I began my education in cabinetry and carpentry, attended junior high, and started high school.

We moved again to Monticello just before my junior year of high school. That was the first time in my life when I didn't have daily farm chores to do. It was strange to live in town, and I greatly missed the open country space, horses, and farm life. Monticello was, however, the first and only time in my life where a school teacher actually took the time and energy to prove that I was personally important to him.

He was my wrestling coach, Joe Wolfe Davis. I wasn't the only one to recognize his genuine kindness and acceptance; a few of my team-mates also expressed similar feelings. Coach Davis single-handedly took our small band of half-wit, scraggly, trouble-making, mediocre wrestlers and turned us into a phenomenon. During that year, we won first place in every dual meet and tournament we participated in, which included taking first place in both Region and State tournaments. Though he was my coach for only one season, I learned much from him. Like many of the lessons I learned from the farm however, it wasn't until several years later that I really began to understand the crucial life lessons he uncovered and left for us to discover. Outside my own family, Coach Davis was my first real positive role model that I would have followed into battle and died for.

After my junior year, our family moved to Wellington, a "big" town of approximately 1,000 people, (and, yes, I mean 1,000!) where I graduated from

Carbon High in nearby Price. From Wellington, I left and served a two-year mission in Scotland for my church.

In the summers between school, before my mission and for a few years after I returned, I switched back and forth between working for my brother, Byron, as a carpenter and my brother-in-law, Randy Bird, as a lumberjack. Later on, for a couple of years, I also drove semi-truck for another brother-in-law, Elden Pace. When I was 25, my oldest brother, Jerald, invited me to California to be a carpenter's foreman for his company. Only a couple of weeks after I arrived, Jerald's business partner and brother-in-law, Terry Leib, came to the job site and asked me, almost frantically, "Eldon, have you ever danced before?" I had not and had no plan to do so but, after days of pleading I agreed to join a ballroom dance festival with a girl whose partner became unavailable. About eight and a half months later, Jackie became my permanent partner.

At 32, my little family moved back to Wellington, Utah, where we purchased an old, vacant apartment building. We tore out the inside and remodeled it into Eldon Grant's Custom Cabinets. Within a few years however, I found myself caught in a deadly tail-spin. Every area of my life seemed to be crumbling all around me. I was on the verge of losing virtually everything of significant value to me —my wife, kids, health, friends, income, business, spirituality, and self-esteem. I was desperate for solutions, but I didn't know where to turn or who to talk to. This was the lowest point of my life, and I was in a major panic.

One of the most frightening things I could imagine was that someone else would find out I had problems, so I didn't want to talk about my troubles with anyone. At the same time, I also knew that if I didn't get help, things would only get worse and that was not an option. I finally forced myself to ask a few people I considered to be successful for advice. Disappointingly, they had plenty of their own problems hidden behind the facade of what only seemed to be a perfect life. It also became clear that their achievements stemmed from advantages that I never had, and so their successes were not realistic for me to duplicate. That experience left me even more frustrated and desperate than ever.

After an entire year of dead-end searching, major frustration and anger welled up in my heart and soul, reaching the breaking point. I looked toward heaven, tears in my eyes, and cried, "Heavenly Father, I've been asking for your help for an entire year. I've also been asking everyone else I can find, and I feel further away from answers now than ever before. My faith is dwindling fast. But just for the record, as I shook my fist, I will find answers to every one of my problems or I will die trying—and I don't care what comes first!"

A few nights later, I was awake about 1:00 AM with terrible insomnia. I was flipping through channels on the TV, trying to find something to relieve my pent-up emotions and aching spirit. At that time of the night, nothing was on that I wanted to watch. Suddenly, though, as I skipped past an infomercial, I heard a voice say as clear as a bell, "Watch this guy."

Three distinct, different times, the voice returned. I shifted uncomfortably and finally began to watch. To my surprise, I was intrigued. Robert G. Allen was talking about real estate investment and, after watching him for a while, I thought, "I could do that," so I ordered his book.

To that point, I had only read about ten books in my whole life, mostly in elementary school. In fact, after high school, I had vowed that I'd never read another book for the rest of my life and I was succeeding at that, if nothing else. So, ordering this book was no small leap of faith. I will forever remember the powerful feelings that stirred my soul as Allen's words twisted in my mind and seemed to address me personally.

"Eldon," I heard Mr. Allen say, "I can teach you all the techniques and strategies to become a successful real estate investor, but it won't do you any good until you change the way you think about and value yourself. Your life will never improve until you begin to feel worthy of the improvements you think you want. Now, I'm an expert in real estate, not personal development. However, I have travelled the world, and I know the world's leading experts. In fact, I've put together a set of cassette tapes from them specifically for you, and I suggest you start here."

I'd never heard anyone talk like that before, and yet it had such a familiar ring. I believed him and ordered the tapes. When they arrived, I opened them up, still a little apprehensive. I looked over the twelve authors and titles. I'd never heard of any of these people before. I pulled out a tape that sounded intriguing: *Seeds of Greatness* by Denis Waitley. I was not prepared for what I heard and could never have imagined the journey I had just begun, let alone the huge shifts it would enable me to make in my life.

For the next 45 minutes, that man captivated my attention like nothing I had ever before experienced. He addressed virtually every question I had been asking for the previous year and introduced me into a world that I had never imagined. Tape after tape, I was so enthralled that I couldn't stop listening. These people instantly became my role models and mentors. I was completely obsessed. I listened to them everywhere I went and became their devoted apprentice.

I searched out and found a lot more authors and trainers and studied everything I could get my hands on. After a couple of years, I reached another major fork in my road. I began to recognize that just because somebody had written a book or two or ten and might even be famous, did not mean that they actually knew what they were talking about. Why did real experts caution me to be careful about whose advice I follow? Because many of those additional books and programs I'd found and studied taught ideas that sounded good but were contrary to what I'd learned working with animals and crops on the farm or in the cabinet shop and on construction jobsites.

I finally figured out that the principles I'd learned as a child also governed relationships, health, organizations, families, money, time management, business, and even our emotional and spiritual well-being. They are what we are divinely-intended to discover through this experience on Earth. They provide solutions to every problem we ever face.

These ideas, the laws and principles which govern the universe, are cause-and-effect. They are what makes things die and what makes them grow, what wastes our resources and what creates a return-on-investment. I made a new, iron-clad pact with myself that I would never again study anyone's work until I determined who they are and verified that they are creating extraordinary—even miraculous results for themselves in what they teach. These potential role models and mentors couldn't offer just temporary illusions of success but the kind of real success that compounds on itself forever.

I immersed myself in hundreds and hundreds more tapes, books, training programs, and courses from the kind of people who practice what they preach. I learned that almost everything I had accepted as truth about success was completely backwards! I had to relearn much of what I had been accepting as truth previous to that time in my life. I learned that real truth, not the stuff most people peddle, has been documented since the beginning of recorded history and verified by the results they have created in many people's lives.

It wasn't until I found the courage to face my fears and take the ultimate risk to stop searching for answers but instead, figure out how to consistently ask better questions, to give up my false sense of security, and allow myself to be vulnerable enough to push myself to expand my potential, that real solutions began to open up. Like the old Chinese proverb, "When the student is ready, the teacher shall appear." Finally, I was ready.

As I began to really apply these principles, a detailed map of miraculous success, in every area of life began to emerge. These principles have enabled me to turn every problem in my life into opportunities and solve them while washing away the fears lurking in the dark corners of my mind—fears about my own lack of worth, capability, and effectiveness. My life, of course, hasn't become problem-free or effortless but I finally, absolutely love being me and I love the daily challenge of creating a better tomorrow.

Do I claim to know everything? Absolutely not; I really claim to know very little except that I'm unquestionably on the right track.

These experiences have enabled me to share my story and these secret, ancient and crucial life principles with many audiences over the years. They have brought me to where I am today; to publish this first in a series of books and launch my business to teach ultimate problem-solving skills.

I echo the words of Theodore Roosevelt, who said, "Far better it is to dare mighty things, to win glorious triumphs, even though checked by failure than to take rank with those poor souls who neither enjoy much, nor suffer much, who live in that grey twilight that knows neither victory nor defeat."

I am totally excited that you have chosen to join me on this journey, and I promise that as we continue to discover these ultimately powerful principles that earth life has to teach us, apply them in our lives, and hold each other accountable, we will solve every problem that comes our way and live a life of miracles, guaranteed!

Contact us:

info@SolveEveryProblem.com
www.SolveEveryProblem.com
(704) Solve-It (704) 765-8348 -Office
(704) 765-8631 - - - - - - -Fax
(844) Eldon-Gr(ant) (844) 353-6647 Toll Free (US, Canada only)

Made in the USA
San Bernardino, CA
11 May 2017